Taste of Home
the busy family
COOKBOOK

Taste of Home
B O O K S

REIMAN MEDIA GROUP, INC. • GREENDALE, WISCONSIN

Taste of Home   Reader's Digest

A TASTE OF HOME/READER'S DIGEST BOOK

Editor: Janet Briggs
Art Directors: Edwin Robles, Jr., Lori Arndt
Layout Designers: Kathy Crawford, Catherine Fletcher
Proofreaders: Linne Bruskewitz, Jean Steiner
Editorial Assistant: Barb Czysz
Food Director: Diane Werner RD
Recipe Testing and Editing: Taste of Home Test Kitchen
Food Photography: Reiman Photo Studio
Cover Photo Photographer: Dan Roberts
Cover Photo Food Stylist: Jennifer Janz
Cover Photo Set Stylist: Jennifer Bradley Vent

Senior Editor, Retail Books: Jennifer Olski
Creative Director: Ardyth Cope
Vice President, Executive Editor/Books: Heidi Reuter Lloyd
Senior Vice President, Editor in Chief: Catherine Cassidy
President, Food & Entertaining: Suzanne M. Grimes
President and Chief Executive Officer: Mary G. Berner

Pictured on front cover: Turkey Florentine (p. 110) and Lemon Angel Hair (p. 207)

Pictured on spine: Jalapeno Swiss Burgers (p. 24)

Pictured on back cover: Personal Pizza (p. 39)

International Standard Book Number (10): 0-89821-664-8
International Standard Book Number (13): 978-0-89821-664-6
Library of Congress Control Number: 2007935262

For other Taste of Home books and products, visit www.tasteofhome.com.
For more Reader's Digest products and information, visit
www.rd.com (in the United States)
www.rd.ca (in Canada)

Printed in China
7 9 10 8 6

Table of Contents

Introduction   4

Beef   7

Pork   47

Poultry   83

Seafood   133

Meatless   163

Sides & Salads   185

Desserts   225

Indexes   249

Dinnertime Solutions Designed for Your Family

The kids are in a frenzy and bickering. You've worked all day and the stress is mounting. Everyone is tired and hungry.

It's the crazy hour—that frantic time between heading home and sitting down to dinner. You need to feed the family...and fast!

So take a deep breath and reach for **The Busy Family Cookbook.** It's packed with scrumptious dishes your family will love to eat and you'll enjoy making.

Each fast-to-the-table idea features a short ingredient list, simple prep techniques, no-fuss cooking methods and easy-to-follow directions. With readily available ingredients and everyday cooking appliances, you can whip up nutritious, delicious meals in no time flat!

To help you make the most of every minute, each chapter is arranged with the quickest recipes first. Flip through and browse by cooking time, conveniently displayed at the top of every page with at-a-glance icons, pictured at right.

Also, look near each recipe name for icons to find microwave shortcuts and plan-ahead recipes requiring extra time for marinating, chilling, freezing or standing. To lend a hand in planning, prep and cook times are given in 5-minute increments and are rounded up.

10 minute recipes = 10 minutes or less from start to table.

20 minute recipes = Up to 20 minutes or less from start to table.

30 minute recipes = Up to 30 minutes or less from start to table.

30+ minute recipes = Up to 60 minutes or less from start to table.

micro wave

plan ahead

Get Cooking with a Well-Stocked Kitchen

In a perfect world you would plan out weekly or even monthly menus and have all the ingredients on hand to make each night's dinner. The reality, however, is you likely haven't thought about dinner until you've walked through the door.

With a reasonably stocked pantry, refrigerator and freezer, you'll still be able to serve a satisfying meal in short order. Consider these tips:

- **Quick-cooking meats** like boneless chicken breasts, chicken thighs, pork tenderloin, pork chops, ground meats, Italian sausage, sirloin and flank steaks, fish fillets and shrimp should be stocked the freezer. Wrap them individually (except shrimp), so you can remove only the amount you need. For the quickest defrosting, wrap meats for freezing in small thin packages.

- **Frozen vegetables** prepackaged in plastic bags are a real time-saver. Simply pour out the amount needed. No preparation is required!

- **Pastas, rice, rice mixes and couscous** are great staples to have in the pantry—and they generally have a long shelf life. Remember, thinner pastas, such as angel hair, cook faster than thicker pastas. Fresh (refrigerated) pasta cooks faster than dried.

- **Dairy products** like milk, sour cream, cheeses (shredded, cubed or crumbled), eggs, yogurt and butter or margarine are more perishable, so check the use-by date on packages and replace as needed.

- **Condiments** such as ketchup, mustard, mayonnaise, salad dressings, salsa, taco sauce, soy sauce, stir-fry sauce, lemon juice, etc. add flavor to many dishes. Personalize the list to suit your family's needs.

- **Fresh fruit and vegetables** can make a satisfying predinner snack. Oranges and apples are not as perishable as bananas. Ready-to-use salad greens are great for an instant salad.

- **Dried herbs, spices, vinegars** and seasoning mixes add flavor and keep for months.

- **Pasta sauces, olives, beans,** broths, canned tomatoes, canned vegetables, and canned or dried soups are great to have on hand for a quick meal...and many of these items are common recipe ingredients.

- **Get your family into the habit** of posting a grocery list. When an item is used up or is almost gone, just add it to list for next shopping trip. This way you won't completely run out of an item, and you'll also save time when writing your grocery list.

Make the Most of Your Time Every Night

With recipes in hand and your kitchen stocked, you're well on your way to a relaxing family meal. Here are some pointers to help you get dinner on the table fast:

- **When using an oven or grill,** preheat it before starting on the recipe.

- **Pull out all the ingredients,** mixing tools and cooking tools before beginning any prep work.

- **Whenever possible,** use convenience items, such as prechopped garlic, onion and peppers, shredded or cubed cheese, seasoning mixes, jarred sauces, etc.

- **Multi-task!** While the meat is simmering for a main dish, toss a salad, cook a side dish or start on dessert.

- **Encourage helpers.** Have younger children set the table. Older ones can help with ingredient preparation or even assemble simple recipes themselves.

- **Take care of two meals in one night** by planning main dish leftovers or making a double batch of favorite sides.

6 Tricks to Tame Hunger

If rumbling tummies can't wait for dinner, calm the kids' appetites with some nutritious, yet not too filling presupper snacks.

1 | **Start them with a salad** tossed using their favorite dressing. Try a ready-to-serve salad mix and add a little protein like cubed cheese or julienned slices of deli meat.

2 | **Cut up an apple** and smear a little peanut butter on each slice. Or offer other fruits such as seedless grapes, cantaloupe, oranges or bananas. For variety, give kids a vanilla yogurt or reduced-fat ranch dressing as a dipper for the fruit or combine a little reduced-fat sour cream with a sprinkling of brown sugar. Too tired to cut up the fruit? A fruit snack cup will do the trick, too.

3 | **Raw veggies,** such as carrots, cucumbers, mushrooms, broccoli and cauliflower, are tasty treats, especially when served with reduced-fat dressing for dipping. Plus, many of these vegetables can be purchased precut.

4 | **Give kids a small serving of cheese and crackers.** Look for presliced cheese and cut the slices into smaller squares to fit the crackers. Choose a cracker that is made from whole wheat, such as an all-natural, 7-grain cracker.

5 | **A snack-size serving of yogurt** with a sprinkle of granola for some crunch might settle down their hunger.

6 | **During the cold months,** a small mug of soup with a few oyster crackers will hit the spot.

Beef

Jalapeno Swiss Burgers (p. 24)

Mozzarella Beef Sandwiches

Prep Time: 10 min.

This is a great supper when we're short on time. I simply jazz up deli roast beef with cheese and jarred spaghetti sauce.
—Erica Svejda, Janesville, Wisconsin

1 loaf (1 pound, 20 inches) unsliced French bread
1-1/4 pounds thinly sliced deli roast beef
1 cup meatless spaghetti sauce
1-1/4 cups (5 ounces) shredded part-skim mozzarella cheese

Cut bread in half lengthwise; cut widthwise into five portions. On each bread bottom, layer the beef, spaghetti sauce and cheese.

Place on an ungreased baking sheet. Broil 4 in. from the heat for 1-2 minutes or until cheese is melted; replace tops.
Yield: 5 servings.

Chipped Beef on Toast   micro wave

Prep Time: 10 min.

A creamy sauce that's prepared in the microwave is the base to this fast-to-fix dish, which makes a light dinner or hearty breakfast. Serve it over toast or in puff pastry shells. —Jane Fry, Lancaster, Pennsylvania

1/4 cup butter, cubed
1/4 cup all-purpose flour
2 cups milk
2 packages (2-1/2 ounces *each*) thinly sliced dried beef
4 slices bread, toasted and halved

In a microwave-safe bowl, microwave butter on high for 35 seconds or until melted. Stir in flour until smooth. Gradually stir in milk.

Microwave, uncovered, on high for 2-3 minutes or until thickened, stirring every minute. Stir in beef; cook on high for 1 minute or until heated through. Serve on toast.
Yield: 4 servings.

Editor's Note: This recipe was tested in a 1,100-watt microwave.

Corned Beef and Cabbage Sandwiches

Prep Time: 10 min.

You don't have to wait for St. Patrick's Day to serve these festive sandwiches. Your family is sure to enjoy the creamy cabbage and tender corned beef piled high on a hard roll any time of year. —Taste of Home Test Kitchen

1/3 cup mayonnaise
1 tablespoon white vinegar
1/4 teaspoon ground mustard
1/4 teaspoon celery seed
1/4 teaspoon pepper
1-1/2 cups thinly shredded raw cabbage
4 kaiser *or* hard rolls, split
3/4 to 1 pound fully cooked corned beef, sliced

In a small bowl, combine the mayonnaise, vinegar, mustard, celery seed and pepper. Stir in cabbage. Spoon onto the bottom halves of rolls. Cover with corned beef; replace roll tops.
Yield: 4 servings.

Steak Diane

Prep: 20 min.

When I want to provide a memorable dinner but don't want to spend hours in the kitchen, this is the recipe I rely on. I've used it many times on holidays or other occasions for a quick, impressive main dish. We relish the savory sauce poured over the steaks. —Phoebe Carre, Mullica Hill, New Jersey

4 beef rib eye steaks (1/2 inch thick and 8 ounces *each*)
1/4 teaspoon pepper
1/8 teaspoon salt
2 tablespoons finely chopped green onion
1/2 teaspoon ground mustard
4 tablespoons butter, *divided*
1 tablespoon lemon juice
1-1/2 teaspoons Worcestershire sauce
1 tablespoon minced fresh parsley
1 tablespoon minced fresh chives

Sprinkle steaks on both sides with pepper and salt. In a large skillet, cook onion and mustard in 2 tablespoons butter for 1 minute. Add steaks; cook for 2-5 minutes on each side or until the meat reaches desired doneness (for medium-rare, a meat thermometer should read 145°; medium, 160°; well-done, 170°).

Remove steaks to a serving platter and keep warm. In the same skillet, add the lemon juice, Worcestershire sauce and remaining butter; cook and stir for 2 minutes or until thickened. Add parsley and chives. Serve with steaks.
Yield: 4 servings.

Teriyaki Sirloin Steak

plan ahead

Prep: 10 min. + marinating | Grill: 10 min.

Since a co-worker shared this recipe with me, I seldom make steak any other way. It's an excellent entree for folks who really savor tasty meat, and it's earned me many compliments on my cooking.
—Nilah Lewis, Calgary, Alberta

1/2 cup soy sauce
1/4 cup vegetable oil
1/4 cup packed brown sugar
2 teaspoons ground mustard
2 teaspoons ground ginger
1 teaspoon garlic powder
1 to 1-1/2 pounds boneless beef sirloin steak (3/4 inch thick)

In a large resealable plastic bag, combine the first six ingredients; add the steak. Seal bag and turn to coat; refrigerate for 8 hours or overnight.

Preheat grill.

Drain and discard marinade. Grill steak, covered, over medium heat for 5-8 minutes on each side or until meat reaches desired doneness (for medium-rare, a meat thermometer should read 145°; medium, 160°; well-done, 170°).
Yield: 4-6 servings.

Editor's Note: Marinate steak the night before or first thing in the morning. The steak can also be broiled.

Chili Burgers

Prep: 20 min.

Chili Burgers are hearty, easy-to-assemble sandwiches. The savory chili and french-fried onions are a fun alternative to traditional burger toppings like ketchup and mustard. —Sue Ross, Casa Grande, Arizona

1 pound ground beef
1-1/2 teaspoons chili powder
1 can (15 ounces) chili with beans
4 hamburger buns, split and toasted
1/2 cup shredded cheddar cheese
1 can (2.8 ounces) french-fried onions

In a large bowl, combine beef and chili powder. Shape into four patties. Pan-fry, grill or broil until meat is no longer pink and a thermometer reads 160°.

Meanwhile, in a small saucepan, bring chili to a boil. Reduce heat; simmer for 5 minutes or until heated through. Place burgers on bun bottoms; top with chili, cheese and onions. Replace bun tops.
Yield: 4 servings.

Mushroom Cheeseburgers
Prep: 20 min.

Instead of topping juicy cheeseburgers with sauteed mushrooms, include some savory 'shrooms in the meat mixture for a new twist! Folks will be pleasantly surprised with these deluxe sandwiches...bite after bite. —Taste of Home Test Kitchen

1 pound ground beef
1/4 cup chopped canned
   mushrooms
1/4 cup finely chopped
   onion
1 teaspoon dried oregano
1/2 teaspoon salt
1/2 teaspoon pepper
4 slices process American
   cheese
4 hamburger buns, split
Lettuce leaves, optional

Preheat grill.

In a large bowl, combine beef, mushrooms, onion, oregano, salt and pepper. Shape into four patties.

Grill burgers, uncovered, over medium heat for 5-7 minutes on each side or until no longer pink. Top each burger with a slice of cheese. Serve on buns with lettuce if desired.
Yield: 4 servings.

Editor's Note: The burgers can also be broiled or cooked with an indoor grill.

Italian Beef Sandwiches
Prep: 20 min.

Italian Beef Sandwiches are ready in a snap. I simply stop at the deli on the way home from work to pick up sliced roast beef and sandwich buns. Served with an au jus created by dressing up canned beef broth, the pepper-topped sandwiches make a perfect weeknight dinner. —Pat Fredericks, Oak Creek, Wisconsin

1 can (14-1/2 ounces) beef broth
2 garlic cloves, minced
1 teaspoon dried oregano
1/8 teaspoon pepper
1 medium green pepper, thinly
   sliced into rings
1 pound thinly sliced deli roast beef
6 hoagie buns, split

In a skillet, add the broth, garlic, oregano and pepper; bring to a boil. Add green pepper. Reduce heat; simmer, uncovered, about 5 minutes or until green pepper is tender. Remove green pepper with a slotted spoon; keep warm.

Return broth to a boil. Add roast beef; cover and remove from the heat. Let stand for 2 minutes or until heated through. Place beef and green pepper on buns; serve with broth for dipping.
Yield: 6 servings.

Zesty Steak Salad

Prep: 20 min.

Add any other of your favorite salad ingredients like shredded cheese, croutons, mushrooms or cucumber to this meaty salad. —Leah Carrell, Quitman, Texas

 1 pound boneless beef top sirloin steak, cut into strips
1/3 cup Worcestershire sauce
 1 medium onion, julienned
 1 medium green pepper, julienned
 1 tablespoon butter
 6 cups shredded lettuce
 6 to 9 cherry tomatoes, halved
Salsa, optional

In a large bowl, combine sirloin and Worcestershire sauce; cover and refrigerate.

Meanwhile, in a large skillet, saute onion and green pepper in butter for 3-4 minutes or until crisp-tender. Add sirloin; stir-fry until meat is no longer pink. Spoon meat and vegetables over lettuce; garnish with tomatoes. Serve with salsa if desired. **Yield: 4-6 servings.**

Editor's Note: To save time, use a package of ready-to-serve salad greens.

Savory Beef and Noodles

Prep: 20 min.

No one can resist a hearty entree like this. It's true comfort food at its finest. The recipe calls for only 1/2 cup gravy. Refrigerate the remainder and serve it with potatoes or leftover roast beef at another meal. —Taste of Home Test Kitchen

1 pound ground beef
1 can (10-1/2 ounces) condensed French onion soup, undiluted
1/2 cup beef gravy
1 can (4 ounces) mushroom stems and pieces, drained
1 tablespoon all-purpose flour
1 tablespoon water
Hot cooked noodles
Minced fresh parsley, optional

In a large skillet, cook beef over medium heat until no longer pink; drain. Stir in the soup, gravy and mushrooms. Bring to a boil. Reduce heat; cover and simmer for 5 minutes.

In a small bowl, combine flour and water until smooth; stir into beef mixture. Bring to a boil; cook and stir for 2 minutes or until thickened. Serve over hot cooked noodles. Garnish with fresh parsley if desired. **Yield: 4 servings.**

Editor's Note: Start heating the water for the noodles before you begin cooking the ground beef.

Barbecue Macaroni Beef

Prep: 20 min.

My husband's Grandma Curten used to make this meal for him when he was a little boy. It's a regular around our house, which is fine with me, because it's easy to fix and so good. The veggies add a nice crunch. —Rose Curten, Modoc, Illinois

8 ounces elbow macaroni
1 pound ground beef
1 bottle (28 ounces) barbecue sauce
1 medium onion, chopped
1 medium green pepper, chopped
3 celery ribs, chopped

Cook the macaroni according to package directions. Meanwhile, in a large skillet, cook beef over medium heat until no longer pink; drain. Drain macaroni. Stir the macaroni, barbecue sauce, macaroni, onion, green pepper and celery into ground beef. Cook, uncovered, until heated through. **Yield: 4 servings.**

The Busy Family Cookbook

Italian Flank Steak

plan ahead

Prep: 10 min. + marinating | Grill: 10 min.

Savory and satisfying, this steak is nice for entertaining or busy days since it marinates overnight and grills in minutes.
—Walajean Saglett, Canandaiqua, New York

2 envelopes (.7 ounce *each*) fat-free Italian salad dressing mix

2 tablespoons vegetable oil

1 tablespoon lemon juice

1 beef flank steak (1 pound)

In a small bowl, combine the salad dressing mix, oil and lemon juice. Brush onto both sides of steak; place in a shallow dish. Cover and refrigerate several hours or overnight.

Preheat grill.

Grill over medium heat for 6-8 minutes on each side until meat reaches desired doneness (for medium-rare a meat thermometer should read 145°; medium, 160°; well-done, 170°). To serve, thinly slice across the grain.
Yield: 4 servings.

Editor's Note: Brush marinade on steak the night before or first thing in the morning. The steak can also be broiled.

Beef Fried Rice

Prep: 20 min.

Years ago, I frequently depended on economical ground beef to feed my three hungry kids. I fixed it every way imaginable. This was one of our favorites.
—Edith Haney, Erie, Pennsylvania

1 pound ground beef

3 eggs

Dash pepper

3 tablespoons vegetable oil, *divided*

2 cups cold cooked long grain rice

2 small onions, chopped

3 tablespoons soy sauce

1 teaspoon sugar

In a skillet, cook beef over medium heat until no longer pink; drain. In a large bowl, beat eggs and pepper. In skillet, heat 1 tablespoon oil over medium-high heat. Pour eggs into skillet. As eggs set, lift edges, letting uncooked portion flow underneath.

When eggs are completely cooked, remove from the skillet; cut into strips

Return to pan. Stir in the remaining ingredients. Cook and stir over medium-low heat in remaining oil for 5 minutes or until heated through.
Yield: 6 servings.

Editor's Note: When cooking rice, make extra. Cooked rice can be refrigerated for up to 7 days and frozen for up to 6 months. For convenience, package a cup or two of rice in refrigerator/freezer bags. Flatten rice out in the bags before freezing. That way it will defrost more quickly.

Grilled Roast Beef Sandwiches

Prep: 15 min.

I first tasted a memorable combination of roast beef and green chilies at a local cafe. In this recipe, the chilies give the quick grilled sandwich a little bite. It's simple and delicious. —Karen Ledbetter, Fort Collins, Colorado

1 can (4 ounces) chopped green chilies, drained
2 tablespoons mayonnaise
1 tablespoon Dijon mustard
10 slices rye bread
5 slices Swiss cheese
10 thin slices cooked roast beef
2 tablespoons butter, softened
Salsa, optional

In a small bowl, combine the chilies, mayonnaise and mustard; spread about 1 tablespoon on one side of each slice of bread. Top five slices of bread with 1 slice of cheese and 2 slices of beef. Cover with remaining bread.

Butter the outsides of bread. In a skillet over medium heat, toast sandwiches for 4-5 minutes on each side or until bread is lightly browned and cheese is melted. Serve with salsa if desired.
Yield: 5 servings.

Gingered Pepper Steak

Prep: 15 min.

This wonderfully tender steak is a treat even for folks not watching their diet. When my mother-in-law shared the recipe, she said it cooks up in no time, and she was right.
—Susan Adair, Muncie, Indiana

2 teaspoons sugar
2 teaspoons cornstarch
1/4 teaspoon ground ginger
1/4 cup reduced-sodium soy sauce
1 tablespoon white wine vinegar
1 pound beef flank steak, thinly sliced
2 medium green peppers, julienned
1 teaspoon vegetable oil
Hot cooked rice, optional

In a large bowl, combine the sugar, cornstarch, ginger, soy sauce and vinegar until smooth. Add beef and toss to coat; set aside.

In a large skillet or wok, stir-fry green peppers in oil until crisp-tender, about 3 minutes. Remove with a slotted spoon and keep warm. Add beef with marinade to pan; stir-fry for 3 minutes or until meat reaches desired doneness. Return peppers to pan; heat through. Serve over rice if desired. **Yield: 4 servings.**

Editor's Note: When minutes count, use instant white or brown rice.

Sloppy Joe Burgers

Prep: 20 min.

Five ingredients and a few minutes is all it takes to whip up this satisfying sandwich.
—Leann Jasper, Newmarket, Ontario

1 pound ground beef
2 tablespoons all-purpose flour
1 can (10-1/2 ounces) condensed French onion soup, undiluted
1/4 teaspoon Worcestershire sauce
6 hamburger buns, split and toasted

In a large skillet, cook beef over medium heat until no longer pink; drain. Stir in the flour, soup and Worcestershire sauce until blended. Bring to a boil; cook and stir over medium heat for 2 minutes or until thickened. Serve on buns. **Yield: 6 servings.**

Pepper Steak Sandwiches

Prep: 20 min.

My family loves these warm sandwiches, which dresses up deli roast beef with sauteed peppers, cheese and Italian salad dressing. Include a salad or soup, and your meal is set.
—Hosanna Miller, Dundee, Ohio

> 1 medium onion, thinly sliced
> 1 medium green pepper, thinly sliced
> 1 medium sweet red pepper, thinly sliced
> 1/2 cup mayonnaise, *divided*
> 3/4 pound thinly sliced deli roast beef
> 1/4 cup Italian salad dressing
> 5 sandwich rolls, split
> 3/4 cup shredded part-skim mozzarella cheese

In a large skillet, saute the onion and peppers in 2 tablespoons mayonnaise until crisp-tender. Remove vegetables and keep warm.

In the same skillet, add the roast beef, Italian dressing and remaining mayonnaise. Cook and stir for 4-5 minutes or until heated through. Place beef and vegetables on rolls; sprinkle with mozzarella cheese. **Yield: 5 servings.**

Editor's Note: Reduced-fat or fat-free mayonnaise is not recommended for this recipe.

Zippy Burgers

Prep: 20 min.

This easy recipe enhances lean ground beef with onion powder, chili powder and red pepper flakes. These satisfying burgers are sure to sizzle in any summer meal.
—Taste of Home Test Kitchen

> 1/4 cup beer *or* beef broth
> 2 tablespoons Worcestershire sauce
> 2 teaspoons chili powder
> 1 teaspoon onion powder
> 1/2 teaspoon crushed red pepper flakes
> 1/4 teaspoon salt
> 1/4 teaspoon pepper
> 1 pound lean ground beef
> 4 hamburger buns, split

Coat grill rack with nonstick cooking spray before starting the grill. Preheat grill.

In a large bowl, combine the first seven ingredients. Crumble beef over mixture and mix well. Shape into four patties.

Grill hamburgers, covered, over medium heat for 6-8 minutes on each side or until meat is no longer pink. Serve on buns. **Yield: 4 servings.**

Editor's Note: These burgers can also be broiled or cooked with an indoor grill.

The Busy Family Cookbook

Taco Sandwich

Prep: 20 min.

This is like a taco on French bread. It's great when you don't have a taco shells or tortillas. The cream cheese-salsa spread adds a pleasant flavor boost.
—Melody Stoltzfus, Parkesburg, Pennsylvania

- 1 pound ground beef
- 1 loaf (1 pound) unsliced Italian bread
- 4 ounces cream cheese, softened
- 1/2 cup salsa
- 2 tablespoons taco seasoning
- 1 cup shredded lettuce
- 1 large tomato, sliced
- 6 slices American cheese

In a large skillet, cook beef over medium heat until no longer pink. Meanwhile, cut bread in half lengthwise; hollow out top and bottom of loaf, leaving a 1/2-in. shell (discard removed bread or save for another use). In a small mixing bowl, beat cream cheese and salsa until blended. Spread inside bread shell; set aside.

Drain beef. Stir in taco seasoning. Layer lettuce and tomato in bottom of bread shell; top with beef mixture and cheese. Replace bread top.
Yield: 6 servings.

Mushroom Beef Tenderloin

Prep: 20 min.

This quick-to-fix dish looks special and tastes delicious. A delightful mushroom sauce nicely complements the juicy beef. I like to serve it with toasted French bread.
—Blanche Stevens, Anderson, Indiana

3/4 pound fresh mushrooms, sliced
  5 tablespoons butter, *divided*
  2 teaspoons all-purpose flour
  1 teaspoon salt
1/4 teaspoon pepper
  1 cup heavy whipping cream
  1 tablespoon minced fresh parsley
  6 beef tenderloin steaks (1-1/2
     inches thick and 4 ounces *each*)

In a large skillet, saute mushrooms in 3 tablespoons butter for 6-8 minutes or until tender. Stir in the flour, salt and pepper until blended. Gradually add the cream. Bring to a gentle boil; cook and stir for 1-2 minutes or until thickened. Stir in parsley; set aside and keep warm.

Meanwhile, in another large skillet, heat the remaining butter over medium-high heat. Cook steaks for 6-7 minutes on each side or until meat reaches desired doneness (for medium-rare, a meat thermometer should read 145°; medium, 160°; well-done, 170°). Serve with the mushroom sauce.
Yield: 6 servings.

Editor's Note: To save time, buy presliced mushrooms.

Bacon Cheeseburger Pasta

Prep: 20 min.

I try to make all my recipes not only kid friendly, but easy to reheat since my husband works long hours and often eats later than our children. If you like, use reduced-fat cheese and ground turkey for a lighter version. —Melissa Stevens, Elk River, Minnesota

- 8 ounces uncooked penne pasta
- 1 pound ground beef
- 6 bacon strips, diced
- 1 can (10-3/4 ounces) condensed tomato soup, undiluted
- 1 cup (4 ounces) shredded cheddar cheese

Barbecue sauce and prepared mustard, optional

Cook pasta according to package directions. Meanwhile, in a large skillet, cook beef over medium heat until no longer pink; drain and set aside.

In the same skillet, cook bacon until crisp. Using a slotted spoon, remove to paper towels; drain discarding drippings. Drain pasta; add to the skillet. Stir in the soup, beef and bacon; heat through. Sprinkle with cheese; cover and cook until the cheese is melted. Serve with barbecue sauce and mustard if desired.
Yield: 4-6 servings.

Editor's Note: To save time, use precooked bacon, which is available in the packaged deli meat section of the supermarket.

Cube Steak Diane

Prep: 20 min.

Dijon mustard and grape juice combine in a flavorful sauce for this easy and economical take on a classic dish. —Lauren Heyn, Oak Creek, Wisconsin

- 4 beef cube steaks
- 1/4 cup butter, cubed
- 1/2 cup white grape juice
- 2 tablespoons Worcestershire sauce
- 4 teaspoons Dijon mustard

Salt and pepper to taste

In a large skillet, saute steaks in butter for 2 minutes on each side or meat is no longer pink; drain.

In a small bowl, combine the grape juice, Worcestershire sauce and mustard; stir into cooking juices. Bring to a boil; cook for 1 minute. Remove steaks and keep warm. Cook the sauce 1-2 minutes longer or until thickened. Season with salt and pepper. Serve over cube steaks.
Yield: 4 servings.

One-for-All Marinated Beef

plan ahead

Prep: 5 min. + marinating | Grill: 15 min. + standing

I use this great marinade not just for beef, but for everything I grill—from pork chops to chicken.—Sue Sauer, Deer River, Minnesota

3/4 cup orange juice
1/4 cup reduced-sodium soy sauce
2 tablespoons brown sugar
2 tablespoons prepared mustard
1 tablespoon canola oil
2 garlic cloves, minced
1 beef flank steak (1-1/2 pounds)

In a large resealable plastic bag, combine the first six ingredients; add steak. Seal bag and turn to coat; refrigerate for 4 hours or overnight.

Coat grill rack with nonstick cooking spray before starting grill. Preheat grill.

Drain and discard marinade. Grill steak, covered, over medium heat 6-8 minutes on each side or until meat reaches desired doneness (for medium-rare, a meat thermometer should read 145°; medium, 160°; well-done, 170°). Let stand for 10 minutes before slicing.
Yield: 6 servings.

Editor's Note: Marinate steak the night before or first thing in the morning. The steak can also be broiled.

Spicy Grilled Steaks

Prep: 20 min.

Rubs are a wonderful way to add flavor to meat when you don't have time to marinate. Meat lovers will be in their glory when they see (and smell!) these steaks sizzling on the grill. —Taste of Home Test Kitchen

1 tablespoon paprika
2 teaspoons dried thyme
1 teaspoon onion powder
1 teaspoon garlic powder
1/2 teaspoon rubbed sage
1/2 teaspoon salt
1/2 teaspoon pepper
1/2 teaspoon cayenne pepper
4 boneless beef top loin steaks (1 inch thick and about 12 ounces *each*)

Preheat grill.

In a small bowl, combine the first eight ingredients. Rub about 1 teaspoon of spice mixture over each side of steaks.

Grill, covered, over medium heat for 7-9 minutes on each side or until meat reaches desired doneness (for medium-rare, a meat thermometer should read 145°; medium, 160°; well-done, 170°).
Yield: 4 servings.

Editor's Note: The steak can also be broiled.

Pepper Steak with Potatoes

micro wave

Prep: 15 min. | Cook: 15 min.

I added potatoes to an Asian favorite to create this well-rounded skillet dish. It's a snap to prepare because the potatoes are cooked in the microwave, plus it's hearty enough to satisfy all the men in our house. —Kristine Marra, Clifton Park, New York

5 medium red potatoes, cut into 1/4-inch slices
1/2 cup water
1 pound boneless beef sirloin steak, thinly sliced
1 garlic clove, minced
2 tablespoons olive oil
1 medium green pepper, julienned
1 small onion, chopped
Pepper to taste
4 teaspoons cornstarch
1 cup beef broth

Place the potatoes and water in a microwave-safe bowl; cover and microwave on high for 5-7 minutes or until tender.

Meanwhile, in a large skillet, saute beef and garlic in oil until meat is no longer pink. Remove and keep warm; drain drippings. In the same skillet, saute green pepper and onion until crisp-tender. Return beef to the pan. Add potatoes and pepper; heat through.

In a small saucepan, combine cornstarch and broth until smooth. Bring to a boil; cook and stir for 2 minutes or until thickened. Drizzle over meat mixture; toss to coat. **Yield: 6 servings.**

Editor's Note: This recipe was tested in a 1,100-watt microwave.

Jalapeno Swiss Burgers

Prep: 10 min. | Grill: 20 min.

Mexican culture greatly influences our cuisine, and we eat a lot of spicy foods. In this recipe, the mellow flavor of Swiss cheese cuts the heat of the jalapenos. —Jeanine Richardson, Floresville, Texas

2 pounds ground beef
4 slices Swiss cheese
1 small onion, thinly sliced
2 to 3 pickled jalapeno peppers, seeded and julienned
4 hamburger buns, split

Preheat grill.

Shape beef into eight thin patties. Top four patties with the cheese, onion and jalapenos. Top with remaining patties; press edges firmly to seal. Grill, covered, over medium heat for 8-9 minutes on each side or until no longer pink. Serve on buns. **Yield: 4 servings.**

Editor's Note: When cutting or seeding hot peppers, use rubber or plastic gloves to protect your hands. Avoid touching your face.

Cold Day Chili

Prep: 5 min. | Cook: 25 min.

I like to make chili from beans I've soaked overnight, but this speedier version tastes just as good on a frosty winter day. The mildly sweet mixture of beef and beans is economical, too. —Lucile Proctor, Panguitch, Utah

1 pound ground beef
1 medium onion, halved and thinly sliced
2 cans (16 ounces *each*) kidney beans, rinsed and drained
1 can (14-1/2 ounces) diced tomatoes, undrained
1/2 to 3/4 cup water
1 to 2 tablespoons brown sugar
1 tablespoon chili powder
1 tablespoon white vinegar
2 teaspoons prepared mustard
1 teaspoon salt
1/8 teaspoon pepper

In a large saucepan, cook beef and onion over medium heat until the meat is no longer pink; drain. Add the remaining ingredients. Bring to a boil; reduce heat. Cover and simmer for 10 minutes or until heated through.
Yield: 4 servings.

Editor's Note: Before cooking the beef and onion, measure out the dry seasonings and place in a custard cup. Place vinegar and mustard in another custard cup. That way, you're ready to add the seasoning when the meat is browned.

Philly Cheese Steak Pizza

Prep: 15 min. | **Bake: 15 min.**

Crescent roll crust is topped with deli beef, mozzarella cheese and sauteed veggies for a tasty meal. The quick combination offers the terrific taste of the traditional sandwich in a fun new way. —Maria Regakis, Somerville, Massachusetts

1 tube (8 ounces) refrigerated crescent rolls
1 medium green pepper, chopped
1 medium onion, chopped
2 tablespoons olive oil
1/4 teaspoon beef bouillon granules
1/2 pound thinly sliced deli roast beef
1 tablespoon prepared Italian salad dressing
1-1/2 cups (6 ounces) shredded part-skim mozzarella cheese

Preheat oven to 375°.

Unroll crescent roll dough into one long rectangle; seal perforations. Press onto the bottom and up the sides of an ungreased 13-in. x 9-in. x 2-in. baking dish. Bake at 375° for 7-10 minutes or until lightly browned.

Meanwhile, in a large skillet, saute the green pepper, onion in oil and bouillon until vegetables are tender; set aside.

Arrange beef over crust. Brush with salad dressing and sprinkle with mozzarella cheese. Bake 4-5 minutes longer or until cheese is melted. Top with green pepper mixture. Cut into squares.
Yield: 6 servings.

Minestrone Macaroni

Prep: 5 min. | Cook: 25 min.

This is by far the easiest, tastiest economical recipe I've found. It seems to taste even better as a leftover. —Diane Varner, Elizabeth, Colorado

1 pound ground beef
2 cans (14-1/2 ounces *each*) Italian diced tomatoes, undrained
2-1/4 cups water
1-1/2 cups uncooked elbow macaroni
2 beef bouillon cubes
1 can (16 ounces) kidney beans, rinsed and drained
1 can (15 ounces) garbanzo beans, rinsed and drained
1 can (14-1/2 ounces) cut green beans, rinsed and drained

In a large skillet, cook beef over medium heat until no longer pink; drain. Add the tomatoes, water, macaroni and bouillon; bring to a boil. Reduce heat; cover and simmer for 12-15 minutes or until macaroni is tender. Stir in beans and cook until heated through.
Yield: 6 servings.

Onion Salisbury Steak

Prep: 5 min. | Cook: 20 min.

I've relied on this stick-to-your-ribs recipe for as long as I can remember. Ground beef patties, tender onions and a rich gravy top toasted bread to make this Depression-era favorite.
—Claudine Moffatt, Manchester, Missouri

1 pound lean ground beef
1/2 teaspoon salt
1/8 to 1/4 teaspoon pepper
2 medium onions, thinly sliced
4 slices bread, toasted
1/4 cup all-purpose flour
1-1/2 cups water
1 tablespoon beef bouillon granules

In a large bowl, combine the beef, salt and pepper; shape into four oval patties. In a large skillet, brown patties on one side. Turn and add onions. Cook until meat is no longer pink.

Place toast on serving plates. Top each with onions and a beef patty; keep warm.

Stir flour into skillet until blended. Gradually add water; stir in bouillon. Bring to a boil; cook and stir for 2 minutes or until thickened and bubbly. Serve with meat and onions. **Yield: 4 servings.**

Reuben Monte Cristos

Prep: 15 min. | Cook: 10 min.

Leftover corned beef is used to make a twist on a traditional Reuben. The sandwiches are dipped in egg and crushed corn chips before grilling them to crunchy perfection. These tasty sandwiches are great with a cup of soup. —Michelle Rhodes, Cleveland, Ohio

2 eggs
1 tablespoon milk
2-1/2 cups corn chips, crushed
8 slices rye bread
1/2 cup Thousand Island salad dressing
12 slices deli corned beef
8 slices Swiss cheese
1 cup sauerkraut, rinsed and well drained

In a shallow bowl, beat the eggs and milk. Place chips in another shallow bowl. Dip one side of four slices of bread in the egg mixture, then in the chips. Place chip side down on a greased baking sheet. Spread salad dressing on each slice. Layer each with 1 slice corned beef, 1 slice Swiss cheese and 1/4 cup sauerkraut.

Dip the one side of the remaining bread slices in egg mixture and chips; place chip side up on sandwiches.

On a large skillet or griddle, toast sandwiches over medium-high heat for 4-5 minutes on each side or until bread is lightly browned and cheese is melted. **Yield: 4 servings.**

Corn Bread Hamburger Pie

Prep: 15 min. | **Bake: 15 min.**

This one-dish skillet supper is a big hit with children. We've added green beans and other vegetables to it and it always turns out. —Carol Ellis, Quartzsite, Arizona

1 pound ground beef
1 medium onion, chopped
1 medium green pepper, chopped
1 package (8-1/2 ounces) corn bread/muffin mix
1 can (10-3/4 ounces) condensed tomato soup, undiluted
1/4 cup salsa
2 tablespoons ketchup
1 tablespoon steak sauce, optional
Minced fresh parsley, optional

Preheat oven to 400°.

In a 10-in. ovenproof skillet, cook the beef, onion and green pepper over medium heat until meat is no longer pink; drain. Meanwhile, prepare corn bread batter according to package directions; let stand for 2 minutes.

Stir next four ingredients into beef mixture. Spoon corn bread batter over beef mixture. Bake, uncovered, at 400° for 15 minutes or until lightly browned. Sprinkle with parsley if desired. **Yield: 4-6 servings.**

Editor's Note: To save time, buy prechopped green pepper and onion. Look for them in the produce or frozen vegetable section of your supermarket.

Almost Stuffed Peppers

Prep: 5 min. | **Cook: 25 min.**

For a quick way to enjoy an old favorite, stir up the makings for stuffed green peppers in a skillet. This easy, one-pan meal is requested so often, I even make it when I'm not in a hurry. —Jan Roat, Red Lodge, Montana

1 pound ground beef
2 cups water
1 can (14-1/2 ounces) diced tomatoes, undrained
1 large green pepper, cut into 1/4-inch slices
1 medium onion, thinly sliced
1-1/2 teaspoons salt
1/2 teaspoon Italian seasoning
1/2 teaspoon pepper
1-1/2 cups uncooked instant rice

In a large skillet, cook beef over medium heat until no longer pink; drain. Remove; set aside and keep warm.

In the same skillet, combine the water, tomatoes, green pepper, onion and seasonings; bring to a boil. Reduce heat; simmer, uncovered, until vegetables are tender. Stir in rice; cover and remove from the heat. Let stand for 5 minutes. Stir in beef; return to the heat and cook until heated through.
Yield: 4-6 servings.

Spicy Flank Steak

Prep: 10 min. | Cook: 20 min.

The cool and creamy sour cream sauce is a wonderful addition to the spicy steak. —Taste of Home Test Kitchen

1/3 cup sour cream

2 tablespoons mayonnaise

1/2 teaspoon garlic powder

1/4 teaspoon celery salt

2 tablespoons chili sauce

1 tablespoon lime juice

1/2 to 1 teaspoon crushed red pepper flakes

1/4 teaspoon salt

1 beef flank steak (1 to 1-1/2 pounds)

In a small bowl, combine the sour cream, mayonnaise, garlic powder and celery salt; cover and refrigerate until serving. Combine the chili sauce, lime juice, pepper flakes and salt; brush on each side of steak.

Broil 2-3 in. from the heat for 6-8 minutes on each side or until meat reaches desired doneness (for medium-rare, a meat thermometer should read 145°; medium, 160°; well-done, 170°). Let stand for 5 minutes. Cut across the grain into thin strips. Serve with the sour cream sauce. **Yield: 6 servings.**

Editor's Note: The steak can also be grilled, uncovered, over medium heat.

One-Dish Spaghetti

Prep: 10 min. | Cook: 20 min.

I rely on this made-in-minutes main dish quite often. You don't even have to precook the spaghetti. Served with a green salad and garlic bread, it makes a quick-and-easy supper. —Trudie Reed, Orange, California

1 pound ground beef

1 large onion, chopped

1 to 2 garlic cloves, minced

2 cans (8 ounces *each*) tomato sauce

1-1/2 cups water

1/2 teaspoon salt

1/2 teaspoon dried oregano

4 ounces uncooked spaghetti, broken into thirds

Grated Parmesan cheese

In a 2-1/2-qt. microwave-safe dish, combine the beef, onion and garlic. Cover and microwave on high for 1-1/2 minutes; stir to crumble meat. Cook 1-2 minutes longer or until meat is no longer pink; drain. Stir in the tomato sauce, water, salt and oregano. Cover and microwave on high for 2-1/2 minutes.

Stir in the spaghetti; toss to coat. Cover and cook on high for 9-11 minutes, stirring twice. Let stand for 5 minutes. Serve with Parmesan cheese. **Yield: 4 servings.**

Editor's Note: This recipe was tested in a 1,100-watt microwave.

Barbecued Onion Meat Loaves

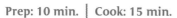

micro wave

Prep: 10 min. | Cook: 15 min.

These moist meat loaves get plenty of flavor from barbecue sauce and dry onion soup mix. The recipe is also handy during the summer when I don't want to turn on the oven.
—Nicole Russman, Lincoln, Nebraska

1 egg, lightly beaten
1/3 cup milk
2 tablespoons plus 1/4 cup barbecue sauce, *divided*
1/2 cup crushed seasoned stuffing
1 tablespoon onion soup mix
1-1/4 pounds lean ground beef

In a bowl, combine the egg, milk, 2 tablespoons barbecue sauce, stuffing and onion soup mix. Crumble beef over mixture and mix well. Shape into five loaves; arrange around the edge of a microwave-safe dish.

Microwave, uncovered, on high for 4-1/2 to 6 minutes or until a meat thermometer reads 160°. Cover and let stand for 5-10 minutes. Top with the remaining barbecue sauce.
Yield: 5 servings.

Editor's Note: This recipe was tested in a 1,000-watt microwave.

Corned Beef Stir-Fry

Prep: 5 min. | Cook: 25 min.

The celery seed really comes through in this colorful combination of carrots, cabbage and corned beef. A woman at church shared the recipe with me. My husband and son love its slightly sweet taste. —Alesah Padgett, Franklin, Georgia

7 tablespoons vegetable oil, *divided*
3 tablespoons white vinegar
2 tablespoons sugar
1 teaspoon celery seed
1/4 teaspoon salt
6 cups coarsely chopped cabbage
1 cup shredded carrots
1/4 cup chopped green onions
1/2 pound thinly sliced corned beef

In a small bowl, whisk 4 tablespoons oil, vinegar, sugar, celery seed and salt until sugar is dissolved; set aside.

In a large skillet, saute the cabbage, carrots and onions in remaining oil for 15 minutes or until crisp-tender. Stir in vinegar-oil mixture and corned beef. Cover and simmer for 10 minutes or until heated through.
Yield: 4-6 servings.

Editor's Note: To save time, buy preshredded carrots.

Cheeseburger Chowder

Prep: 5 min. | Cook: 20 min.

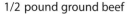

After tasting a wonderful chowder at a restaurant, I dressed up a can of cheese soup to see if I could capture the same flavors. I then took things a step further by adding chilies and Southwestern spices. I hope you enjoy it as much as I do.
—Lori Risdal, Sioux City, Iowa

1/2 pound ground beef
1 can (10-3/4 ounces) condensed cheddar cheese soup, undiluted
1-3/4 cups milk
1 cup frozen shredded hash brown potatoes
1 can (4 ounces) chopped green chilies
1 tablespoon taco seasoning
1 tablespoon dried minced onion
1/2 teaspoon chili powder
Coarsely crushed corn chips, shredded Monterey Jack cheese and chopped green onions, optional

In a large saucepan, cook beef over medium heat until no longer pink; drain. Stir in the soup, milk, potatoes, chilies, taco seasoning, onion and chili powder until blended. Bring to a boil. Reduce heat; simmer, uncovered, for 5 minutes or until heated through. Garnish with corn chips, cheese and green onions if desired. **Yield: 4 servings.**

30
minute recipes

Asian Beef Noodles
Prep: 15 min. | Cook: 15 min.

We've raised beef the majority of our lives, so I like to try new recipes that feature it. This recipe is different and absolutely delicious. —Margery Bryan, Royal City, Washington

1 package (3 ounces) beef-flavored ramen noodles
1 pound boneless beef sirloin steak (3/4 inch thick)
1 jalapeno pepper, seeded and finely chopped
1 tablespoon vegetable oil
2 tablespoons water
1 tablespoon steak sauce
1 medium carrot, shredded
2 tablespoons sliced green onion
1/4 cup peanut halves

Set aside seasoning packet from noodles. Prepare noodles according to package directions; drain and set aside.

While noodles are cooking, cut steak into 3-in. x 1/2-in. strips. In a large skillet, stir-fry the beef and jalapeno in oil for 1-2 minutes or until meat is no longer pink. Remove and keep warm.

In the same skillet, combine the noodles, water, steak sauce, carrot, onion and contents of seasoning packet. Cook and stir until heated through. Return beef to the pan. Sprinkle with peanuts.
Yield: 4 servings.

Editor's Note: When cutting or seeding hot peppers, use rubber or plastic gloves to protect your hands. Avoid touching your face.

Artichoke Beef Steaks

Prep: 10 min. | Cook: 15 min.

Light green artichokes and vibrant pimientos make these colorful steaks perfect. When weather permits, grill the steaks outside.
—Taste of Home Test Kitchen

1 jar (6-1/2 ounces) marinated artichoke hearts

4 boneless beef rib eye steaks (3/4 inch thick and about 8 ounces *each*)

1/2 teaspoon salt

2 tablespoons butter

1 small onion, sliced and separated into rings

1 garlic clove, minced

1 jar (2 ounces) sliced pimientos, drained

Drain artichokes, reserving 1 tablespoon marinade. Coarsely chop artichokes and set aside. Sprinkle steaks with salt.

In a skillet, cook steaks over medium-high heat in butter for 4 minutes on each side or until the meat reaches desired doneness (for medium-rare, a meat thermometer should read 145°; medium, 160°; well-done, 170°). Remove and keep warm.

In same skillet, saute onion and garlic in reserved marinade. Add artichokes and pimientos; heat through. Serve with steaks.
Yield: 4 servings.

Chili Bow Tie Bake

Prep: 5 min. | Cook: 20 min.

Sometimes I'll add canned or frozen corn to this hearty skillet dish to give it more color.
—Rhonda Hogan, Eugene, Oregon

2 cups uncooked bow tie pasta *or* noodles

1 pound ground beef

1/2 cup chopped onion

1 can (16 ounces) kidney beans, rinsed and drained

1 can (15 ounces) tomato sauce

1 can (14-1/2 ounces) stewed tomatoes

1/4 teaspoon garlic powder

1/4 teaspoon salt

1/4 teaspoon pepper

Cook pasta according to package directions. Meanwhile, in a large skillet, cook beef over medium heat until no longer pink; drain. Stir in the beans, tomato sauce, tomatoes, garlic powder, salt and pepper. Bring to a boil. Reduce heat; cover and simmer for 5 minutes. Drain pasta and stir into beef mixture; heat through.
Yield: 6 servings.

Stir-Fried Beef on Lettuce

Prep: 20 min. | Cook: 10 min.

Being from the Philippines, I'm partial to stir-fries. My husband especially likes this refreshing combination of steak and crisp shredded lettuce. —Ninez McConnell, Mill Creek, Washington

1/3 cup reduced-sodium soy sauce
1/3 cup white wine *or* chicken broth
1 pound boneless beef sirloin steak, cut into 1/8-inch strips
1 teaspoon cornstarch
1/2 pound fresh mushrooms, sliced
2 cups fresh snow peas
4 teaspoons vegetable oil, *divided*
4 cups shredded lettuce

In a bowl, combine soy sauce and wine or broth. Reserve 1/4 cup. Pour remaining soy sauce mixture into a large resealable plastic bag; add the beef; seal and turn to coat. Refrigerate for 15 minutes. In a small bowl, combine the cornstarch and reserved soy sauce mixture until smooth; set aside.

In a nonstick skillet, stir-fry mushrooms and snow peas in 2 teaspoons oil for 3-4 minutes or until snow peas are crisp-tender. Remove and keep warm.

Drain and discard marinade. In the same skillet, stir-fry beef in remaining oil for 2 minutes. Stir broth mixture; add to skillet. Bring to a boil; cook and stir for 1-2 minutes or until slightly thickened. Place lettuce on four serving plates. Top with beef mixture and snow pea mixture. **Yield: 4 servings.**

Beef and Pepper Linguine

Prep: 5 min. | Cook: 25 min.

At first I wasn't very interested in this recipe. I didn't make it for years, but decided to give it a try one day. Boy, am I glad I did! —Marilyn Chigas, Peabody, Massachusetts

1 package (16 ounces) linguine
1 pound ground beef
1 large onion, chopped
2 medium green peppers, cubed
4 to 6 tablespoons soy sauce
Dash garlic powder, optional

Cook linguine according to package directions. Meanwhile, in a large skillet, cook the beef, onion and green peppers over medium heat until meat is no longer pink; drain. Remove from the heat.

Drain linguine; add to beef mixture along with the soy sauce; toss to coat. Sprinkle with garlic powder if desired. **Yield: 6 servings.**

T-Bones with Onions

Prep: 10 min. | Grill: 20 min.

Steak gets a dressy treatment when topped with tasty onion slices flavored with honey and mustard. I found this recipe on a bag of charcoal more than 10 years ago. It's terrific with green beans or corn. —Sheree Quate, Cave Junction, Oregon

3 large onions, cut into
1/4-inch-thick slices
2 tablespoons honey
1/2 teaspoon salt
1/2 teaspoon ground mustard
1/2 teaspoon paprika
1/2 teaspoon pepper
4 beef T-bone steaks (1 inch thick
and 12 ounces *each*)
Additional salt and pepper

Preheat grill.

Place onions in the center of a piece of heavy-duty foil (about 20 in. x 18 in.). Drizzle with honey; sprinkle with the salt, mustard, paprika and pepper. Fold foil over onions and seal tightly. Season steaks with additional salt and pepper.

Grill onions and steaks, covered, over medium heat. Grill onions for 10-12 minutes on each side or until tender. Grill steak for 7-10 minutes on each side or until meat reaches desired doneness (for medium-rare, a meat thermometer should read 145°; medium, 160°; well-done, 170°). Let steak stand for 3-5 minutes. Serve with onions.
Yield: 4 servings.

Editor's Note: Place the onion packets on the grill, then season the steaks. After the onions have cooked for about 6 minutes, add the steaks to the grill.

Quicker Boiled Dinner

Prep: 10 min. | Cook: 40 min.

Corned beef dinner is a real home-style treat. This faster version of the classic boiled dinner uses deli corned beef, frozen sliced carrots and coleslaw mix. There's almost no prep! —Taste of Home Test Kitchen

1 pound unsliced deli corned beef
4 small unpeeled red potatoes, quartered
3 cups water
1 to 2 tablespoons pickling spices
1 teaspoon dried minced onion
1 teaspoon garlic salt
1/8 teaspoon dried thyme
2 cups frozen sliced carrots
4 cups coleslaw mix
Prepared horseradish *or* mustard, optional

In a large Dutch oven, combine the corned beef, potatoes and water. Place pickling spices in a double thickness of cheesecloth; bring up corners of cloth and tie with string to form a bag. Add to pan.

Stir in the onion, salt and thyme. Bring to a boil. Reduce heat; cover and simmer for 10 minutes. Add carrots; cover and simmer for 10 minutes or until carrots are crisp-tender. Add coleslaw mix. Bring to a boil. Reduce heat; cover and simmer for 10 minutes or until vegetables are tender.

Discard spice bag. To serve, thinly slice meat across the grain. Serve with the vegetables and horseradish or mustard if desired.
Yield: 4 servings.

Spanish Spirals

Prep: 5 min. | Cook: 45 min.

I usually cook for only me and my husband, so I try to scale down most recipes. But I make this dish just the way it is because my husband loves the leftovers. —Sandy Pelfrey, North Canton, Ohio

1 pound ground beef
1 medium onion, chopped
1 can (28 ounces) diced tomatoes, undrained
2 cups uncooked rotini
2 teaspoons salt
1 teaspoon sugar
1 teaspoon chili powder
1/4 teaspoon garlic powder

In a skillet, cook the beef and onion over medium heat until meat is no longer pink; drain.

Stir in the tomatoes, rotini, salt, sugar, chili powder and garlic powder. Bring to a boil. Reduce heat; cover and simmer for 25-30 minutes or until rotini is tender.
Yield: 4-6 servings.

Sloppy Joe Casserole

Prep: 10 min. | Bake: 35 min.

As a working mom, I need all the time-saving recipes I can get. My two sons prefer this all-in-one dish to sloppy joe sandwiches. —Carol Knight, Norris City, Illinois

1 pound ground beef
3 cups cooked long grain rice
1 can (15-1/2 ounces) sloppy joe sauce
1 can (15-1/4 ounces) whole kernel corn, drained
1 can (4 ounces) mushroom stems and pieces, drained
1 teaspoon seasoned salt
1/2 cup shredded part-skim mozzarella cheese

Preheat oven to 350°.

In a large skillet, cook beef over medium heat until no longer pink; drain. Stir in the rice, sloppy joe sauce, corn, mushrooms and seasoned salt.

Transfer to a greased 2-qt. baking dish. Cover and bake at 350° for 30 minutes. Uncover; sprinkle with cheese. Bake 5-10 minutes longer or until cheese is melted.
Yield: 4-6 servings.

Editor's Note: When cooking rice, make extra to have on hand. Cooked rice can be refrigerated for up to 7 days and frozen for up to 6 months. For convenience, package a cup or two of rice in refrigerator/freezer bags. Flatten rice out in the bags before freezing. That way it will defrost more quickly.

Meat Loaf Pie

Prep: 10 min. | Bake: 25 min.

Everyone enjoys my Meat Loaf Pie—a tasty cross between meat loaf and pizza. Often, I divide it into two pans, bake one for dinner and freeze the other for another day. —Judy Foye, Freeport, Maine

   1 can (5 ounces)
     evaporated milk
1/2 cup dry bread crumbs
1/2 teaspoon garlic salt
   1 pound lean ground beef
1/3 cup ketchup
   1 cup (4 ounces) shredded
     cheddar cheese
1/2 teaspoon dried oregano
   1 tablespoon grated
     Parmesan cheese

Preheat oven to 350°.

In a large bowl, combine the milk, bread crumbs and garlic salt. Crumble beef over mixture and mix well. Press onto the bottom and 1 in. up the sides of a greased 9-in. pie plate.

Bake, uncovered, at 350° for 20 minutes; drain. Spread with ketchup. Sprinkle with the cheddar cheese, oregano and Parmesan cheese. Bake 3-5 minutes longer or until a meat thermometer reads 160°.
Yield: 4 servings.

Creamy Herbed Meatballs

Prep: 15 min. | Cook: 35 min.

Just about everyone likes meatballs. This recipe is one my husband frequently requests. Basil and parsley give a distinct fresh flavor.
—Marilyn Coupland, Portage la Prairie, Manitoba

   1 egg
1/4 cup dry bread crumbs
1/4 cup finely chopped onion
   1 tablespoon dried basil
1/2 teaspoon salt
1/2 teaspoon pepper
   1 pound ground beef
   1 can (10-3/4 ounces) condensed
     cream of mushroom soup,
     undiluted
1/2 cup water
   2 tablespoons minced fresh parsley

In a large bowl, combine the first six ingredients. Crumble beef over mixture and mix well. Shape into 1-1/2-in. balls.

In a large skillet, cook meatballs in batches until browned on all sides and a meat thermometer reads 160°; drain. Stir in the remaining ingredients. Cover and simmer for 20 minutes or until heated through, stirring occasionally.
Yield: 16 meatballs.

Personal Pizza

Prep: 20 min. | Bake: 20 min.

I practically lived on these easy-to-prepare mini pizzas when I was in college. —Julie Beth Lamb, Visalia, California

- 2 packages (6-1/2 ounces *each*) pizza crust mix
- 1 pound ground beef, cooked and drained
- 1-1/2 cups pizza sauce
- 1 medium onion, chopped
- 1 cup chopped green pepper
- 2 cans (2-1/4 ounces *each*) sliced ripe olives, drained
- 2 cups (8 ounces) shredded part-skim mozzarella cheese

Preheat oven to 425°.

Prepare both packages of pizza dough according to directions. On a floured surface, knead dough several times; divide into

six portions. Roll each into an 8-in. circle. Place on greased baking sheets. Bake at 425° for 10 minutes.

Meanwhile, cook beef over medium heat until no longer pink; drain. Spread pizza sauce over crusts. Top with the beef, onion, green pepper, olives and cheese. Bake for 10-15 minutes or until crust is golden brown and cheese is melted.
Yield: 6 servings.

Editor's Note: For added convenience, bake the crusts and freeze until needed. Place the toppings on the frozen crust and bake as directed in recipe.

Pronto Chili

Prep: 10 min. | Cook: 35 min.

If your busy schedule doesn't allow you to have chili simmer all day long on the stove, try this recipe. It can be made in a flash. —Taste of Home Test Kitchen

- 1 pound ground beef
- 1 medium onion, chopped
- 1 medium green pepper, chopped
- 2 to 3 teaspoons chili powder
- 1 teaspoon ground cumin
- 1 teaspoon salt
- 1 can (14-1/2 ounces) Mexican stewed tomatoes
- 1 can (15-3/4 ounces) chili beans in gravy
- 1 cup frozen corn

Shredded cheddar cheese, optional

In a large saucepan, cook the beef, onion and green pepper over medium heat until the meat is no longer pink; drain. Add the chili powder, cumin, salt, tomatoes, beans and corn. Bring to a boil. Reduce heat; cover and simmer for 20 minutes. Serve with cheese if desired.
Yield: 6 servings.

Mini Italian Meat Loaves

Prep: 15 min. | Bake: 45 min.

This was one of the first recipes I tried as a new wife many years ago. These single-serving loaves have been a super hit ever since.
—Ruth Grimm, Rochester, Minnesota

1 egg
1 cup milk
1/2 cup seasoned bread crumbs
1 teaspoon salt
1-1/2 pounds lean ground beef
3/4 cup Italian tomato sauce
Shredded Parmesan cheese, optional

Preheat oven to 350°.

In a large bowl, combine the first four ingredients. Crumble beef over mixture and mix well. Shape into six loaves.

Place in a greased 13-in. x 9-in. x 2-in. baking dish. Bake, uncovered, at 350° for 30 minutes. Spoon tomato sauce over loaves. Bake for 15 minutes or until a meat thermometer reads 160°. Sprinkle with Parmesan cheese.
Yield: 6 servings.

Golden Burger Spirals

Prep: 20 min. | Bake: 30 min.

After a busy day, this recipe makes a convenient meal the whole family enjoys. I also like to take it to potlucks and church socials. —Lisa Sinyard, Lexington, Alabama

1 package (8 ounces) spiral pasta
1 pound ground beef
1 medium onion, chopped
1 medium green pepper, chopped
1 can (10-3/4 ounces) condensed golden mushroom soup, undiluted
1 can (8 ounces) tomato sauce
1-1/2 cups (6 ounces) shredded cheddar cheese, *divided*
1/2 teaspoon salt

Preheat oven to 350.

Cook the pasta according to package directions. Meanwhile, in a large skillet, cook the beef, onion and green pepper over medium heat until the meat is no longer pink; drain. Add the soup, tomato sauce, 1 cup cheese and salt. Drain pasta and stir into beef mixture.

Transfer to a greased 2-1/2-qt. baking dish. Sprinkle with remaining cheese. Bake, uncovered, at 350° for 30 minutes or until bubbly.
Yield: 4-6 servings.

Skillet Steak and Corn

Prep: 10 min. | **Cook: 35 min.**

This skillet dish combines canned vegetables and meat in a savory sauce. The thin strips of steak cook up in minutes. If you like, you can use slices of chicken breast instead of the steak. —Ruth Taylor, Greeneville, Tennessee

1 pound boneless beef top round steak, cut into strips
1 medium onion, cut into 1/4-inch wedges
1/2 teaspoon dried thyme
2 tablespoons vegetable oil
3/4 cup red wine *or* beef broth
1 can (14-1/2 ounces) diced tomatoes, undrained
2 cans (11 ounces *each*) Mexicorn, drained
Hot cooked rice

In a large skillet, cook the steak, onion and thyme in oil over medium-high heat until meat is no longer pink; drain. Add wine or broth; simmer, uncovered, for 10 minutes or until the liquid has evaporated. Stir in tomatoes; cover and simmer for 15 minutes. Add the corn and heat through. Serve with rice.
Yield: 4 servings.

Ranch Stew

Prep: 5 min. | Cook: 30 min.

My husband, our five children and I have enjoyed this easy-to-make stew for years. We especially love the dumplings. Our bachelor son even makes it for himself!
—Margaret Froehling, Wood Dale, Illinois

1 pound ground beef
1 can (16 ounces) kidney beans, undrained
1 can (15-1/4 ounces) whole kernel corn, undrained
1 can (14-1/2 ounces) diced tomatoes, undrained
1 cup biscuit/baking mix
1/3 cup milk

In a large saucepan, cook beef over medium heat until no longer pink; drain. Add the beans, corn and tomatoes; bring to a boil. Reduce heat.

In a small bowl, combine biscuit mix and milk just until moistened. Drop by tablespoonfuls onto simmering stew. Cover and simmer for 12 minutes or until a toothpick inserted in a dumpling comes out clean (do not lift cover while simmering). Serve immediately.
Yield: 4 servings.

Corn Bread Taco Bake

Prep: 20 min. | Bake: 25 min.

The corn bread and beef bake together in the same casserole dish, making this entree convenient. Everyone who tries it likes it.
—Vicki Good, Oscoda, Michigan

- 1-1/2 pounds ground beef
- 1 can (15-1/4 ounces) whole kernel corn, drained
- 1 can (8 ounces) tomato sauce
- 1/2 cup water
- 1/2 cup chopped green pepper
- 1 envelope taco seasoning
- 1 package (8-1/2 ounces) corn bread/muffin mix
- 1 can (2.8 ounces) french-fried onions, *divided*
- 1/3 cup shredded cheddar cheese

Preheat oven to 400°.

In a large skillet, cook beef over medium heat until no longer pink; drain. Stir in the corn, tomato sauce, water, green pepper and taco seasoning; mix well. Spoon into a greased 2-qt. baking dish.

Prepare corn bread mix according to package directions for corn bread. Stir in half of the onions. Spread over beef mixture. Bake, uncovered, at 400° for 20 minutes. Sprinkle with cheese and remaining onions. Bake 3-5 minutes longer or until cheese is melted and a toothpick inserted into corn bread layer comes out clean. **Yield: 6 servings.**

Mexicana Skillet Stew

Prep: 10 min. | Cook: 35 min.

I sometimes serve this hearty mixture in warm flour tortillas. Add some scrambled eggs and you have a terrific breakfast burrito. —Bobby Walker, Lake Isabella, California

- 1 pound ground beef
- 2 large potatoes, peeled and cut into 1/2-inch cubes
- 1 large onion, chopped
- 1 large green pepper, chopped
- 1 can (4 ounces) mushroom stems and pieces, undrained
- 3/4 cup picante sauce
- Garlic powder and pepper, optional

In a large skillet, cook the beef, potatoes, onion, green pepper and mushrooms over medium heat until meat is no longer pink; drain. Reduce heat to low; cover and cook for 20 minutes or until potatoes are tender, stirring occasionally.

Add the picante sauce, garlic salt and pepper. Cook 5 minutes longer or until heated through.
Yield: 4 servings.

Pizza Mac Casserole

Prep: 20 min. | **Bake: 30 min.**

My family enjoys this tasty variation on a basic ground beef and noodle casserole. This satisfying main dish is simple to make because it uses convenient pizza sauce.
—Trish Quinn, Marion, Indiana

1 cup elbow macaroni
1 pound ground beef
1/2 cup chopped onion
1/2 cup chopped green pepper
2 jars (14 ounces each) pizza sauce
2 cups (8 ounces) shredded part-skim mozzarella cheese

Preheat oven to 350°.

Cook the pasta according to package directions. Meanwhile, in a large skillet, cook beef over medium heat until no longer pink; drain. Drain macaroni and add to the beef along with the onion, green pepper and pizza sauce.

Pour into a greased 2-1/2-qt. baking dish. Cover and bake at 350° for 20 minutes. Uncover; sprinkle with cheese. Bake 10-15 minutes longer or until the cheese is melted. **Yield: 6 servings.**

Editor's Note: While the water for the pasta is being brought to a boil, chop the onion and green pepper. Then cook the beef.

Meatballs Monte Carlo

Prep: 15 min. | **Cook: 40 min.**

You'll need just one pan to prepare this easy entree. Once the meatballs have browned, the egg noodles cook in the tomatoey sauce right along with them.
—Margaret Wilson, Hemet, California

1/3 cup evaporated milk
1/4 cup dry bread crumbs
1 small onion, chopped
1/4 teaspoon salt
Dash pepper
1 pound ground beef
1 envelope spaghetti sauce mix
4 cans (11-1/2 ounces *each*) tomato juice
1 cup water
5 cups uncooked wide egg noodles
1 can (2-1/4 ounces) sliced ripe olives, drained

In a large bowl, combine the milk, bread crumbs, onion, salt and pepper. Crumble beef over mixture and mix well. Shape into 1-1/2-in. balls.

In a large skillet over medium-high heat, brown meatballs; drain. Combine the spaghetti sauce mix, tomato juice and water; pour over the meatballs. Bring to a boil. Stir in the noodles and olives. Reduce heat; cover and simmer for 20-25 minutes or until noodles are tender, stirring occasionally.
Yield: 6 servings.

Fabulous Beef Fajitas

Prep: 35 min. | Cook: 15 min.

Since this is such a breeze to prepare, it makes frequent appearances on our dinner table. The sweet peppers add garden-fresh color and crispness to this tasty mixture. If you prefer, pork tenderloin or chicken is a delicious replacement for the beef.
—Lorna Nault, Chesterton, Indiana

1/2 cup Italian salad dressing, *divided*
1/2 teaspoon chili powder
1 pound boneless beef sirloin steak, cut into 1/4-inch strips
1 medium sweet red pepper, sliced
1 medium green pepper, sliced
1 medium onion, sliced and separated into rings
6 flour tortillas (8 inches), warmed

In a large resealable plastic bag, combine 1/4 cup salad dressing and chili powder; add steak. Seal and turn to coat; chill for 30 minutes.

In a large skillet, saute peppers and onion in remaining salad dressing until crisp-tender. Remove and keep warm.

Drain steak, discarding marinade. In the skillet, saute steak for 6-8 minutes or until no longer pink; drain. Return vegetables to pan; heat through. Spoon meat and vegetables down the center of tortillas; fold in sides.
Yield: 6 servings.

Editor's Note: Use the time the steak marinates, to slice the peppers and onion. Begin cooking the vegetables, a few minutes before the steak is finished marinating.

Skillet Beef Stew

Prep: 10 min. | Cook: 25 min.

Think you can't prepare a hot and hearty stew in under 45 minutes? This super stew recipe uses frozen vegetables and prepared gravy, so you can serve up steaming bowlfuls in no time.
—Taste of Home Test Kitchen

1 pound boneless beef top sirloin steak

2 tablespoons vegetable oil

1 bag (16 ounces) frozen vegetables for stew

1 jar (12 ounces) beef gravy

2 tablespoons Worcestershire sauce

1/2 teaspoon dried thyme

1/4 teaspoon pepper

1/4 teaspoon garlic powder

Cut steak into 2-in. x 1/4-in. strips. In a large skillet, cook beef over medium heat until no longer pink. Drain if necessary. Stir in remaining ingredients; bring to a boil. Reduce heat; cover and simmer for 15 minutes or until heated through. **Yield: 4 servings.**

Saucy Beef Casserole

Prep: 10 min. | Bake: 30 min.

I rely on canned soups and crunchy chow mein noodles to flavor this hearty ground beef bake. —Ferne Spielvogel, Fairwater, Wisconsin

1 pound ground beef

1 medium onion, chopped

1 can (10-3/4 ounces) condensed cream of chicken soup, undiluted

1 can (10-3/4 ounces) condensed vegetable soup, undiluted

3/4 cup chow mein noodles

Preheat oven to 350°.

In a skillet, cook beef and onion over medium heat until meat is no longer pink; drain. Stir in soups.

Transfer to a greased 8-in. square baking dish. Cover and bake at 350° for 25-30 minutes or until heated through. Uncover; sprinkle with chow mein noodles. Bake 5 minutes longer or until noodles are crisp. **Yield: 4 servings.**

The Busy Family Cookbook

Pork

Oriental Pork Cabbage Stir-Fry (p. 62)

Apricot Ham Steaks

Prep: 10 min.

Ham is a versatile main menu item that's a standby with all country cooks. One of the best and easiest ways to serve ham slices is topped off with a slightly sweet glaze, like this apricot version.—Taste of Home Test Kitchen

4 individual boneless fully cooked ham steaks (about 5 ounces *each*)
2 tablespoons butter, *divided*
1/2 cup apricot preserves
1 tablespoon cider vinegar
1/4 teaspoon ground ginger
Dash salt

In a large skillet, saute ham slices in 1 tablespoon of butter until lightly browned on each side.

Meanwhile, in a large saucepan, combine the preserves, vinegar, ginger, salt and remaining butter. Cook over medium heat until heated through. Serve ham with the apricot sauce.
Yield: 4 servings.

Sweet and Sour Pork Chops

Prep: 10 min.

It's hard to believe that the flavorful sauce for these tender pork chops calls for only a handful of items. They're nice enough for company.—Deborah Anderson, Spooner, Wisconsin

3 tablespoons chili sauce
3 tablespoons honey
2 tablespoons soy sauce
8 boneless pork loin chops (1/4 inch thick and 4 ounces *each*)

In a small bowl, combine the chili sauce, honey and soy sauce. Brush over both sides of pork. Broil 4-6 in. from the heat for 3-4 minutes on each side, or until a meat thermometer reaches 160°. **Yield: 4 servings.**

Editor's Note: If using thicker pork chops, the cooking time will need to be increased.

Barbecued Ham Buns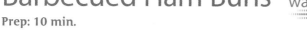

Prep: 10 min.

The recipe for these hot ham sandwiches came from a best friend's mother. I often prepare them as a quick lunch for my husband and me. The versatile recipe can be increased and prepared on the stovetop or slow cooker to feed a crowd.
—Janet Gregory, Spring Creek, Pennsylvania

1/3 cup ketchup
1/3 cup water
3 tablespoons brown sugar
3 tablespoons sweet pickle relish
1 tablespoon prepared mustard
1 tablespoon white vinegar
1 pound fully cooked ham, thinly sliced
6 hamburger buns, split

In a large microwave-safe dish, combine the first six ingredients. Stir in ham. Cover and microwave on high for 1-1/2 minutes; stir. Microwave 1-2 minutes longer or until heated through. Serve on buns. **Yield: 6 servings.**

Editor's Note: This recipe was tested in a 1,100-watt microwave.

Italian Subs

Prep: 10 min.

Use this sandwich for dinner or lunch. Kaiser rolls or hard onion rolls can be used in place of the French bread. I've also used chicken breast or roast beef for the meat.—Nanci Keatley, Salem, Oregon

1 loaf (8 ounces) French bread
6 slices part-skim mozzarella cheese, *divided*
12 thin slices fully cooked ham *or* turkey
1 medium tomato, thinly sliced
1 tablespoon olive oil
2 teaspoons red wine vinegar
2-1/2 teaspoons dried basil
1/8 teaspoon pepper
1/8 teaspoon dried rosemary, crushed

Cut bread in half horizontally; set top aside. Place three slices of cheese on bottom half; layer with ham and tomato.

In a small bowl, combine the oil, vinegar, basil, pepper and rosemary; drizzle over tomato. Top with remaining cheese.

Broil 4 in. from the heat for 2-3 minutes or until cheese is melted. Replace bread top. Cut into four pieces; serve immediately.
Yield: 4 servings.

Spiced Ham Steak

Prep: 10 min.

I turn orange marmalade, mustard and a hint of ginger into a fast-to-fix glaze for ham. The mouth-watering entree may be short on time, but it's definitely long on flavor.
—Connie Moore, Medway, Ohio

1 bone-in fully cooked ham steak (about 1 pound)
1/4 cup orange marmalade
2 tablespoons water
1 tablespoon butter
1 tablespoon prepared mustard
1 teaspoon corn syrup
1/8 to 1/4 teaspoon ground ginger

In a large skillet coated with nonstick cooking spray, cook ham for 4 minutes on each side or until lightly browned; drain.

While ham is cooking, combine the remaining ingredients in a saucepan; bring to a boil. Spoon over ham. Cover and cook for 1-2 minutes or until heated through.
Yield: 4 servings.

The Busy Family Cookbook

Dilly Pork Chops

Prep: 10 min.

Everyone who tastes these tender chops loves them. In fact, they're so good that I often cook extra and freeze them for another busy night. The savory mixture of butter, mustard and dill is wonderful on chicken or fish, too.
—Robin Hightower Parker, Church Hill, Tennessee

1/4 cup butter, melted
1 tablespoon Dijon mustard
1 to 1-1/2 teaspoons dill weed
1/8 teaspoon garlic powder
1 teaspoon Worcestershire sauce
6 boneless pork loin chops (1/2 inch thick and 4 ounces *each*)

In a small bowl, combine the first five ingredients; spoon over both sides of pork. Broil 4-6 in. from the heat for 4 minutes on each side or until a meat thermometer reads 160°.
Yield: 6 servings.

Editor's Note: If using thicker pork chops, the cooking time will need to be increased.

20 minute recipes

Flavorful Mac and Cheese

Prep: 15 min.

It's a snap to stir together this zesty macaroni and cheese dish, thanks to the Mexican-seasoned process cheese sauce. If your family prefers a little less zip, use the original flavor for equally satisfying results.—Sandy Buchanan, Lake Alfred, Florida

1 package (7 ounces) elbow macaroni
1 jar (8 ounces) mild Mexican cheese sauce *or* process cheese sauce
1-1/2 cups chopped fully cooked ham
1 can (8 ounces) crushed pineapple, drained
1/2 cup chopped green pepper
1/4 cup finely chopped onion

Cook macaroni according to package directions; drain. Stir in the cheese sauce until combined. Add remaining ingredients. Transfer to a serving bowl; serve immediately.
Yield: 4 servings.

Editor's Note: While the macaroni is cooking, chop the ham, green pepper and onion.

No-Fuss Ham Patties

Prep: 20 min.

Folks always want more whenever I make these ham patties. They're fast and easy to make, too, which is why I reach for the recipe regularly.—Mrs. Ernest Schoeff, Huntington, Indiana

1 egg, lightly beaten
1/4 cup milk
3 tablespoons sweet pickle relish
8 tablespoons dry bread crumbs, *divided*
1-1/2 teaspoons ground mustard
10 ounces ground fully cooked ham
3 tablespoons butter

In a large bowl, combine the egg, milk, pickle relish, 6 tablespoons bread crumbs and mustard. Crumble ham over mixture and mix well. Shape into four patties. Sprinkle each side with remaining bread crumbs.

In a large skillet, cook patties over medium heat in butter for 4 to 5 minutes on each side or until a meat thermometer reaches 160°.
Yield: 4 servings.

Bacon Cheddar Quiche micro wave

Prep: 20 min.

Whenever company comes to stay over, I make this wonderful dish for breakfast. They think I've worked for hours when it takes only about 20 minutes, start to finish. It also great for a fast dinner.—Val Forsythe, Albert Lea, Minnesota

14 bacon strips, cooked and crumbled
1 cup (4 ounces) shredded cheddar cheese
1 jar (6 ounces) sliced mushrooms, drained
1 tablespoon dried minced onion
5 eggs
1 can (5 ounces) evaporated milk
1/4 teaspoon cayenne pepper

In a greased 9-in. microwave-safe pie plate, layer the bacon, cheese, mushrooms and onion. In a large bowl, beat the eggs, milk and cayenne; pour over the onion.

Microwave, uncovered, on high for 4-1/2 minutes, stirring twice. Cook 1-2 minutes longer or until a knife inserted near the center comes out clean. Let stand for 5 minutes or until set. Cut into wedges.
Yield: 4-6 servings.

Editor's Note: This recipe was tested in a 1,100-watt microwave. To save time, use precooked bacon, which is available in the packaged deli meat section of the supermarket.

Honey-Mustard Pork Scallopini

Prep: 20 min.

This is one of the quickest main-dish entrees I have, and one of the most delicious. My family loves honey and mustard. Pounding the boneless chops tenderizes them and makes them cook quickly.
—Stephanie Moon, Green Bay, Wisconsin

4 boneless butterflied pork chops (4 ounces *each*)
2 tablespoons honey
2 tablespoons spicy brown mustard
1/3 cup crushed butter-flavored crackers (about 8 crackers)
1/3 cup dry bread crumbs
1 tablespoon vegetable oil
1 tablespoon butter

Flatten pork to 1/8-in. thickness. In a small bowl, combine honey and mustard; brush over both sides of pork. In a shallow bowl, combine cracker and bread crumbs; add pork and turn to coat.

In a large skillet, cook pork over medium heat in oil and butter for 2-3 minutes on each side or until crisp and juices run clear. **Yield: 4 servings.**

Sausage Corn Chili

Prep: 20 min.

Nicely spiced Italian sausage and crunchy corn distinguish this thick chili from usual offerings. My daughter won a national contest with this zesty recipe.
—Rhea Lease, Colman, South Dakota

1 pound bulk Italian sausage
1 tablespoon dried minced onion
1 can (16 ounces) kidney beans, rinsed and drained
1 can (15-1/4 ounces) whole kernel corn, drained
1 can (15 ounces) tomato sauce
2/3 cup picante sauce
1/3 to 1/2 cup water
1 teaspoon chili powder

In a large saucepan, cook sausage and onion over medium heat until meat is no longer pink; drain. Stir in the remaining ingredients; bring to a boil. Reduce heat; simmer, uncovered, for 5-10 minutes or until heated through. **Yield: 6 servings.**

Tortellini Carbonara

Prep: 20 min.

Only five ingredients are needed for this creamy pasta, which comes together in mere moments. A rich bacon and Parmesan cheese sauce is simmered in one pan while packaged tortellini boils to perfection in another. —Cathy Croyle, Davidsville, Pennsylvania

8 bacon strips, diced
1 cup heavy whipping cream
1/2 cup minced fresh parsley
1/2 cup grated Parmesan cheese
1 package (9 ounces) refrigerated cheese tortellini

In a large saucepan, cook bacon over medium heat until crisp. Using a slotted spoon, remove to paper towels; drain and discard grease.

Return bacon to saucepan; add the cream, parsley and cheese.

Cook, uncovered, over medium heat until heated through.

Meanwhile, prepare tortellini according to package directions; drain and transfer to a serving bowl. Drizzle cheese sauce over tortellini and toss to coat. Serve immediately.
Yield: 4 servings.

Editor's Note: Heat water for tortellini while bacon is cooking. To save time, use precooked bacon, which is available in the packaged deli meat section of the supermarket.

Barbecue Kielbasa

Prep: 15 min.

I serve this mouth-watering main dish with corn bread and green beans. It can easily be tripled for potlucks. Serve the sweet sauce-covered sausage over cooked instant rice, or for an appealing appetizer, cut it into bite-size pieces.—Gina Slaven, Canfield, Ohio

1 medium onion, halved and thinly sliced
1 tablespoon butter
1 pound smoked kielbasa *or* Polish sausage, cut into 1/4-inch slices
1 cup ketchup
1/3 to 1/2 cup packed brown sugar
2 tablespoons Worcestershire sauce

In a large skillet, saute onion in butter until tender. Stir in the remaining ingredients. Bring to a boil. Reduce heat; simmer, uncovered, for 3 minutes or until sauce is slightly thickened, stirring occasionally.
Yield: 4 servings.

Editor's Note: If serving over instant rice, bring water to a boil while the onion is sauteing.

Pork

Spicy Cajun Stew

Prep: 20 min.

Packed with flavor, this dish is surprisingly quick and easy since it has just five ingredients.—Elizabeth Freise, Kansas City, Missouri

1 package (16 ounces) smoked Polish sausage *or* kielbasa, cut into 1/4-inch pieces
2 cans (10 ounces *each*) diced tomatoes and green chilies, undrained
1 can (14-1/2 ounces) chicken broth
1 package (10 ounces) frozen chopped spinach, thawed and squeezed dry
1/2 to 3/4 cup uncooked instant rice

In a large skillet, cook sausage over medium heat until lightly browned; drain. Add tomatoes and broth; bring to a boil. Stir in spinach. Return to a boil; cook for 2 minutes. Stir in the rice. Cover and remove from the heat. Let stand for 5 minutes. Stir with a fork.
Yield: 5 servings.

Pork Lo Mein

Prep: 20 min.

My husband teases me about using him as the guinea pig in the kitchen. But he's always an eager participant whenever I present attractive, tasty meals like this at dinnertime.
—Billie Bethel, Waynesville, North Carolina

1 pound ground pork
1 cup thinly sliced carrots
1 cup chopped onion
1 garlic clove, minced
2 packages (3 ounces *each*) Oriental *or* Chicken-flavored Ramen noodles
1-1/2 cups water
1 cup frozen peas
6 cups shredded romaine

In a large skillet coated with nonstick cooking spray, cook the pork, carrots, onion and garlic over medium heat until pork is no longer pink; drain.

Break noodles into skillet, stir in seasoning packets. Stir in water and peas; bring to a boil. Reduce heat; simmer, uncovered, for about 6-8 minutes or until noodles and vegetables are tender, stirring several times. Add romaine; heat and stir until wilted.
Yield: 4 servings.

Greek Ham Wraps

Prep: 15 min.

Feta cheese and black olives give Greek flavor to julienned ham in these tasty, handheld specialties. I sometimes add slices of roasted red pepper before wrapping everything in the tortillas. Use the green onion tie when you want to turn an ordinary lunch into something special.—Marilou Robinson, Portland, Oregon

6 tablespoons mayonnaise
2 tablespoons minced fresh basil *or* 2 teaspoons dried basil
6 flour tortillas (8 inches), room temperature
6 lettuce leaves
3 cups julienned fully cooked ham (about 1-1/2 pounds)
1 can (4-1/2 ounces) sliced ripe olives, drained
6 tablespoons crumbled feta cheese
6 green onions, chopped
Additional green onions, optional
1 cup water, optional

In a small bowl, combine the mayonnaise and basil; spread over each tortilla. Top with lettuce, ham, olives, feta cheese and chopped onions; roll up.

For optional onion ties, cut white portion off additional onions; save for another use. In a saucepan, bring water to a boil. Add green onion tops; boil for 1 minute or until softened. Drain and immediately place onion tops in ice water; drain and pat dry. Tie around wraps.
Yield: 6 servings.

Festive Pork

Prep: 20 min.

Slices of tender pork are dressed up in a tangy sauce in this quick recipe. The pretty sauce gives the pork a mouth-watering touch.—Marilyn Paradis, Woodburn, Oregon

1 pork tenderloin (3/4 pound)
1 tablespoon olive oil
1/2 cup reduced-sodium beef broth, *divided*
2 tablespoons dried cranberries
1-1/2 teaspoons Dijon mustard
1 teaspoon cornstarch
1 tablespoon orange juice concentrate

Cut tenderloin into 12 slices; flatten to 1/4-in. thickness. In a large skillet, brown pork on both sides over medium heat in oil. Add 1/4 cup beef broth; reduce heat. Cover and simmer for 5-10 minutes or until meat is no longer pink. Remove meat to a serving dish and keep warm.

In the same skillet, add the cranberries, mustard and remaining broth. Combine cornstarch and orange juice concentrate until smooth; gradually add to broth mixture. Bring to a boil; cook and stir for 1-2 minutes or until thickened. Serve with pork.
Yield: 4 servings.

Walnut Ham Linguine

Prep: 20 min.

I think this dish has just the perfect amount of garlic. It really has a pleasing combination of textures and flavors.
—Mike Pickerel, Columbia, Missouri

1 package (16 ounces) linguine
2 to 4 garlic cloves, minced
1/4 cup olive oil
1/2 cup coarsely chopped walnuts
1/2 pound fully cooked ham slices, cut into 1/2-inch strips
1/3 cup grated Parmesan cheese
1/4 cup minced fresh parsley

Cook linguine according to package directions. Meanwhile, in a large skillet, saute garlic in oil for 1 minute. Add walnuts; saute for 2 minutes longer. Stir in ham; cook 2 minutes or until heated through.

Drain pasta. Add to ham mixture; toss to coat. Sprinkle with Parmesan and parsley. **Yield: 4-6 servings.**

Cajun Chops

Prep: 20 min.

If you like spicy foods, you'll surely want to try these chops. I've never served them to friends without being asked for the recipe before the meal ended!
—Cindy Schaefer, Carey, North Carolina

4 boneless pork chops (1-1/2 inches thick and 4 ounces *each*)
4 teaspoons paprika
2 teaspoons salt
2 teaspoons rubbed sage
3/4 teaspoon cayenne pepper
3/4 teaspoon pepper
3/4 teaspoon garlic powder
2 tablespoons butter

Make a horizontal cut through each pork chop from one side to within 1/4 in. of the opposite side. Open chops and flatten to 1/4-in. thickness.

In a large resealable plastic bag, combine the seasonings. Add pork, a few pieces at a time, and shake to coat. In a large heavy skillet, heat butter on medium until hot. Cook the chops for 2-3 minutes on each side or meat juices run clear. **Yield: 4 servings.**

Editor's Note: Heat the butter while you are coating the pork with the seasonings.

Herbed Pork Medallions

Prep: 20 min.

This effortless entree tastes as good as it looks. The pork slices have a nice blend of seasonings and broil in just minutes. This is special enough for company.—Jodie Arkin, Waconia, Minnesota

1-1/2 pounds pork tenderloin
  2 tablespoons butter, melted
1/4 teaspoon garlic powder
1/2 teaspoon salt
1/2 teaspoon dried tarragon
1/2 teaspoon dried thyme
1/2 teaspoon paprika
1/8 teaspoon pepper
1/8 teaspoon cayenne pepper
  1 tablespoon honey

Cut pork into 1/2-in. slices and pound to flatten. Combine butter and garlic powder; brush over pork. Combine the seasonings; sprinkle over pork.

Broil 4-6 in. from the heat for 4 minutes on each side. Brush with honey; broil for 1 minute longer or until meat juices run clear.
Yield: 6 servings.

Parmesan Ham Pasta

Prep: 20 min.

I always keep the ingredients for this pasta dish on hand so I can whip it up pronto. People who try it always ask for the recipe.—Nancy Ringer, Dwight, Illinois

  1 package (16 ounces) bow tie pasta
  2 cups cubed fully cooked ham
  1 can (4 ounces) mushroom stems and pieces, drained
1/2 cup butter
1/2 cup all-purpose flour
1/2 teaspoon salt
  2 cups milk
  1 package (10 ounces) frozen chopped spinach, thawed and squeezed dry
  1 cup (4 ounces) shredded Parmesan cheese

Cook pasta according to package directions. Meanwhile, in a large skillet, saute ham and mushrooms in butter. Stir in flour and salt until blended. Gradually add milk. Bring to a boil; cook and stir for 2 minutes or until thickened.

Reduce heat. Stir in spinach and cheese. Cook and stir until cheese is melted. Drain pasta; stir into the ham mixture.
Yield: 6 servings.

The Busy Family Cookbook

Toasted Cheese Supreme

Prep: 15 min.

I serve these flavorful hot ham and cheese sandwiches by themselves for lunch or a simple dinner. For a heartier meal, I like to serve them with steaming bowls of clam chowder. —Wanda Evans, Tacoma, Washington

- 8 slices white bread
- 2 tablespoons mayonnaise
- 6 ounces thinly sliced fully cooked ham
- 4 slices cheddar cheese
- 2 slices red onion, separated into rings
- 2 tablespoons horseradish sauce
- 1/4 cup butter, softened

Spread four slices of bread with mayonnaise. Layer each with the ham, cheese and onion. Spread horseradish sauce on remaining bread; place bread with horseradish side down over onion. Spread butter on the outside of each sandwich.

In a large skillet over medium heat, toast sandwiches for 4-5 minutes on each side or until bread is lightly browned and cheese is melted.
Yield: 4 servings.

Pork

Oriental Pork Cabbage Stir-Fry

Prep: 10 min. | Cook: 15 min.

Pork paired with crisp cabbage and carrots makes a stirring combination in this tasty main dish. It's a quick-fix dish when unexpected company arrives. I got the recipe from a friend when I was in college.—Jane Goldsmith, Bloomfield, Indiana

6 cups chopped cabbage, cut into 1-inch pieces
3 teaspoons vegetable oil, *divided*
4 medium carrots, julienned
1 pork tenderloin (1 pound), cut into 3/4-inch pieces
2 tablespoons minced fresh gingerroot
1 cup reduced-sodium chicken broth, *divided*
1/4 cup reduced-sodium soy sauce
4 teaspoons cornstarch
Hot cooked rice, optional

In a large nonstick skillet or wok, stir-fry cabbage in 1 teaspoon oil for 1-2 minutes or until crisp-tender. Add carrots; stir-fry 3-4 minutes longer or until carrots are crisp-tender. Remove and keep warm.

In the same pan, stir-fry pork in remaining oil for 2 minutes. Add ginger and stir-fry for 2 minutes or until pork is lightly browned. Stir in 3/4 cup broth and soy sauce. Bring to a boil. Reduce heat; cover and simmer for 3 minutes or until meat juices run clear.

Combine cornstarch and remaining broth until smooth. Gradually stir into pan. Stir in the cabbage mixture. Bring to a boil; cook and stir for 2-3 minutes or until thickened. Serve with rice if desired. **Yield: 4 servings.**

Pork Chops with Onions and Apples

Prep: 10 min. | Grill: 20 min.

I've always liked pork chops made with apples or onions. I decided to combine both ingredients to create this delicious recipe. Many family members and friends have requested it.
—Lou Ann Marques-Bambera, Attleboro, Massachusetts

2 teaspoons coarsely ground pepper
1/2 teaspoon salt
1/2 teaspoon garlic powder
4 bone-in center-cut pork loin chops (1 inch thick and 8 ounces *each*)
2 medium onions, thinly sliced
2 medium tart apples, peeled and chopped
2 tablespoons butter
2 tablespoons brown sugar

Preheat grill.

In a small bowl, combine the pepper, salt and garlic powder. Rub over pork chops. Grill chops, covered, over medium heat for 8-10 minutes on each side or until a meat thermometer reads 160°.

Meanwhile, in a large skillet, saute onions and apples in butter until tender. Stir in brown sugar; cook until thickened and bubbly. Serve with pork chops. **Yield: 4 servings.**

Raspberry Pork Chops

Prep: 5 min. | Cook: 20 min.

A yummy glaze made with mustard, vinegar and jam covers these succulent pork chops. Fixed fast in a skillet, these tender chops are great for everyday or special occasions.—Janette Hutchings, Festus, Missouri

4 boneless pork loin chops (5 ounces *each*)
1 tablespoon vegetable oil
1/4 cup cider vinegar
1/4 cup seedless raspberry jam
1 tablespoon prepared mustard

In a large skillet, brown pork chops on both sides over medium heat in oil. Stir in the vinegar, jam and mustard. Reduce heat; cover and simmer for 10-15 minutes or until juices run clear.

Remove chops and keep warm. Bring sauce to a boil; cook until liquid is reduced by half, stirring occasionally. Serve with pork chops. **Yield: 4 servings.**

Pork

Pork 'n' Snow Pea Stir-Fry micro wave

Prep: 10 min. | Cook: 15 min.

You don't need a wok to make this stir-fry. A fast-to-fix sauce coats strips of pork and vegetables.—Verona Koehlmoos, Pilger, Nebraska

2 tablespoons vegetable oil
1 pound boneless pork, cut into 1/4-inch strips
2 tablespoons soy sauce
1/8 teaspoon garlic powder
1 package (6 ounces) frozen snow peas, thawed
1 cup thinly sliced green onions
2 tablespoons cornstarch
1 cup beef broth
Hot cooked rice, optional

In a 2-qt. microwave-safe glass dish, heat oil at 70% power for 1-1/2 minutes. Add the pork, soy sauce and garlic powder; toss to coat. Cover and microwave on high for 5-6 minutes or until meat is no longer pink.

Stir in peas and onions. Cover and microwave at 70% power for 2-1/4 minutes. Combine cornstarch and broth until smooth; gradually stir into pork mixture. Cover and microwave on high for 1-1/2 minutes; stir. Cover; microwave 3-4 minutes longer or until thickened, stirring every minute. Serve with rice if desired.
Yield: 4 servings.

Editor's Note: This recipe was tested in a 1,100-watt microwave.

Italian Sausage Skillet

Prep: 5 min. | Cook: 25 min.

This garden-fresh dish gets extra color from a can of stewed tomatoes. The Italian sausage has so many wonderful flavors you don't need to add any other seasonings. —Eve Gauger Vargas, Prairie Village, Kansas

1-1/4 pounds uncooked Italian sausage links
3 small zucchini *or* yellow summer squash, cubed
1/2 cup chopped onion
1 can (14-1/2 ounces) stewed tomatoes
Hot cooked rice *or* pasta

In a large skillet, cook the sausage over medium heat until no longer pink; drain. Remove from the pan; cool slightly before cutting into 1/4-in. slices; return to the pan. Add zucchini and onion; cook and stir for 2 minutes. Stir in tomatoes. Reduce heat; cover and simmer for 10-15 minutes or until the zucchini is tender. Serve with rice or pasta.
Yield: 4-6 servings.

Editor's Note: If serving with rice or noodles, start heating the water for the rice before you begin cooking the sausage. You can cube the squash while the sausage is browning.

Pork Parmesan

Prep: 10 min. | Cook: 15 min.

I came up with this entree by substituting pork for veal. You could even use chicken.—Kenna Robinson, Sault Ste. Marie, Ontario

- 1/2 cup dry bread crumbs
- 1/4 cup grated Parmesan cheese
- 1/4 teaspoon salt
- 1/8 teaspoon pepper
- 1/8 teaspoon paprika
- 1 egg
- 6 boneless pork loin chops (1/2 inch thick and 4 ounces *each*)
- 2 tablespoons vegetable oil
- 1/2 cup tomato sauce
- 6 slices part-skim mozzarella cheese

In a shallow bowl, combine the bread crumbs, Parmesan cheese, salt, pepper and paprika. In another bowl, beat egg. Dip each pork chop in egg, then coat with crumb mixture.

In a large skillet, cook pork chops over medium heat in oil for 6-8 minutes on each side or until juices run clear. Top each chop with tomato sauce and cheese; cover and simmer for 1 minute or until cheese is melted.
Yield: 6 servings.

Sausage Stroganoff

Prep: 10 min. | Cook: 20 min.

This recipe calls for sausage instead of beef, making it an enticing, economical meal. My family loves this dish served with salad and oven-fresh rolls.
—Barbara Berkow, Northbrook, Illinois

- 1 pound bulk pork sausage
- 1 medium onion, chopped
- 1/2 pound fresh mushrooms, sliced
- 1-1/4 cups chicken broth, *divided*
- 1 tablespoon Worcestershire sauce
- 1/4 teaspoon pepper
- 1/4 cup all-purpose flour
- 1 cup (8 ounces) sour cream
- 2 tablespoons minced fresh parsley, optional

Hot cooked noodles

In a large skillet, cook sausage and onion over medium heat until meat is no longer pink; drain. Stir in mushrooms; cook for 1 minute. Add 1 cup broth, Worcestershire sauce and pepper. Bring to a boil. Reduce heat; cover and simmer for 5 minutes or until heated through.

In a small bowl, combine flour and remaining broth until smooth. Gradually stir into skillet. Bring to a boil; cook and stir for 2 minutes. Reduce heat; add sour cream. Stir until heated through (do not boil). Add parsley if desired. Serve with noodles.
Yield: 4 servings.

Editor's Note: Start heating the water for the noodles before you begin cooking the sausage.

Breaded Pork Roll-Ups

Prep: 10 min. | Cook: 15 min.

Pretty swirls of ham and a golden coating make these eye-appealing roll-ups a delightful main course. They are also perfect for company.—Ron Gardner, Grand Haven, Michigan

　　1 egg
　1/3 cup milk
1-1/4 cups dry bread crumbs
　　1 teaspoon seasoned salt
　　4 boneless pork loin chops
　　　　(1/4 inch thick and 4
　　　　ounces *each*)
　　4 thin slices deli ham
　　2 tablespoons vegetable
　　　　oil

In a shallow bowl, lightly beat egg and milk. In another shallow bowl, combine bread crumbs and seasoned salt. Flatten pork chops to 1/8-in. thickness; place a ham slice on each. Fold sides and ends over ham and roll up; secure each with a toothpick. Dip roll-ups in egg mixture, then roll in crumbs.

In a large skillet, cook the chops in oil over medium heat for 2-3 minutes on each side or until chops are lightly browned; Cook, uncovered, for 10-12 minutes longer or until meat is no longer pink, turning occasionally. Discard toothpicks. **Yield: 4 servings.**

Sausage Jumble

Prep: 5 min. | Cook: 25 min.

Mother always served this dish with coleslaw and homemade biscuits or corn bread.
—Patsye Yonce, Ovid, New York

　　1 pound bulk pork sausage
　1/2 cup chopped onion
　　2 cups fresh *or* frozen whole kernel
　　　　corn, thawed
　　1 can (28 ounces) chopped
　　　　tomatoes, undrained
　　1 cup uncooked instant rice
　3/4 cup water
　　1 teaspoon salt
　1/2 teaspoon pepper
　2/3 cup shredded cheddar cheese
　1/3 cup shredded part-skim
　　　　mozzarella cheese

In a large skillet, cook sausage and onion over medium heat until meat is no longer pink; drain.

Add the corn, tomatoes, rice, water, salt and pepper. Bring to a boil. Reduce heat; cover and simmer for 10 minutes or until rice is tender. Sprinkle with cheddar and mozzarella cheese. Cook, uncovered, 5 minutes longer or until cheese is melted. **Yield: 4-6 servings.**

Bean and Ham Pasta

Prep: 5 min. | Cook: 25 min.

This pasta medley is brimming with ham, corn and black beans. If you'd like, you can thicken the juices with cornstarch to make a sauce.
—Maureen De Garmo, Concord, California

1 can (14-1/2 ounces) chicken broth
1-1/2 cups uncooked spiral pasta
1 can (15 ounces) black beans, rinsed and drained
1-1/2 cups frozen corn
1 cup cubed fully cooked ham
1/4 teaspoon dried thyme
Salt and pepper to taste
Dash ground cumin
1/4 cup shredded Parmesan cheese

In a large saucepan, bring broth to a boil. Add the pasta; cook, uncovered, for 10 minutes or until tender. Do not drain. Stir in the beans, corn, ham and seasonings; heat through. Sprinkle with cheese. **Yield: 4 servings.**

Editor's Note: While the pasta is cooking, measure out the remaining ingredients.

Pork with Garlic Cream Sauce

Prep: 15 min. | Broil: 10 min.

This quick-cooking dish is a garlic lover's delight. The tender pork medallions are dressed in a creamy garlic sauce and sprinkled with sesame seeds. It's a family favorite that's oh so good!
—Elisa Lochridge, Aloha, Oregon

1 pork tenderloin (1 pound)
2 teaspoons vegetable oil
2 teaspoons sesame seeds, toasted, *divided*
1 to 2 garlic cloves, minced
1 tablespoon butter
1/3 cup 1% milk
3 ounces reduced-fat cream cheese
1 tablespoon minced chives

Cut pork into 1-in. slices; flatten to 1/2-in. thickness. Place in a 15-in. x 10-in. x 1-in. baking pan coated with nonstick cooking spray. Brush oil over all sides of pork; sprinkle with half of the sesame seeds.

Broil 4-6 in. from the heat for 3-5 minutes; turn and sprinkle with remaining sesame seeds. Broil 3-5 minutes longer or until meat juices runs clear.

Meanwhile, in a saucepan, saute garlic in butter for 1 minute. Stir in milk and cream cheese. Reduce heat; cook and stir until blended and smooth. Stir in chives. Serve with pork. **Yield: 4 servings.**

Hurry-Up Ham 'n' Noodles

Prep: 10 min. | Cook: 20 min.

I created this rich-tasting entree. It is ready to serve in almost the time it takes to cook the noodles. I've made it for luncheons and potlucks, but mostly I make it on days when I'm in a hurry to get something on the table.—Lucille Howell, Portland, Oregon

5 to 6 cups uncooked wide egg noodles
1/4 cup butter, cubed
1 cup heavy whipping cream
1-1/2 cups julienned fully cooked ham
1/2 cup grated Parmesan cheese
1/4 cup thinly sliced green onions
1/4 teaspoon salt
1/8 teaspoon pepper

Cook noodles according to package directions. Meanwhile, in a large skillet, melt butter over medium heat. Gradually whisk in cream. Bring to a boil, stirring constantly; cook and stir for 2 minutes longer or until thickened.

Add the ham, cheese, onions, salt and pepper; cook, uncovered, until heated through. Drain noodles; add to ham mixture. Toss to coat; heat through. **Yield: 4 servings.**

Basil Orange Chops

Prep: 5 min. | Cook: 20 min.

Only one pan is required for this easy-to-prepare dish, making cleanup a snap. The orange sauce nicely dresses up the tender chops.—Lori Blevins, Douglasville, Georgia

4 boneless pork loin chops (1/2 inch thick and 4 ounces *each*)
1 green onion, sliced
1 tablespoon vegetable oil
1 cup orange juice
1 tablespoon grated orange peel
2 teaspoons dried basil
2 teaspoons cornstarch
2 teaspoons water

In a large skillet, brown pork chops and onion over medium heat in oil. Stir in the orange juice, peel and basil. Bring to a boil. Reduce heat; cover and cook 10-15 minutes until meat juices run clear. Remove chops and keep warm.

In a small bowl, combine the cornstarch and water until smooth; add to the skillet. Bring to a boil; cook and stir for 2 minutes or until thickened. Serve with the chops. **Yield: 4 servings.**

Pork Fajita Pasta

Prep: 10 min. | Cook: 20 min.

One night, my husband and I started making fajitas before we realized we didn't have any tortillas. We improvised and served the pork mixture over noodles instead. It's become a family favorite.—Janice Thompson, Lansing, Michigan

1 package (7 ounces) angel hair pasta
4 boneless pork loin chops (1/2 inch thick and 4 ounces *each*), cut into thin strips
1 medium green pepper, julienned
1 medium onion, sliced and separated into rings
1 envelope (1.4 ounces) fajita seasoning
1/3 cup water
1 cup (4 ounces) shredded cheddar cheese
1 medium tomato, seeded and chopped

Cook pasta according to package directions. Meanwhile, in a large skillet, cook pork over medium heat until juices run clear. Add green pepper and onion; cook and stir for 1-2 minutes or until vegetables are crisp-tender. Stir in fajita seasoning and water; cook 1 minute longer. Drain pasta. In a large bowl, layer the pasta, pork mixture, cheese and tomato.
Yield: 4 servings.

Editor's Note: While the water for the pasta is being brought to a boil, cut up the pork, pepper, onion and tomato.

Pork with Apples And Sweet Potatoes

Prep: 10 min. | **Bake: 40 min.**

Here's a meal-in-one that is quick, delicious and nutritious. The tenderloin is rubbed with a few simple seasonings. Baked apples and sweet potatoes round out the dinner perfectly.—Linda Lacek, Winter Park, Florida

1 teaspoon salt
1/2 teaspoon ground cinnamon
1/2 teaspoon ground cardamom
1/4 teaspoon pepper
4-1/2 cups cubed peeled sweet potatoes (about 1-1/2 pounds)
4 teaspoons olive oil, *divided*
2 pork tenderloins (3/4 pound *each*)
4 large tart apples, peeled

Preheat oven to 425°.

In a small bowl, combine the salt, cinnamon, cardamom and pepper. Place sweet potatoes in a large bowl. Sprinkle with 1 teaspoon spice mixture and 3 teaspoons oil; toss to coat. Arrange potatoes in a single layer in a 15-in. x 10-in. x 1-in. baking pan coated with nonstick cooking spray. Bake, uncovered, at 425° for 10 minutes.

Rub the remaining oil over pork; rub with remaining spice mixture. Place over the sweet potatoes. Bake for 15 minutes.

Cut each apple into eight wedges. Turn pork; arrange apples around meat. Bake 15 minutes longer or until a meat thermometer reads 160°.
Yield: 6 servings.

Sausage-Topped Polenta

Prep: 5 min. | **Cook: 25 min. + cooling**

My Italian grandmother and mother have relied on this recipe for years. Many sauces can be served with polenta, but this tomato and sausage topping is our favorite.—Joyce Riskedal, Earlville, Illinois

1 pound bulk pork sausage
1 can (6 ounces) tomato paste
1-1/2 cups water
1 tablespoon minced fresh parsley
1 teaspoon sugar
1/2 teaspoon dried basil

POLENTA:
2 cups water
1 teaspoon salt
1 cup cornmeal
1 cup cold water
1 cup (4 ounces) shredded brick *or* part-skim mozzarella cheese

In a large skillet, cook sausage over medium heat until no longer pink; drain. Stir in the next five ingredients. Bring to a boil. Reduce heat; cover and simmer for 3 minutes, stirring occasionally.

Meanwhile, in a saucepan, bring water and salt to a boil. Combine cornmeal and cold water until blended; stir into boiling water. Return to a boil, stirring constantly. Reduce heat; cover and simmer for 15 minutes, stirring occasionally.

Spoon polenta into a greased 9-in. round baking pan. Cool for 15-20 minutes or until set. Cut into wedges. Sprinkle with cheese and top with sausage mixture.
Yield: 6 servings.

Pizzeria Burgers

Prep: 15 min. | **Cook: 20 min.**

I strive to find meals my kids like but that require little work on my part, and this recipe fits the bill.—Amy LaPointe, North Fond du Lac, Wisconsin

3/4 cup pizza sauce, *divided*
1/4 cup dry bread crumbs
1/4 teaspoon dried oregano
1 teaspoon salt
Dash pepper
1-1/2 pounds ground beef
1/4 pound bulk pork sausage
6 slices part-skim mozzarella cheese
6 sandwich rolls, split

In a large bowl, combine 1/2 cup pizza sauce, bread crumbs, oregano, salt and pepper. Crumble beef and sausage over mixture and mix well. Shape into six patties.

In a large skillet, cook patties over medium heat until no longer pink. Top with remaining pizza sauce and the mozzarella cheese. Cover and cook 2 minutes longer or until cheese is melted. Serve on rolls.
Yield: 6 servings.

Teriyaki Tenderloin

plan
ahead →

Prep: 10 min. + marinating | Bake: 35 min.

The marinade for this tender pork entree is so good that it's hard to believe it calls for only three ingredients. You can easily double or triple the recipe to accommodate larger gatherings without much effort.—Tara Brouwer, Zeeland, Michigan

1/2 cup soy sauce
1/4 cup sugar
2 tablespoons ketchup
1 pork tenderloin
(1 pound)

In a large resealable plastic bag, combine the soy sauce, sugar and ketchup. Add the pork tenderloin; seal bag and turn to coat. Refrigerate for 8 hours or overnight.

Preheat oven to 425°.

Drain and discard marinade. Place pork in a greased 13-in. x 9-in. x 2-in. baking dish. Bake, uncovered, at 425° for 35-40 minutes or until a meat thermometer reads 160°. Let stand for 5 minutes before slicing.
Yield: 4 servings.

Editor's Note: Marinate pork the night before or first thing in the morning.

Bacon Cheese Frittata

Prep: 10 min. | Bake: 25 min.

I always serve this attractive frittata to overnight guests in our home. It also makes a simple dinner. To cut down on last-minute preparation, I keep cooked bacon in the freezer. —Diana Bullock, Hanover, Maryland

6 eggs
1 cup milk
2 tablespoons butter, melted
1/2 teaspoon salt
1/4 teaspoon pepper
1/4 cup chopped green onions
5 bacon strips, cooked and crumbled
1 cup (4 ounces) shredded cheddar cheese

Preheat oven to 350°.

In a large bowl, whisk the eggs, milk, butter, salt and pepper until blended. Pour into a greased 11-in. x 7-in. x 2-in. baking dish. Sprinkle with onions, bacon and cheese.

Bake, uncovered, at 350° for 25-30 minutes or until a knife inserted near the center comes out clean.
Yield: 6 servings.

Editor's Note: To save time, use precooked bacon, which is available in the packaged deli meat section of the supermarket.

The Busy Family Cookbook

Maple-Glazed Kabobs

Prep: 20 min. | Grill: 20 min.

A friend who makes his own maple syrup shared this recipe with me. My family often requests these slightly sweet kabobs for our summer dinner cookout.
—Sue Gronholz, Columbus, Wisconsin

- 8 small new potatoes *or* 1 large potato, cut into 8 chunks
- 3 carrots, cut into 8 pieces (2 inches each)
- 1 pork tenderloin (1 pound)
- 1 large green *or* large sweet red pepper
- 8 large mushrooms
- 1/4 cup butter, cubed
- 1/4 cup maple syrup
- 1-1/2 teaspoons grated orange peel

Preheat grill.

Place potatoes in a large saucepan and cover with water. Bring to a boil. Reduce heat; cover and cook for 10-15 minutes or until crisp-tender. Drain.

While potatoes are cooking, cut pork into 12 equal pieces and pepper into eight chunks. Onto four metal or soaked wooden skewers, thread meat and vegetables alternately; set aside.

In a small saucepan, combine the butter, syrup and orange peel; cook and stir over low heat until butter is melted.

Grill kabobs, uncovered, over medium heat for 5 minutes; turn and baste with butter mixture. Cook for 12-14 minutes longer or until the meat juices run clear, turning and basting frequently.
Yield: 4 servings.

30+

Pork with Pineapple Salsa

Prep: 10 min. | Bake: 30 min.

Not only does this easy entree taste awesome, but it's good for you, too. A little brown sugar, ground ginger and Dijon mustard help give the moist tenderloin its incredible flavor, and the tangy salsa can be made in no time.—Nicole Pickett, Oro Valley, Arizona

1 can (20 ounces) unsweetened pineapple tidbits
1 pork tenderloin (1-1/4 pounds)
3 tablespoons brown sugar, *divided*
2 tablespoons Dijon mustard
1 teaspoon paprika
1/2 teaspoon ground ginger
1/3 cup finely chopped sweet red *or* green pepper
1/4 cup chopped green onions
1/8 teaspoon crushed red pepper flakes, optional

Preheat oven to 450°.

Drain pineapple, reserving 1/4 cup juice. Set aside 1 cup of pineapple (save remaining pineapple for another use). Place the pork on a rack in a shallow roasting pan. Combine 2 tablespoons brown sugar, mustard, paprika and ginger. Spread half over the pork.

Bake, uncovered, at 450° for 15 minutes. Spread with remaining brown sugar mixture. Bake 15-20 minutes longer or until a meat thermometer reads 160°.

Meanwhile, for salsa, in a small bowl, combine the red pepper, onions, pepper flakes if desired, remaining brown sugar, reserved pineapple and juice. Let pork stand for 5 minutes before slicing. Serve with salsa.
Yield: 4 servings.

Pork 'n' Green Chili Tortillas

Prep: 15 min. | **Cook: 40 min.**

This tortilla recipe is a big hit with my family. I'm often asked to make it for special occasions.—Bobbi Jones, Claypool, Arizona

1/3 cup all-purpose flour
1 teaspoon salt
1/2 teaspoon pepper
2 pork tenderloins
  (1 pound *each*), cubed
1/4 cup vegetable oil
6 cans (4 ounces *each*)
  chopped green chilies
1/2 cup salsa
12 flour tortillas (8 inches),
  warmed
Shredded cheddar cheese

In a large resealable plastic bag, combine the flour, salt and pepper. Add pork cubes; toss to coat.

In a large skillet, cook pork over medium heat in oil until no longer pink. Add chilies and salsa. Bring to a boil. Reduce heat; cover and simmer for 30 minutes or until meat is tender. Spoon 1/2 cup pork mixture down the center of each tortilla. Sprinkle with cheese; roll up.
Yield: 6 servings.

Mexican Pork and Pasta

Prep: 10 min. | **Cook: 35 min.**

On a cold Midwestern evening, this hot and spicy dish really warms us up. It's a fun, festive change from spaghetti. Plus, everyone loves the leftovers...if there are any!
—Phyllis Brooks, Auburn, Illinois

1 pound bulk hot pork sausage
1 medium onion, chopped
1/2 cup chopped green pepper
1 can (14-1/2 ounces) stewed
  tomatoes
1 can (8 ounces) tomato sauce
1 cup uncooked spiral pasta
2 tablespoons brown sugar
1 to 2 teaspoons chili powder
1 teaspoon salt
Parmesan cheese, optional

In a large skillet, cook sausage over medium heat until no longer pink; drain. Add onion and green pepper; cook until tender.

Stir in the tomatoes, tomato sauce, pasta, brown sugar, chili powder and salt; cover and simmer for 20 minutes or until pasta is tender. Sprinkle with Parmesan cheese if desired.
Yield: 4 servings.

Au Gratin Taters 'n' Chops

Prep: 10 min. | Bake: 25 min.

Children and adults alike will enjoy this cheesy chop and potato combination. I made it often as a college student, decreasing the number chops to two so I would have great-tasting leftovers for lunch or dinner the next day.—Laura Starkey, Manhattan, Kansas

6 boneless pork loin chops (3/4 inch thick and 4 ounces *each*)
1 tablespoon vegetable oil
1 package (4.9 ounces) au gratin potatoes
1/2 cup shredded cheddar cheese
4 bacon strips, cooked and crumbled

Preheat oven to 375°.

In a large skillet, brown pork chops in oil on both sides. Meanwhile, in a large bowl, combine potatoes and sauce mix according to package directions. Spoon into a greased 13-in. x 9-in. x 2-in. baking dish. Arrange chops over potatoes.

Bake, uncovered, at 375° for 20-25 minutes or until meat juices run clear and potatoes are tender. Sprinkle cheese and bacon over chops. Bake 2-3 minutes longer or until cheese is melted. **Yield: 6 servings.**

Editor's Note: Cook bacon while the chops are baking. To save time, use precooked bacon, which is available in the packaged deli meat section of the supermarket.

Marinated Pork Loin   plan ahead

Prep: 15 min. + marinating | Broil: 20 min.

One of my favorite dinners is this tender, juicy pork. It's easy to make and is special enough to serve to guests.—Jean Heady, Naples, Florida

1/2 cup reduced-sodium chicken broth
1/2 cup ketchup
2 tablespoons cider vinegar
2 tablespoons Worcestershire sauce
2 tablespoons brown sugar
2 garlic cloves, minced
1/2 teaspoon salt
1/4 teaspoon pepper
1/8 teaspoon cayenne pepper
1 boneless whole pork loin roast (2 pounds)

In a large saucepan, combine the first nine ingredients. Bring to a boil. Reduce heat; simmer, uncovered, for 5 minutes. Remove from the heat; cool slightly. Place 2/3 cup marinade in a bowl for basting; cover and chill. Pour remaining marinade into a large resealable plastic bag. Cut pork into five slices, about 1 in. each; add to bag. Seal and turn to coat; refrigerate overnight.

Drain and discard marinade. Broil 4-5 in. from the heat for 10 minutes on each side or until juices run clear, brushing with reserved marinade occasionally. **Yield: 5 servings.**

Editor's Note: Marinate pork the night before or first thing in the morning.

Spinach Ravioli Bake

Prep: 5 min. | Bake: 40 min.

This pasta bake is unbelievably simple to prepare yet tastes delicious. The fact that you use frozen ravioli—straight from the bag without boiling or thawing—saves so much time.—Susan Kehl, Pembroke Pines, Florida

2 cups spaghetti sauce
1 package (25 ounces) frozen Italian sausage ravioli *or* ravioli of your choice
2 cups (8 ounces) shredded part-skim mozzarella cheese
1 package (10 ounces) frozen chopped spinach, thawed and squeezed dry
1/4 cup grated Parmesan cheese

Preheat oven to 350°.

Place 1 cup spaghetti sauce in a greased shallow 2-qt. baking dish. Top with half of the ravioli, mozzarella cheese, spinach and Parmesan cheese. Repeat layers.

Bake, uncovered, at 350° for 40-45 minutes or until heated through and cheese is melted.
Yield: 4-6 servings.

Sausage Hash

Prep: 10 min. | Cook: 35 min.

We always have plenty of pork sausage around, so when I need a quick supper, I use this handy recipe. The colorful vegetables give this dish a perky look to match its flavor.—Virgina Krites, Cridersville, Ohio

1 pound bulk pork sausage
1 medium onion, chopped
2 medium carrots, grated
1 medium green pepper, chopped
3 cups diced cooked potatoes
1/2 teaspoon salt
1/4 teaspoon pepper

In a large skillet, cook the sausage over medium heat until no longer pink; drain. Add the onion, carrots and green pepper; cook until tender. Stir in the potatoes, salt and pepper. Reduce heat; cook and stir for 20 minutes or until lightly browned and heated through.
Yield: 6 servings.

Editor's Note: To save time, cook extra potatoes a day or two before you plan on making this dish, or use precooked potatoes, which are available in the refrigerated case in the supermarket.

Pepper-Crusted Pork Tenderloin

Prep: 10 min. | Bake: 50 min.

Family and guests will be impressed by this elegant entree and its golden-crumb coating with peppery pizzazz. The meat slices up so moist and tender, you can serve it without sauce and still have a succulent, taste-tempting main dish.—Taste of Home Test Kitchen

2 pork tenderloins (3/4 pound *each*)
3 tablespoons Dijon mustard
1 tablespoon buttermilk
2 teaspoons minced fresh thyme
1 to 2 teaspoons coarsely ground pepper
1/4 teaspoon salt
2/3 cup soft bread crumbs

Preheat oven to 425°.

Place tenderloins side by side and tie together with kitchen string. In a small bowl, combine the mustard, buttermilk, thyme, pepper and salt; spread over surface of meat. Press crumbs onto meat.

Place on a rack in a shallow roasting pan. Cover and bake at 425° for 15 minutes. Uncover; bake 35-40 minutes longer or until a meat thermometer reads 160°. Let stand for 5 minutes. Remove string before slicing. **Yield: 6 servings.**

Pasta Ham Hot Dish

Prep: 20 min. | Bake: 30 min.

I brought this simple casserole to a potluck at work and it was a hit. You can use a pound of browned ground beef in place of ham.—Judie Porath, Black Duck, Minnesota

4 ounces uncooked spaghetti, broken into 2-inch pieces
1/4 cup chopped onion
1 tablespoon butter
2 cups cubed fully cooked ham
1 can (15-1/4 ounces) whole kernel corn, drained
1 can (14-3/4 ounces) cream-style corn
1 cup cubed process cheese (Velveeta)
1/2 teaspoon seasoned salt

Cook the spaghetti according to package directions. Meanwhile, in a small skillet, saute onion in butter until tender. Drain spaghetti; place in a large bowl. Add the ham, corn, cheese, seasoned salt and onion mixture.

Transfer to a greased 2-qt. baking dish. Cover and bake at 350° for 30-35 minutes or until cheese is melted, stirring once. **Yield: 4-6 servings.**

Editor's Note: While the water is heating for the spaghetti, chop the onion and cube the ham and cheese.

Pork

Pork Chops with Apple Stuffing

Prep: 20 min. | **Bake: 35 min.**

Here's an easy way to dress up plain old pork chops—top them with a moist apple stuffing! —Alta Looney, Howard, Ohio

1/2 cup all-purpose flour
1-1/2 teaspoons salt, *divided*
6 boneless pork loin chops (5 ounces *each*)
3 cups day-old cubed bread, toasted
1-1/2 cups chopped peeled tart apples
1/2 cup chopped celery
1/2 cup chopped onion
1 teaspoon poultry seasoning
1/4 teaspoon pepper
1/3 cup boiling water
1 teaspoon butter, melted

Preheat oven to 350°.

In a large resealable plastic bag, combine flour and 1/2 teaspoon salt. Add pork chops; toss to coat. In a nonstick skillet coated with nonstick cooking spray, brown chops for about 3 minutes on each side. Transfer to a shallow 2-1/2-qt. baking dish.

In a large bowl, combine the bread cubes, apples, celery, onion, poultry seasoning, pepper and remaining salt; toss to coat. Add water and butter; toss to coat.

Place 1/2 cup of stuffing on each pork chop. Cover and bake at 350° for 30 minutes. Uncover; bake 5-10 minutes longer or until a meat thermometer reads 160°. **Yield: 6 servings.**

Golden Pork Chops

Prep: 10 min. | **Bake: 35 min.**

I've had this recipe for several years and really don't remember where I first got it. I have a large family and am always looking for easy recipes that will please all of them. This is definitely one of those.—Betty Sparks, Windsor, Connecticut

1 can (14-3/4 ounces) cream-style corn
1/2 cup finely chopped onion
1/2 cup finely chopped celery
1/2 teaspoon paprika
1-1/2 cups crushed corn bread stuffing
4 boneless pork loin chops (3/4 inch thick and 6 ounces *each*)
1 tablespoon brown sugar
1 tablespoon spicy brown mustard

Preheat oven to 400°.

In a large bowl, combine the corn, onion, celery and paprika. Stir in stuffing. Transfer to a greased 11-in. x 7-in. x 2-in. baking dish.

Arrange pork chops over stuffing. Combine brown sugar and mustard; spread over chops. Bake, uncovered, at 400° for 35-40 minutes or until meat thermometer reads 160°.
Yield: 4 servings.

Spiral Stromboli

Prep: 10 min. | Bake: 25 min.

I frequently fix this speedy sandwich on days we return from our cabin and it's suppertime when we get home. The stuffed loaf takes advantage of refrigerated dough, so it's easy to assemble for a meal, appetizer or late-night snack.
—Jean Gruenert, Burlington, Wisconsin

1 tube (11 ounces) refrigerated crusty French loaf
3/4 to 1 cup shredded part-skim mozzarella cheese
3/4 to 1 cup shredded cheddar cheese
1/4 pound *each* thinly sliced deli salami and ham
1/4 cup chopped roasted red peppers *or* 1 jar (2 ounces) pimientos, drained
1 tablespoon butter, melted
2 to 3 tablespoons shredded Parmesan cheese

Preheat oven to 375°.

Unroll the dough and pat into a 14-in. x 12-in. rectangle. Sprinkle with mozzarella and cheddar cheese to within 1/2 in. of edges; top with meat and red peppers. Roll up jelly-roll style, starting with a short side; seal seam and tuck ends under.

Place seam side down on an ungreased baking sheet. Brush with butter; sprinkle with Parmesan cheese. Bake at 375° for 25-30 minutes or until golden brown. Slice with a serrated knife.
Yield: 4 servings.

Pork

Spinach Pork Tenderloin

Prep: 25 min. | Bake: 25 min. + standing

Stuffed with fresh spinach and artichoke hearts, these pork slices look fancy enough for guests. A sweet-sour sauce enhances the entree.—Linda Rae Lee, San Francisco, California

    2 cups torn fresh baby
      spinach
  1/4 cup water
  1/2 cup frozen artichoke
      hearts, thawed and
      chopped
  1/3 cup shredded Parmesan
      cheese
  1/4 teaspoon dried rosemary,
      crushed
    1 pork tenderloin
      (1 pound)
  1/2 teaspoon salt, *divided*
  1/8 teaspoon pepper

SAUCE:
  1/2 cup apple-cranberry juice
      concentrate
  1/4 cup balsamic vinegar
    1 tablespoon sugar

Preheat oven to 425°.

In a large nonstick skillet, cook the spinach in water over medium heat for 3-4 minutes or until wilted; drain well. In a large bowl, combine the spinach, artichokes, Parmesan cheese and rosemary; set aside.

Cut a lengthwise slit down center of tenderloin to within 1/2 in. of bottom. Open meat so it lies flat; cover with plastic wrap. Flatten pork to 1/4-in. thickness; remove plastic. Sprinkle meat with 1/2 teaspoon salt; top with spinach mixture.

Close meat; tie with kitchen string and secure ends with toothpicks. Sprinkle with pepper and remaining salt. Place in a shallow baking pan. Bake at 425° for 15 minutes.

Meanwhile, in a small saucepan, combine the sauce ingredients. Bring to a boil over medium heat. Reduce heat; simmer, uncovered, for 15 minutes. Pour sauce over the meat. Bake 10 minutes longer or until a meat thermometer reads 160°. Let stand for 10 minutes before slicing. Discard toothpicks.
Yield: 4 servings.

Editor's Note: Start making the sauce while you are stuffing the pork tenderloin. If the sauce is done simmering before the pork is ready to be glazed, just set it aside until it's needed.

Poultry

Aloha Chicken (p. 99)

Corny Chicken Wraps

Prep: 10 min.

My girls like these tortilla roll-ups very much—they ask for them practically every week. Tender chicken combines with canned corn and salsa for a fast-to-fix main dish.
—Sue Seymour, Valatie, New York

2 cups cubed cooked chicken breast
1 can (11 ounces) whole kernel corn, drained
1 cup salsa
1 cup (4 ounces) shredded cheddar cheese
8 flour tortillas (6 inches), warmed

In a large saucepan, combine the chicken, corn and salsa. Cook over medium heat until heated through.

Sprinkle cheese over tortillas. Place about 1/2 cup chicken mixture down the center of each tortilla; roll up and secure with toothpicks.
Yield: 4 servings.

Family-Favorite Chicken Salad

Prep: 10 min.

Red grapes add color to this kid-pleasing chicken salad.
—Taste of Home Test Kitchen

2 cups cubed cooked chicken
1 cup frozen peas, thawed
1 cup halved seedless red grapes
1/2 cup sliced celery
1/4 cup sliced green onions
2 tablespoons minced fresh parsley
3/4 cup mayonnaise
1 teaspoon lemon juice
1/4 teaspoon salt
Leaf lettuce, optional

In a large bowl, combine the first six ingredients. In a small bowl, combine the mayonnaise, lemon juice and salt. Pour over chicken mixture; stir to coat. Serve in a lettuce-lined bowl if desired. **Yield: 4-6 servings.**

Editor's Note: If you don't have leftover chicken, buy a cooked rotisserie chicken from the supermarket and cut it up for the chicken. You'll get about 3 cups of meat from a 3-1/2 pound chicken.

Chicken Salad Clubs

Prep: 10 min.

Mondays have always been soup and sandwich night at our house. One evening, I embellished a regular chicken salad sandwich with some not-so-usual ingredients, like rye bread and honey-mustard dressing. The results were delicious.
—Sarah Smith, Edgewood, Kentucky

8 bacon strips
4 lettuce leaves
8 slices rye *or* pumpernickel bread
1 pound prepared chicken salad
4 slices Swiss cheese
8 slices tomato
1/3 cup honey-mustard salad dressing

In a large skillet, cook bacon over medium heat until crisp. Remove to paper towels to drain. Place lettuce on four slices of bread; layer each with chicken salad, two bacon strips, one cheese slice and two tomato slices. Spread salad dressing on one side of remaining bread; place over tomatoes. **Yield: 4 servings.**

Editor's Note: To save time, use precooked bacon, which is available in the packaged deli meat section of the supermarket.

Poultry

Broiled Chicken Cordon Bleu

Prep: 20 min.

I like to make this flavorful chicken when I am having an especially hectic day—it's so quick to make. You can vary it by using Monterey Jack or cheddar cheese and by replacing the ham with another type of cold cut. —Hope Meece, Ambia, Indiana

4 boneless skinless chicken breasts (4 ounces *each*)
1/4 cup butter, melted
4 thin slices deli ham
4 tablespoons honey-Dijon salad dressing
4 thin slices Swiss cheese

Broil chicken 4-6 in. from the heat for 3 minutes on each side. Brush with butter. Broil 4 minutes longer or until meat juices run clear, turning and basting occasionally.

Place a ham slice on each chicken breast; broil for 1-2 minutes. Spread each with 1 tablespoon dressing; top with cheese. Broil for 30 seconds or until cheese is melted.
Yield: 4 servings.

Teriyaki Chicken Sandwiches

Prep: 20 min.

Lemon juice, soy sauce, garlic, ginger and a little brown sugar combine to make a lip-smacking sauce that seasons shredded cooked chicken. —Pam May, Auburn, Alabama

2-1/2 cups shredded cooked chicken
1/4 cup lemon juice
1/4 cup soy sauce
2 tablespoons sugar
1 tablespoon brown sugar
3/4 teaspoon minced garlic
1/2 teaspoon ground ginger
4 sandwich buns, split

In a large saucepan, combine the first seven ingredients. Bring to a boil. Reduce heat; simmer, uncovered, for 3-4 minutes or until heated through. Spoon chicken mixture onto each bun bottom; replace tops.
Yield: 4 servings.

Fiesta Chicken 'n' Stuffing

micro wave

Prep: 20 min.

My mother gave me this recipe at my bridal shower, and I've been making it ever since. Mom knew that every new bride needs recipes for good food that is super easy to make.
—Angela Peppers, Memphis, Tennessee

3 eggs
3/4 cup milk
2 cups crushed stuffing mix
1-1/2 cups cubed cooked chicken
1 large tomato, chopped
3 tablespoons chopped green chilies
3 tablespoons chopped green onions
Sour cream and salsa, optional

In a large bowl, combine eggs and milk. Stir in the stuffing mix, chicken, tomato, chilies and onions.

Transfer to a greased microwave-safe 9-in. pie plate. Microwave, covered, on high for 2-1/2 minutes; stir. Microwave for 2-1/2 minutes; stir. Cook 2-3 minutes longer or until set and a meat thermometer reads 160°. Let stand for 5 minutes before serving. Garnish with sour cream and salsa if desired.
Yield: 4 servings.

Editor's Note: This recipe was tested in a 1,000-watt microwave.

Poultry

Colorful Chicken Croissants

Prep: 15 min.

This fruity chicken salad was created by a friend of mine. I've made it many times, and guests are always surprised at the pleasant blend of tastes and textures. It's handy to take in a cooler to a picnic, where you can assemble the croissants on site.
—Shelia Lammers, Englewood, Colorado

1/4 cup diced celery
1/4 cup golden raisins
1/4 cup dried cranberries
1/4 cup sliced almonds
3/4 cup mayonnaise
  2 tablespoons chopped red onion
1/4 teaspoon pepper
1/4 teaspoon salt, optional
  2 cups cubed cooked chicken breast
  4 croissants, split

In a large bowl, combine the first seven ingredients and salt if desired. Stir in the chicken. Spoon about 1/2 cup into each croissant.
Yield: 4 servings.

Editor's Note: Plan ahead for this salad and the next time you make chicken breasts, cook extra. You can cube and freeze the meat until you're ready to make the salad.

Smothered Chicken

Prep: 20 min.

You can't go wrong when serving this speedy skillet dish. Tender chicken breasts are topped with mushrooms, bacon, green onions and cheese for a swift and savory sensation that's sure to become a family favorite. —Penny Walton, Westerville, Ohio

4 boneless skinless chicken breast halves (4 ounces *each*)

Garlic powder and seasoned salt to taste

1 tablespoon vegetable oil

1 jar (4-1/2 ounces) sliced mushrooms, drained

1 cup (4 ounces) shredded Mexican cheese blend

1/2 cup chopped green onions

1/2 cup bacon bits

Flatten chicken to 1/4-in. thickness. Sprinkle with garlic powder and seasoned salt.

In a large nonstick skillet, brown chicken over medium heat in oil for 4 minutes; turn. Top with the mushrooms, cheese, green onions and bacon. Cover and cook 4 minutes longer or until chicken juices run clear and cheese is melted.
Yield: 4 servings.

Parmesan Chicken

Prep: 20 min.

People can't believe it when I tell them how little time it takes to fix this delicious chicken. It's very moist inside and so pretty to serve with its lovely basil-flecked coating. —Mollie Hall, San Ramon, California

4 boneless skinless chicken breast halves (4 ounces *each*)

1/2 cup seasoned bread crumbs

1/4 cup grated Parmesan cheese

1/2 teaspoon dried basil

1 egg

1 tablespoon butter

1 tablespoon vegetable oil

Flatten chicken to 1/4-in. thickness. In a shallow bowl, combine the bread crumbs, Parmesan cheese and basil. In another shallow bowl, beat the egg. Dip chicken into egg, then coat with crumb mixture.

In a large skillet, brown chicken over medium heat in butter and oil for 3-5 minutes on each side or until juices run clear.
Yield: 4 servings.

Poultry

Chicken Mushroom Fettuccine

Prep: 20 min.

I depend on this recipe when I get home late from work and my hungry family wants something scrumptious for dinner. It's quick, too, because it uses canned chicken and fresh mushrooms that I buy presliced. —Susanne Stevens, Cedar City, Utah

1 package (16 ounces) fettuccine
1 pound fresh mushrooms, sliced
4 garlic cloves, minced
1/4 cup butter, cubed
2 cans (5 ounces *each*) chunk white chicken, drained
1/2 cup milk
1-1/3 cups grated Parmesan cheese

Cook fettuccine according to package directions. Meanwhile, in a large skillet, saute mushrooms and garlic in butter for 2-3 minutes or until crisp-tender. Stir in the chicken and milk; cook for 5-7 minutes or until heated through.

Drain fettuccine; add to skillet. Sprinkle with the cheese; toss to coat.
Yield: 6 servings.

Breaded Turkey Breasts

Prep: 20 min.

A tasty crumb coating seasoned with Parmesan cheese and Italian herbs gives turkey slices a delicious flavor. I saw this recipe demonstrated on TV, but modified it to reduce fat. The thin turkey slices take just a few minutes on the stovetop, so be careful not to overcook them. —Rhonda Knight, Hecker, Illinois

1 cup dry bread crumbs
1/4 cup grated Parmesan cheese
2 teaspoons Italian seasoning
1 cup milk
8 turkey breast slices (2 ounces *each*)
1/4 cup olive oil

In a shallow bowl, combine the bread crumbs, Parmesan cheese and Italian seasoning. Pour milk into another shallow bowl. Dip turkey in milk, then roll in crumbs.

In a large skillet, cook turkey over medium heat in oil for 4-5 minutes on each side or until juices run clear. Drain on paper towels.
Yield: 4 servings.

Raspberry Thyme Chicken

Prep: 20 min.

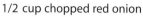

Here's an easy way to dress up chicken. I guarantee you won't miss the fat and calories when you taste this tender poultry with berry sauce.
—Lenita Schafer, Princeton, Massachusetts

1/2 cup chopped red onion
2 teaspoons vegetable oil
1-1/2 teaspoons minced fresh thyme *or* 1/2 teaspoon dried thyme
1/2 teaspoon salt, *divided*
4 boneless skinless chicken breast halves (4 ounces *each*)
1/3 cup seedless raspberry preserves
2 tablespoons balsamic vinegar
1/8 teaspoon pepper

In a nonstick skillet, saute onion in oil until tender. Meanwhile, sprinkle thyme and 1/4 teaspoon salt over chicken; add to skillet. Cook for 5 minutes on each side or until chicken juices run clear. Remove to a serving plate and keep warm.

In the same skillet, add the preserves, vinegar, pepper and remaining salt. Cook and stir over medium-low heat until preserves are melted and sauce is heated through. Serve with chicken.
Yield: 4 servings.

Poultry

Mustard Chicken Breasts

micro wave

Prep: 20 min.

Curry powder, lemon juice, honey and mustard make a lip-smacking sauce for paprika-sprinkled chicken that is cooked in the microwave. This made-in-minutes main dish is a favorite with my family, and I'm sure it will be with yours, too.
—Tina Footen, Nampa, Idaho

4 bone-in chicken breast halves (6 ounces *each*), skin removed
1 teaspoon paprika
1 medium lemon, thinly sliced
1/3 cup spicy brown mustard
1/3 cup honey
1 teaspoon dried minced onion
1/2 teaspoon curry powder
1/2 teaspoon lemon juice

Arrange chicken in a 9-in. or 10-in. microwave-safe pie plate, with the thickest side toward the outside of the plate. Sprinkle with paprika; top with lemon slices. Cover and microwave, on high for 6-8 minutes, rotating dish a half turn once.

In a small microwave-safe bowl, combine the remaining ingredients. Microwave, uncovered, on high for 1 to 1-1/2 minutes or until heated through; stir.

Drain chicken; top with sauce. Cover and cook on high for 1-1/2 minutes until a meat thermometer reads 170°.
Yield: 4 servings.

Editor's Note: This recipe was tested in a 1,100-watt microwave.

Chicken Salsa Pizza

Prep: 20 min.

This zippy chicken pizza is sure to become the most-requested version in the house. The cooked chicken and a prebaked crust make it quick, easy and oh-so-good.
—Mrs. Guy Turnbull, Arlington, Massachusetts

1 prebaked Italian bread shell crust (14 ounces)

2 cups (8 ounces) shredded cheddar cheese, *divided*

1 jar (11 ounces) salsa

1 cup cubed cooked chicken

Preheat oven to 450°.

Place bread shell on an ungreased 12-in. pizza pan. Sprinkle with 3/4 cup cheese. Top with the salsa, chicken and remaining cheese. Bake at 450° for 8-10 minutes or until cheese is bubbly.
Yield: 4 servings.

Chicken a la King

Prep: 20 min.

If you have leftover cooked cubed chicken or turkey in the freezer, this speedy entree is even easier to prepare. Defrost in the microwave for last-minute meals.
—Polly Hurst, Flemingsburg, Kentucky

1/4 cup butter, cubed

1/3 cup all-purpose flour

1/2 teaspoon salt

1 cup chicken broth

1 cup milk

2 cups cubed cooked chicken

1 can (4 ounces) mushroom stems and pieces, drained

1 jar (2 ounces) diced pimientos, drained

Toast points

In a large saucepan, melt butter; stir in flour and salt until smooth; gradually add the broth and milk. Bring to a boil over medium heat; cook and stir for 2 minutes or until thickened. Stir in the chicken, mushrooms and pimientos; heat through. Serve over toast points.
Yield: 4 servings.

Editor's Note: Toast the bread while you are making the sauce.

Poultry

Chicken Stroganoff

micro wave

Prep: 20 min.

I concocted this recipe for those evenings when I'm running late and everyone is hungry. Even my finicky child asks for seconds. For a no-fuss beef Stroganoff, substitute leftover steak. —Phyllis Brittenham, Garwin, Iowa

4 cups uncooked egg noodles
2 cups cubed cooked chicken
1-1/2 cups (12 ounces) sour cream
1 can (10-3/4 ounces) condensed cream of mushroom soup, undiluted
1/2 teaspoon seasoned salt
1/4 teaspoon pepper
Minced fresh parsley, optional

Cook noodles according to package directions; drain. In a greased 2-qt. microwave-safe dish, combine the chicken, sour cream, soup, seasoned salt and pepper. Stir in the noodles.

Cover and microwave on high for 3-6 minutes or until heated through. Sprinkle with parsley if desired. Let stand for 5 minutes before serving.
Yield: 4-6 servings.

Editor's Note: This recipe was tested in a 1,100-watt microwave.

Asian Turkey Burgers

Prep: 20 min.

Garlic, ginger and soy sauce are used to turn ground turkey into moist tender patties. They're winners at my house. —Jeanette Saskowski, Antioch, Tennessee

1 egg white
1 tablespoon soy sauce
1/2 cup dry bread crumbs
1 tablespoon finely chopped onion
1 garlic clove, minced
1/4 teaspoon ground ginger
1/8 teaspoon pepper
12 ounces ground turkey

In a large bowl, combine the first seven ingredients. Crumble turkey over mixture and mix just until combined. Shape into four patties.

In a nonstick skillet coated with nonstick cooking spray, cook burgers over medium heat for 6-8 minutes on each side or until a meat thermometer reaches 165°.
Yield: 4 servings.

Soft Chicken Tacos

Prep: 20 min.

I came up with this healthy chicken and bean filling for tacos since my husband needs to watch his cholesterol level. Sliced radishes make a unique crunchy topping.
—Ruth Peterson, Jenison, Michigan

1 pound boneless skinless chicken breasts, cut into 1-inch cubes

1 can (15 ounces) black beans, rinsed and drained

1 cup salsa

1 tablespoon taco seasoning

6 fat-free flour tortillas (8 inches), warmed

Shredded lettuce, shredded reduced-fat cheddar cheese, sliced radishes, chopped tomatoes, sliced green onions and fat-free sour cream, optional

In a large skillet coated with nonstick cooking spray, cook chicken over medium heat until juices run clear. Stir in the beans, salsa and taco seasoning; heat through. Spoon the chicken mixture down the center of each tortilla; roll up. Serve with toppings of your choice.
Yield: 6 servings.

Cajun Chicken Club

Prep: 20 min.

It takes just minutes to assemble these sandwiches. Cajun seasoning gives them a zippy flavor. —Mrs. J.M. Andrews, Marcellus, New York

8 bacon strips
4 boneless skinless chicken breast halves (4 ounces *each*)
1/2 to 1 teaspoon Cajun seasoning
1 tablespoon vegetable oil
4 slices Swiss cheese
1/4 cup prepared creamy Parmesan salad dressing
4 sandwich rolls, split and toasted
8 tomato slices

In a large skillet, cook bacon over medium heat until crisp; drain on paper towels.

While bacon is cooking, flatten the chicken to 3/8-in. thickness; sprinkle with Cajun seasoning. In another large skillet, cook chicken over medium heat in oil for 5 minutes on each side or until juices run clear. Place cheese over chicken. Remove from the heat; cover and let stand for 1 minute or until cheese begins to melt.

Spread dressing over both halves of rolls. Layer bottom halves with two slices of tomato, chicken and two strips of bacon; replace tops.
Yield: 4 servings.

Editor's Note: To save time, use precooked bacon, which is available in the packaged deli meat section of the supermarket.

Cranberry-Orange Turkey Cutlets

Prep: 20 min.

*Every time I make this, my husband suggests it would be a great
company dish. It is easy to prepare, but looks elegant.*
— Joan Tweed, Irmo, South Carolina

4 turkey breast tenderloins
(4 ounces *each*)
1 cup dry bread crumbs
1 egg white
1 tablespoon fat-free milk
1/2 teaspoon salt
3/4 cup cranberry-orange *or*
whole-berry cranberry
sauce
1 tablespoon olive oil

Flatten turkey to 1/4-in. thickness. Place bread crumbs in a shallow bowl. In another shallow bowl, beat the egg white, milk and salt. Dip turkey into egg white mixture, then coat with crumbs. Refrigerate turkey, uncovered, for 10 minutes.

Meanwhile, in a small saucepan, heat cranberry-orange sauce. In a large nonstick skillet, brown turkey in oil for 3-4 minutes on each side or until juices run clear. Serve sauce with turkey. **Yield: 4 servings.**

Editor's Note: This recipe was tested with Ocean Spray Cranberry-Orange sauce. Look for it in the canned fruit section of your grocery store.

Barbecued Chicken Pizza

Prep: 20 min.

*My daughter loves creating smiling faces on this pizza with shredded cheese and fresh
veggie toppings. —Patricia Richardson, Verona, Ontario*

1 prebaked Italian bread shell crust
(14 ounces)
2/3 cup honey garlic barbecue sauce
1 small red onion, chopped
1 cup cubed cooked chicken
2 cups (8 ounces) shredded
part-skim mozzarella cheese

Preheat oven to 350°.

Place the crust on a 14-in. pizza pan. Spread barbecue sauce to within 1/2 in. of edges. Sprinkle with the onion, chicken and cheese. Bake at 350° for 10 minutes or until cheese is melted. **Yield: 4 servings.**

Poultry

Ranch Turkey Pasta Dinner

Prep: 20 min.

This entree is a great way to finish up a holiday turkey. At times, I use chicken if I have that on hand instead. Try sprinkling grated cheese over the top of each helping for extra flavor.
—Peggy Key, Grant, Alabama

2-1/2 cups uncooked penne pasta
6 to 8 tablespoons butter, cubed
1 envelope ranch salad dressing mix
1 cup frozen peas and carrots, thawed
3 cups cubed cooked turkey

Cook pasta according to package directions. Meanwhile, in a large skillet, melt butter. Stir in salad dressing until smooth. Add peas and carrots; cook and stir for 2-3 minutes. Drain pasta and add to skillet. Stir in turkey, cook for 3-4 minutes or until heated through.
Yield: 4 servings.

Honey-Mustard Chicken

Prep: 20 min.

I get bored with the same old chicken, so I came up with this simple recipe. The coating adds fast flavor to tender chicken cooked on the stovetop.
—Laura Theofilis, Leonardtown, Maryland

4 boneless skinless chicken breast halves (4 ounces *each*)
1 cup dry bread crumbs
1 teaspoon plus 2 tablespoons Dijon mustard, *divided*
3 tablespoons honey
2 tablespoons butter

Flatten chicken to 1/4-in. thickness. In a shallow bowl, combine bread crumbs and 1 teaspoon mustard. In another shallow bowl, combine honey and remaining mustard. Dip chicken in honey-mustard mixture, then coat with crumbs.

In a nonstick skillet, cook chicken over medium heat in butter for 4-6 minutes on each side or until juices run clear.
Yield: 4 servings.

Aloha Chicken

Prep: 20 min.

I'm always on the lookout for low-fat recipes that are scrumptious, too, like this one. In this dish, quick-cooking chicken breasts get wonderful sweet flavor from pineapple, honey and teriyaki sauce. —Jenny Reece, Lowry, Minnesota

- 4 boneless skinless chicken breast halves (4 ounces *each*)
- 1 tablespoon all-purpose flour
- 1 tablespoon vegetable oil
- 2 cans (8 ounces *each*) unsweetened pineapple chunks
- 1 teaspoon cornstarch
- 1 tablespoon honey
- 1 tablespoon reduced-sodium teriyaki sauce *or* reduced-sodium soy sauce
- 1/8 teaspoon pepper

Hot cooked rice

Flatten chicken to 1/4-in. thickness. Place flour in a large resealable plastic bag; add chicken and toss to coat.

In a large skillet, brown chicken over medium heat in oil for 3-5 minutes on each side or until juices run clear. Remove and keep warm.

Drain pineapple, reserving 1/4 cup juice. (Discard remaining juice or save for another use.) In a small bowl, combine cornstarch and reserved juice until smooth. Gradually add to skillet. Stir in the honey, teriyaki sauce and pepper. Bring to a boil; cook and stir for 30 seconds or until thickened. Add pineapple and chicken; heat through. Serve with rice.

Yield: 4 servings.

Editor's Note: If serving with rice, begin cooking the rice before you flatten the chicken breast, or make instant rice while the chicken is cooking.

20
minute recipes

Chicken Veggie Casserole
Prep: 20 min.

This casserole is a hot, satisfying and complete meal in one dish.
—Martha Balser, Cincinnati, Ohio

1 can (10-3/4 ounces) condensed cream of chicken soup, undiluted
1/2 cup milk
1/4 teaspoon dried thyme
1/4 teaspoon salt
1/4 teaspoon pepper
2 cups cubed cooked chicken
1 can (15-1/4 ounces) whole kernel corn, drained
2 cups frozen cut green beans, thawed
2 cups sliced cooked potatoes

Preheat oven to 400°.

In a large bowl, combine the soup, milk, thyme, salt and pepper. Stir in the chicken, corn, beans and potatoes.

Pour into a greased 1-1/2-qt. baking dish. Bake, uncovered, at 400° for 15 minutes or until heated through.
Yield: 6 servings.

Editor's Note: To save time, purchase precooked potatoes from the refrigerated section of the grocery store.

Turkey Salad on Wheat

Prep: 15 min.

Inspired by the turkey salad at a local deli, I developed this version to suit my family's tastes. You can serve it on whole-grain bread for a filling meal or on croissants for an elegant luncheon. Precooked bacon and leftover turkey make it a snap to fix.
—Merrijane Rice, Bountiful, Utah

  2 cups chopped romaine
1-1/4 cups diced cooked turkey
  1/2 cup shredded Swiss cheese
  2 green onions, thinly sliced
  6 bacon strips, cooked and crumbled
  1/3 cup frozen peas, thawed
  1/2 cup mayonnaise
  1/4 teaspoon pepper
  12 slices whole wheat bread

In a large bowl, combine the first six ingredients. Add mayonnaise and pepper; toss to coat. Spread on six slices of bread; top with remaining bread. Serve immediately.
Yield: 6 servings.

Curried Chicken 'n' Broccoli micro wave

Prep: 20 min.

You can't beat this dish since it's easy, nutritious and delicious. I've received many compliments on it. —Esther Shank, Harrisonville, Virginia

  1 package (14 ounces) frozen broccoli florets, thawed
  2 cups cooked chicken strips
  1 can (10-3/4 ounces) condensed cream of chicken soup, undiluted
  1/2 cup mayonnaise
  1 tablespoon lemon juice
  1/4 to 1/2 teaspoon curry powder
  1/4 teaspoon salt
  1/2 cup shredded cheddar cheese
Hot cooked rice

Place the broccoli in a 1-1/2-qt. microwave-safe dish. Top with the chicken. In a small bowl, combine the soup, mayonnaise, lemon juice, curry powder and salt. Spoon over chicken. Sprinkle with cheese. Cover and microwave at 70% power for 6-8 minutes. Serve with rice.
Yield: 4 servings.

Editor's Note: This recipe was tested in a 1,100-watt microwave. Reduced-fat or fat-free mayonnaise is not recommended for this recipe. If serving with rice, begin cooking the rice before you make the chicken, or use instant rice.

Poultry

Chicken Chili

Prep: 5 min. | Cook: 25 min.

I got this instant chili recipe from my aunt. To save time, I usually cook and cube the chicken the night before or use leftovers. The next day, it's simple to simmer the ingredients on the stovetop. I serve the hearty results with crunchy corn chips or warm bread. —Yvonne Morgan, Grand Rapids, Michigan

2 cans (15 ounces *each*) great northern beans, rinsed and drained
2 jars (16 ounces *each*) picante sauce
4 cups cubed cooked chicken
1 to 2 teaspoons ground cumin
Shredded Monterey Jack cheese

In a large saucepan, combine the beans, picante sauce, chicken and cumin. Bring to a boil. Reduce heat; cover and simmer for 20 minutes. Sprinkle with cheese.
Yield: 6 servings.

Bow Tie Turkey Bake micro wave

Prep: 20 min. | Cook: 10 min.

This convenient casserole can be assembled the night before and refrigerated to cook the next day. It's so easy to make. —Betty Aiken, Bradenton, Florida

2-1/2 cups uncooked bow tie pasta
8 ounces turkey Italian sausage links, casings removed
1 jar (26 ounces) spaghetti sauce
3/4 cup 4% cottage cheese, drained
1/4 cup grated Parmesan cheese
1 package (10 ounces) frozen chopped spinach, thawed and squeezed dry
1 tablespoon shredded Parmesan cheese

Cook the pasta according to package directions. Meanwhile, in a large skillet, cook sausage over medium heat until no longer pink; drain. Drain the pasta.

Spread 1/4 cup spaghetti sauce in a greased 2-qt. microwave-safe dish. Layer with half of the pasta, a third of the remaining sauce and half of the cottage cheese, sausage and grated Parmesan. Top with spinach. Repeat layers. Top with remaining sauce. Sprinkle with shredded Parmesan.

Cover and microwave on high for 6-7 minutes or until heated through.
Yield: 4-6 servings.

Editor's Note: This recipe was tested in a 1,100-watt microwave.

Cheddar Chicken Spirals

micro wave

Prep: 20 min. | Cook: 10 min.

My granddaughters just love this chicken dish. I try to make it every time they come to visit. Lucky for me, it goes together quick as a wink.
—Miriam Christophel, Battle Creek, Michigan

1-1/2 cups uncooked spiral pasta
1/2 cup mayonnaise
1/3 cup milk
1/2 teaspoon salt
1/2 teaspoon dried basil
2 cups frozen mixed vegetables, thawed
1-1/2 cups cubed cooked chicken
1-1/2 cups (6 ounces) shredded cheddar cheese, *divided*

Cook the pasta according to package directions. Meanwhile, in a large bowl, combine the mayonnaise, milk, salt and basil. Stir in the vegetables, chicken and 1 cup cheese. Drain pasta; stir into vegetable mixture.

Transfer to a greased 1-1/2-qt. microwave-safe dish. Sprinkle with remaining cheese. Cover and microwave on high for 4-5 minutes or until heated through and the cheese is melted. Let stand for 5 minutes before serving.
Yield: 4 servings.

Editor's Note: Reduced-fat or fat-free mayonnaise is not recommended for this recipe. This recipe was tested in a 1,000-watt microwave.

30
minute recipes

Chicken with Peach Stuffing

Prep: 5 min. | Cook: 25 min.

This is my favorite kind of recipe...something that tastes so good, yet requires a minimum of preparation. This half-hour dish fits the bill.
—Theresa Stewart, New Oxford, Pennsylvania

1 can (15-1/4 ounces) sliced peaches
4 boneless skinless chicken breast halves (4 ounces *each*)
2 tablespoons vegetable oil
2 tablespoons butter
1 tablespoon brown sugar
1 tablespoon cider vinegar
1/8 teaspoon ground allspice
3 cups instant chicken-flavored stuffing mix

Drain peaches, reserving juice; set the peaches aside. Add enough water to juice to measure 1 cup; set aside.

In a large skillet, brown chicken on both sides in oil. Gradually stir in the peach juice mixture, butter, brown sugar, vinegar and allspice. Bring to a boil. Reduce heat; cover and simmer for 5 minutes or until chicken juices run clear.

Stir in stuffing mix and peaches. Cover and remove from the heat. Let stand for 5 minutes or until liquid is absorbed.
Yield: 4 servings.

Baked Garlic Chicken

Prep: 10 min. | Bake: 20 min.

I think this is a quick recipe for lovely golden breaded chicken breasts. The meat is always moist and well-seasoned. I hope you and your family will agree.
—Mary Lou Wayman, Salt Lake City, Utah

1/3 cup mayonnaise
1/4 cup grated Parmesan cheese
3 to 4 tablespoons savory herb with garlic soup mix
4 boneless skinless chicken breast halves (4 ounces *each*)
2 tablespoons dry bread crumbs

Preheat oven to 400°.

In a small bowl, combine the mayonnaise, Parmesan cheese and soup mix.

Place the chicken in a greased 11-in. x 7-in. x 2-in. baking dish. Spread with the mayonnaise mixture. Sprinkle with bread crumbs. Bake, uncovered, at 400° for 20-25 minutes or until juices run clear and a meat thermometer reads 170°.
Yield: 4 servings.

Editor's Note: Reduced-fat or fat-free mayonnaise is not recommended for this recipe.

Swiss Mushroom Chicken

Prep: 15 min. | Cook: 10 min.

Everyone enjoys these golden chicken breasts topped with ham, melted Swiss cheese and fresh mushrooms. They're easy to prepare but look and taste special. —Jan Baxter, Humarock, Massachusetts

- 4 skinless chicken breast halves (4 ounces *each*)
- 1 egg
- 1 cup crushed butter-flavored crackers (about 25 crackers)
- 3/4 teaspoon salt
- 1/2 pound fresh mushrooms, sliced
- 2 tablespoons butter, *divided*
- 4 slices deli ham *or* thinly sliced hard salami
- 4 slices Swiss cheese

Flatten chicken to 1/4-in. thickness. In a shallow bowl, lightly beat the egg. Combine cracker crumbs and salt in another shallow bowl. Dip chicken in egg, then roll in crumbs; set aside.

In a large ovenproof skillet, saute mushrooms in 1 tablespoon butter until tender; remove and set aside. In the same skillet, cook chicken over medium heat in remaining butter for 3-4 minutes on each side or until juices run clear.

Top each chicken breast half with a ham slice, mushrooms and a cheese slice. Broil 4-6 in. from the heat for 1-2 minutes or until cheese is melted. **Yield: 4 servings.**

Chicken Stir-Fry Bake

Prep: 5 min. | Bake: 25 min.

One night, I opted to use frozen vegetables in my chicken stir-fry. Not wanting to stand watch over the stovetop, I baked the entree in the oven. People say this tastes like it's hot from the skillet. —Carly Carter, Nashville, Tennessee

- 2 cups uncooked instant rice
- 1 can (8 ounces) sliced water chestnuts, drained
- 2 cups cubed cooked chicken
- 1 package (16 ounces) frozen stir-fry vegetables, thawed
- 1 can (14-1/2 ounces) chicken broth
- 1/4 cup soy sauce
- 1 garlic clove, minced
- 1/2 to 3/4 teaspoon ground ginger

Preheat oven to 375°.

Place rice in a greased 11-in. x 7-in. x 2-in. baking dish. Layer with water chestnuts, chicken and vegetables. Combine the remaining ingredients; pour over top. Cover and bake at 375° for 25 minutes or until rice is tender. **Yield: 4 servings.**

Poultry

Easy Italian Chicken

Prep: 10 min. | Cook: 15 min.

When we want a hearty Italian dish but I don't want to spend hours cooking, this is the recipe I choose. Boneless skinless chicken breasts are convenient to have in the freezer because they thaw and cook quickly. Plus, I always have the other ingredients in my pantry. —Joan Rose, Langley, British Columbia

4 boneless skinless chicken breast
   halves (4 ounces *each*)
1 can (14-1/2 ounces) Italian stewed
   tomatoes
1 can (4 ounces) mushroom stems
   and pieces, drained
1/2 teaspoon dried basil
1/4 teaspoon garlic powder
1 tablespoon cornstarch
1/3 cup cold water
Hot cooked spaghetti

In a large skillet coated with nonstick cooking spray, cook chicken for 5-6 minutes on each side or until the juices run clear.

Meanwhile, in a saucepan over medium heat, combine the tomatoes, mushrooms, basil and garlic powder; bring to a boil. Combine cornstarch and water until smooth; gradually add to tomato mixture. Cook and stir for 2 minutes or until thickened. Serve chicken with spaghetti; top with tomato sauce.
Yield: 4 servings.

Pesto Chicken Pasta

Prep: 5 min. | Cook: 20 min.

Because my job shift ends at 7 p.m., I need to get dinner on the table fast. I double this dish for my family. It's great hot or cold. Try it with cooked shrimp instead of chicken. —Linda Sweet, Newark, Delaware

8 ounces uncooked ziti *or* uncooked small tube pasta
1 cup frozen peas and carrots
1 envelope pesto sauce mix
1 tablespoon cornstarch
1-1/2 cups milk
1 cup cubed cooked chicken
1/4 teaspoon salt
1/4 teaspoon pepper
1/4 cup chopped walnuts

Cook pasta according to package directions; add peas and carrots during the last 2 minutes of cooking. Meanwhile, in a small saucepan, whisk the pesto mix, cornstarch and milk until smooth. Bring to a boil; cook and stir for 2 minutes or until thickened. Stir in the chicken, salt and pepper.

Drain pasta mixture; place in a large serving bowl. Add the chicken mixture; toss to coat. Sprinkle with walnuts.
Yield: 4 servings.

Editor's Note: While the water is being brought to a boil, cube the chicken. If you don't have leftover chicken, buy a cooked rotisserie chicken from the supermarket and cut it up for the chicken. You'll get about 3 cups of meat from a 3-1/2 pound chicken.

Honey Garlic Chicken

Prep: 5 min. | Cook: 20 min.

The mellow flavor of chicken pairs well with honey, orange juice and garlic. Broiling for a few minutes gives the chicken a little golden color. —Taste of Home Test Kitchen

4 boneless skinless chicken breast halves (4 ounces *each*)
2 tablespoons honey
2 tablespoons orange *or* lemon juice
1 tablespoon vegetable oil
1/2 teaspoon salt
Dash pepper
1 to 2 garlic cloves, minced

Preheat oven to 400°.

Place chicken in a greased 13-in. x 9-in. x 2-in. baking pan. In a small bowl, combine the remaining ingredients; pour over chicken.

Bake, uncovered, at 400° for 15 minutes. Broil 4-6 in. from the heat for 5-7 minutes or until juices run clear, brushing occasionally with sauce.
Yield: 4 servings.

Poultry

Smoked Turkey Sausage with Pasta

Prep: 10 min. | Cook: 20 min.

Chock-full of sausage, mushrooms, tomatoes and basil flavor, this quick recipe satisfies the toughest critics. It's one of my husband's favorite dishes, and he has no idea it's lower in fat. Add a green salad for a delicious meal. —Ruth Ann Ruddell, Shelby Township, Michigan

4 ounces uncooked angel hair pasta

1/2 pound smoked turkey kielbasa, cut into 1/2-inch slices

2 cups sliced fresh mushrooms

2 garlic cloves, minced

4-1/2 teaspoons minced fresh basil *or* 1-1/2 teaspoons dried basil

1 tablespoon olive oil

2 cups julienned seeded plum tomatoes

1/8 teaspoon salt

1/8 teaspoon pepper

Cook pasta according to package directions. Meanwhile, in a large nonstick skillet, saute the sausage, mushrooms, garlic and basil in oil until mushrooms are tender.

Drain pasta; add to the sausage mixture. Add the tomatoes, salt and pepper; toss gently. Heat through.
Yield: 4 servings.

Chicken Amandine

Prep: 10 min. | Bake: 20 min.

These chicken breasts are coated with a nicely seasoned nut mixture. While they bake, you can prepare the rest of your meal. —Taste of Home Test Kitchen

1-1/2 cups sliced almonds

3/4 cup dry bread crumbs

2 tablespoons dried parsley flakes

1/2 teaspoon salt

1/4 teaspoon pepper

2 eggs

1 tablespoon water

4 boneless skinless chicken breast halves (4 ounces *each*)

Preheat oven to 400°.

In a food processor, cover and process almonds until finely chopped. Place in a shallow bowl. In another shallow bowl, combine the bread crumbs, parsley, salt and pepper. In a third bowl, beat the eggs and water.

Roll chicken in crumb mixture, then dip in egg mixture and coat with almonds. Place on a greased baking sheet. Bake at 400° for 20-25 minutes or until juices run clear.
Yield: 4 servings.

Chicken with Apple Cream Sauce

Prep: 5 min. | Cook: 25 min.

Topping chicken with an apple cream sauce is a unique and delicious way to serve it. We think the sauce is absolutely wonderful. —Victoria Casey, Coeur d'Alene, Idaho

4 boneless skinless chicken breast halves (6 ounces *each*)
1 tablespoon vegetable oil
1 cup apple juice
1 teaspoon lemon juice
1/4 to 1/2 teaspoon dried rosemary, crushed
1/2 teaspoon salt
1/8 teaspoon pepper
1 tablespoon cornstarch
1/2 cup heavy whipping cream
1 tablespoon minced fresh parsley
Hot cooked rice

In a skillet, brown the chicken in oil over medium heat for 4 minutes on each side.

Combine the apple juice, lemon juice, rosemary, salt and pepper; pour over chicken. Reduce heat; cover and simmer for 10 minutes or until chicken juices run clear. Remove chicken and keep warm.

Combine cornstarch and cream until smooth; stir into cooking liquid in skillet. Bring to a boil; cook and stir for 2 minutes or until thickened. Add parsley. Return chicken to skillet and heat through. Serve over rice.
Yield: 4 servings.

Editor's Note: If serving with rice, start heating the water for the rice before you begin cooking the chicken. When minutes count, use instant white or brown rice.

30

minute recipes

Turkey Florentine

Prep: 15 min. | Bake: 15 min.

Swiss cheese and spinach are tucked into browned turkey slices, then topped with spaghetti sauce. I usually serve these roll-ups with pasta, a green salad and rolls.
—Lillian Butler, Stratford, Connecticut

1 cup seasoned bread crumbs
8 slices uncooked turkey breast
2 tablespoons vegetable oil
4 slices Swiss cheese, cut in half
1 package (10 ounces) frozen chopped spinach, thawed and squeezed dry
3 cups meatless spaghetti sauce

Preheat oven to 400°.

Place bread crumbs in a large resealable plastic bag; add turkey in batches and shake to coat. In a large skillet, brown turkey in oil over medium heat. Remove from the skillet.

Place half a cheese slice and 2 tablespoons spinach down the center of each turkey slice. Fold turkey over filling; secure with toothpicks.

Place in a greased 11-in. x 7-in. x 2-in. baking dish. Top with spaghetti sauce. Bake, uncovered, at 400° for 12-15 minutes or turkey juices run clear. Discard toothpicks.
Yield: 4 servings.

Peanut Chicken Stir-Fry

Prep: 10 min. | **Cook: 20 min.**

Peanut butter is one of my husband's favorite foods. I love that I can use it to make a delicious meal. —Diane Kelly, Puyallup, Washington

1/2 cup plus 1 tablespoon water, *divided*
1/4 cup peanut butter
3 tablespoons soy sauce
1 tablespoon brown sugar
1 tablespoon cornstarch
2 to 3 garlic cloves, minced
2 tablespoons vegetable oil
1 pound boneless skinless chicken breasts, cubed
3 cups fresh broccoli florets
Hot cooked rice *or* noodles

In a small bowl, combine 1/2 cup water, peanut butter, soy sauce and brown sugar until smooth; set aside. Combine cornstarch and remaining water until smooth; set aside.

In a skillet or wok, stir-fry garlic in oil for 30 seconds. Add the chicken; stir-fry for 5 minutes or until no longer pink. Add the broccoli; stir-fry for 5 minutes. Stir in the peanut butter mixture; cook and stir for 2-3 minutes or until sauce is smooth and broccoli is crisp-tender. Stir cornstarch mixture; gradually add to skillet. Bring to a boil; cook and stir for 2 minutes or until thickened. Serve with rice. **Yield: 4 servings.**

Editor's Note: Reduced-fat or generic brands of peanut butter are not recommended for this recipe.

Sweet 'n' Sour Sausage Stir-Fry

Prep: 15 min. | **Cook: 15 min.**

My family truly enjoys this quick meal. I can have it on the table in about 30 minutes with no thawing and no planning.—Wendy Wendler, Satellite Beach, Florida

1 package (14 ounces) smoked turkey sausage, cut into 1/2-inch slices
2 small onions, quartered and separated
1 cup shredded carrots
1 can (8 ounces) unsweetened pineapple chunks
1 tablespoon cornstarch
1/2 to 1 teaspoon ground ginger
6 tablespoons water
2 tablespoons soy sauce
Hot cooked rice, optional

In a large nonstick skillet, stir-fry sausage for 3-4 minutes or until lightly browned. Add onions and carrots; stir-fry until crisp-tender. Drain pineapple, reserving juice. Add pineapple to sausage mixture.

In a small bowl, combine cornstarch and ginger. Stir in the water, soy sauce and reserved pineapple juice until smooth. Add to the skillet. Bring to a boil; cook and stir for 1-2 minutes or until thickened. Serve over rice if desired. **Yield: 4 servings.**

Poultry

Spaghetti with Homemade Turkey Sausage

plan ahead

Prep: 10 min. + chilling | Cook: 20 min.

This speedy and hearty dish is quite tasty. You get the rich flavor by allowing the turkey and spices to blend overnight. Don't skip this step! —Shirley Goodson, West Allis, Wisconsin

1 pound ground turkey
1 teaspoon fennel seed, crushed
1 teaspoon water
1/2 teaspoon salt
1/2 teaspoon pepper
12 ounces uncooked spaghetti
1 jar (27 ounces) spaghetti sauce

In a large bowl, combine the turkey, fennel seed, water, salt and pepper. Cover and refrigerate overnight.

Cook pasta according to package directions. Crumble turkey into bite-size pieces into a large skillet. Cook over medium heat until no longer pink; drain if necessary. Stir in spaghetti sauce and heat through. Drain pasta and serve with sauce. **Yield: 6 servings.**

Quick Barbecued Chicken

Prep: 10 min. | Cook: 20 min.

Cooking outdoors is a great way to make dinner when time is tight. While the grill is heating up, you can quickly simmer the sauce. To prevent the sauce from burning while grilling, brush it on only during the last few minutes.
—Taste of Home Test Kitchen

1 cup ketchup
1/4 cup packed brown sugar
2 tablespoons red wine vinegar
2 teaspoons soy sauce
1 tablespoon dried minced onion
1/4 teaspoon celery seed
1/2 teaspoon salt, *divided*
1/4 teaspoon crushed red pepper flakes, optional
Dash Liquid Smoke, optional
4 boneless skinless chicken breast halves (6 ounces *each*)
1 tablespoon vegetable oil

Preheat grill.

In a saucepan, combine the first six ingredients; add 1/4 teaspoon salt and pepper flakes and Liquid Smoke if desired. Bring to a boil. Reduce heat; cook and stir over low heat for 10 minutes or until thickened.

While sauce is simmering, rub chicken with oil and sprinkle with remaining salt. Grill, covered, over medium heat for 3 minutes on each side.

Set aside 1/2 cup barbecue sauce for serving. Brush half of the remaining sauce over chicken. Grill, covered, 7-12 minutes longer or until chicken juices run clear, turning and basting occasionally with sauce. Serve with reserved sauce. **Yield: 4 servings.**

Apricot Salsa Chicken

Prep: 5 min. | **Cook: 25 min.**

In an unusual but tongue-tingling combination, apricots and salsa smother pieces of chicken with a sweet and spicy sauce in this recipe.
—Grace Yaskovic, Branchville, New Jersey

1/2 cup all-purpose flour
1 teaspoon salt
1/4 teaspoon pepper
1/4 teaspoon paprika
6 boneless skinless chicken breast halves (4 ounces *each*)
3 tablespoons vegetable oil
1 jar (16 ounces) salsa
1 jar (12 ounces) apricot preserves
1/2 cup apricot nectar
Hot cooked rice

In a large resealable plastic bag, combine the first four ingredients; add chicken in batches. Seal bag and shake to coat.

In a large skillet, cook chicken over medium heat in oil until browned on each side; drain. Stir in the salsa, preserves and nectar; bring to a boil. Reduce heat; simmer, uncovered, for 15 minutes or until sauce thickens and meat juices run clear. Serve with rice.
Yield: 6 servings.

Editor's Note: If serving with rice, start heating the water for the rice before you begin cooking the chicken. When minutes count, use instant white or brown rice.

Poultry

113

Crispy Chicken

Prep: 10 min. | Bake: 20 min.

One of my favorite quick-cooking cuts of meat is boneless chicken breast. The crushed rice cereal gives it a unique, but tasty crust. Have one of your kids coarsely crush the cereal for you.
— Coleen Martin, Brookfield, Wisconsin

1-1/2 cups crisp rice cereal, coarsely crushed
2 tablespoons all-purpose flour
1/2 teaspoon salt
1/4 teaspoon dried thyme
1/4 teaspoon poultry seasoning
1/4 cup butter, melted
4 boneless skinless chicken breast halves (4 ounces *each*)

Preheat oven to 400°.

In a shallow bowl, combine the cereal, flour and seasonings. Place butter in another shallow bowl. Dip chicken in butter, then roll in cereal mixture.

Place in a greased 11-in. x 7-in. x 2-in. baking pan. Drizzle with remaining butter. Bake, uncovered, at 400° for 20-25 minutes or until juices run clear.
Yield: 4 servings.

Italian Turkey Burgers

Prep: 15 min. | Grill: 15 min.

Seasoned with oregano and Parmesan cheese, these plump burgers are a delicious change-of-pace entree. I like to serve them on crusty Italian bread with warmed spaghetti sauce. —Mary Tallman, Arbor Vitae, Wisconsin

1/4 cup canned crushed tomatoes
2 tablespoons grated Parmesan cheese
1/2 teaspoon garlic powder
1/2 teaspoon dried oregano
1/4 teaspoon salt
1/4 teaspoon pepper
1 pound ground turkey
8 slices Italian bread, toasted
1/2 cup meatless spaghetti sauce, warmed

Coat grill rack with nonstick cooking spray before starting the grill. Preheat grill.

In a large bowl, combine the first six ingredients. Crumble turkey over mixture and mix well. Shape into four 3/4-in.-thick oval-shape patties.

Grill patties, uncovered, over medium heat for 6-8 minutes on each side or until a meat thermometer reaches 165°. Place a patty on each of four slices of bread. Drizzle with spaghetti sauce; top with remaining bread.
Yield: 4 servings.

The Busy Family Cookbook

Honey Chicken Stir-Fry

Prep: 15 min. | **Cook 15 min.**

When I was a new mom, my schedule was very dependent upon our young son. So I like meals that can be ready in as little time as possible. This all-in-one stir-fry with a hint of sweetness is a big time-saver. —Caroline Sperry, Shelby Township, Michigan

1 pound boneless skinless chicken breasts, cut into 1-inch pieces

1 garlic clove, minced

3 teaspoons olive oil, *divided*

3 tablespoons honey

2 tablespoons reduced-sodium soy sauce

1/8 teaspoon salt

1/8 teaspoon pepper

1 package (16 ounces) frozen broccoli stir-fry vegetable blend

2 teaspoons cornstarch

1 tablespoon cold water

Hot cooked rice

In a large nonstick skillet, stir-fry chicken and garlic in 2 teaspoons oil. Add honey, soy sauce, salt and pepper. Cook and stir until chicken is lightly browned and juices run clear. Remove and keep warm.

In the same pan, stir-fry the vegetables in remaining oil for 4-5 minutes or until tender. Return chicken to the pan; stir to coat. Combine cornstarch and cold water until smooth; gradually stir into chicken mixture. Bring to a boil; cook and stir for 1 minute or until thickened. Serve with rice. **Yield: 4 servings.**

Editor's Note: If serving with rice, start heating the water for the rice before you begin cooking the chicken. When minutes count, use instant white or brown rice.

30+ Cashew Chicken

Prep: 10 min. | **Bake: 45 min.**

I love to cook and bake for my family and friends. This chicken and rice casserole is seasoned with ground ginger. Some cashews are stirred in for added crunch.
—Bonnie DeVries, Brainerd, Minnesota

1 pound boneless skinless chicken breasts, cut into 1-inch cubes
1 medium onion, chopped
2 cups frozen broccoli cuts
1-3/4 cups boiling water
1 cup uncooked long grain rice
1 jar (6 ounces) sliced mushrooms, drained
1 tablespoon chicken bouillon granules
1/2 to 1 teaspoon ground ginger
Pepper to taste
3/4 cup salted cashews, *divided*

Preheat oven to 375°.

In a large bowl, combine the first nine ingredients. Transfer to a greased shallow 1-1/2-qt. baking dish.

Cover and bake at 375° for 45-55 minutes or until rice is tender and chicken is no longer pink. Stir in 1/2 cup of cashews. Sprinkle with remaining cashews.
Yield: 4 servings.

Onion Turkey Meatballs

Prep: 20 min. | Cook: 35 min.

This is one of my experiments. I came up with it when trying to figure out a new taste for ground turkey since we eat a lot of it. I didn't want to run to the grocery store, so I used ingredients I had on hand. It's now one of our family's favorites.
—Regina Davis, Griffin, Georgia

1 cup soft bread crumbs
1 envelope onion soup mix, *divided*
1-1/2 pounds ground turkey
3 cups water, *divided*
3 tablespoons all-purpose flour
Hot cooked noodles *or* rice

In a large bowl, combine the bread crumbs, and half of the soup mix. Crumble meat over mixture and mix well. Shape into 1-in. balls.

In a large skillet, cook meatballs in batches until browned on all sides and a meat thermometer reads 165°; drain. Stir in 2-1/2 cups water and remaining soup mix. Bring to a boil. Reduce heat; cover and simmer for 10 minutes or until juices run clear.

In a small bowl, combine flour and remaining water until smooth; gradually add to the skillet. Bring to a boil; cook and stir for 2 minutes or until thickened. Serve with noodles or rice. **Yield: 6 servings.**

Editor's Note: Start heating the water for the noodles as you are browning the meatballs.

Chicken 'n' Chips

Prep: 10 min. | Bake: 25 min.

My husband is always ready to try a new recipe, so I surprised him with this creamy chicken casserole sprinkled with crushed tortilla chips. He loves the flavor, and I like that it's the perfect size for our small family. —Kendra Schneider, Grifton, North Carolina

1 can (10-3/4 ounces) condensed cream of chicken soup, undiluted
1 cup (8 ounces) sour cream
2 tablespoons taco sauce
1/4 cup chopped green chilies
3 cups cubed cooked chicken
12 slices process American cheese
4 cups broken tortilla chips

Preheat oven to 350°.

In a bowl, combine the soup, sour cream, taco sauce and chilies. In an ungreased shallow 2-qt. baking dish, layer half of the chicken, soup mixture, cheese and tortilla chips. Repeat layers.

Bake, uncovered, at 350° for 25-30 minutes or until bubbly. **Yield: 4-6 servings.**

Poultry

Bacon-Wrapped Chicken

Prep: 25 min. | Bake: 35 min.

Tender chicken gets a special treatment when spread with a creamy filling and wrapped with tasty bacon strips. This easy entree is frequently requested by my bunch.
—MarlaKaye Skinner, Tucson, Arizona

6 boneless skinless chicken breast halves (4 ounces *each*)
1 carton (8 ounces) spreadable chive and onion cream cheese
1 tablespoon butter
Salt to taste
6 bacon strips

Preheat oven to 400°.

Flatten chicken to 1/2-in. thickness. Spread 3 tablespoons cream cheese over each. Dot with butter and sprinkle with salt; roll up. Wrap each with bacon strip.

Place seam side down in a greased 13-in. x 9-in. x 2-in. baking pan. Bake, uncovered, at 400° for 35-40 minutes or until juices run clear. Broil 6 in. from the heat for 5 minutes or until bacon is crisp.
Yield: 6 servings.

Golden Chicken and Autumn Vegetables

Prep: 10 min. | Cook: 35 min.

This comforting combination is sure to warm you up on a chilly day. Tender chicken breasts, sweet potatoes and green beans are cooked in a simple broth seasoned with rosemary, garlic and thyme. —Taste of Home Test Kitchen

4 bone-in chicken breast halves (8 ounces *each*), skin removed
2 large sweet potatoes, peeled and cut into large chunks
2 cups fresh *or* frozen cut green beans
1 cup chicken broth
1 tablespoon minced fresh parsley
1/2 teaspoon garlic powder
1/2 teaspoon dried rosemary, crushed
1/4 teaspoon dried thyme

In a large nonstick skillet, brown chicken on both sides over medium-high heat. Add sweet potatoes and beans. In a small bowl, combine the remaining ingredients; pour over chicken and vegetables. Bring to a boil. Reduce heat; cover and cook over low heat for 20 minutes or until chicken juices run clear.
Yield: 4 servings.

The Busy Family Cookbook

Chicken Parmigiana

Prep: 15 min. | Bake: 25 min.

My family loves Italian food, and Chicken Parmigiana is one of our favorites. Since most of the recipes I found were time-consuming, I came up with this version, which bakes in about a half hour. —Robin Stevens, Cadiz, Kentucky

4 boneless skinless chicken breast halves (4 ounces *each*)
1 can (6 ounces) tomato paste
3/4 cup water
2 garlic cloves, minced
1 tablespoon dried parsley flakes
1 teaspoon salt
1/4 teaspoon pepper
1/2 teaspoon Italian seasoning
1/2 teaspoon dried oregano
1/4 teaspoon crushed red pepper flakes, optional
2 cups (8 ounces) shredded part-skim mozzarella cheese
1/4 cup grated Parmesan cheese

Preheat oven to 400°.

Place the chicken in a greased 8-in. square baking dish. In a small saucepan, combine the tomato paste, water, garlic and seasonings; bring to a boil. Pour over chicken.

Bake, uncovered, at 400° for 15-20 minutes or until chicken juices run clear. Sprinkle with cheeses; bake 10 minutes longer or until the cheese is melted. **Yield: 4 servings.**

30+

minute recipes

Chicken with Mushroom Sauce

Prep: 15 min. | **Bake: 20 min.**

This tender, quick-to-assemble chicken dish features a rich flavorful sauce made with convenient canned soup and mushrooms. —Virginia Conley, Wauwatosa, Wisconsin

4 boneless skinless chicken breast halves (4 ounces *each*)
2 tablespoons butter
1 can (10-3/4 ounces) condensed cream of mushroom soup, undiluted
1 cup (8 ounces) sour cream
1 can (4 ounces) mushroom stems and pieces, drained
1/4 cup white wine *or* chicken broth
1/2 teaspoon garlic powder
1/2 teaspoon salt
1/2 teaspoon pepper
Hot cooked noodles *or* rice
Sliced almonds, toasted, optional

Preheat oven to 375°.

In a large skillet, brown chicken on both sides in butter; drain. Place in a greased 11-in. x 7-in. x 2-in. baking dish. In a large bowl, combine the soup, sour cream, mushrooms, wine or broth, garlic powder, salt and pepper; pour over the chicken.

Bake, uncovered, at 375° for 20 minutes or until meat juices run clear. Serve chicken and sauce with noodles or rice. Sprinkle with almonds if desired.
Yield: 4 servings.

Turkey Tetrazzini

Prep: 20 min. | **Bake: 35 min.**

This tasty main dish is popular with everyone. A delicious layer of melted cheese tops this hearty, creamy casserole.
—Sue Ross, Casa Grande, Arizona

2 cups uncooked spaghetti (broken into 2-inch pieces)
1 teaspoon chicken bouillon granules
3/4 cup boiling water
1 can (10-3/4 ounces) condensed cream of mushroom soup, undiluted
1/8 teaspoon celery salt
1/8 teaspoon pepper
1-1/2 cups cubed cooked turkey
1 small onion, finely chopped
2 tablespoons diced pimientos, drained
1-1/2 cups (6 ounces) shredded cheddar cheese, *divided*

Cook spaghetti according to package directions. Meanwhile, in a large bowl, dissolve bouillon in water. Add the soup, celery salt and pepper. Drain spaghetti; add to soup mixture. Stir in the turkey, onion, pimientos and 1/2 cup cheese.

Transfer to a greased 8-in. square baking dish. Top with remaining cheese. Bake, uncovered, at 350° for 35-40 minutes or until heated through.
Yield: 6 servings.

Thanksgiving in a Pan

Prep: 15 min. | **Bake: 30 min.**

This meal-in-one tastes like a big holiday dinner without the work. It's a great way to use up leftover turkey, but I often use thick slices of deli turkey instead.
—Lynne Hahn, Temecula, California

1 package (6 ounces) stuffing mix
2-1/2 cups cubed cooked turkey
2 cups frozen cut green beans, thawed
1 jar (12 ounces) turkey gravy
Pepper to taste

Preheat oven to 350°.

Prepare stuffing mix according to package directions. Transfer to a greased 11-in. x 7-in. x 2-in. baking dish. Top with turkey, beans, gravy and pepper. Cover and bake at 350° for 30-35 minutes or until heated through.
Yield: 6 servings.

Poultry

Tasty Turkey Skillet

Prep: 10 min. | Cook: 35 min.

I like using boxed rice and pasta mixes as the basis for quick meals. This colorful dish is simple to cook on the stovetop using fried rice mix, tender turkey and convenient frozen vegetables. —Betty Kleberger, Florissant, Missouri

1 pound turkey breast tenderloins, cut into 1/4-inch strips
1 package (5.3 ounces) Oriental fried rice mix
1 tablespoon butter
2 cups water
1/8 teaspoon cayenne pepper
1-1/2 cups frozen corn, thawed
1 cup frozen broccoli cuts, thawed
2 tablespoons chopped sweet red pepper, optional

In a nonstick skillet coated with nonstick cooking spray, cook turkey over medium heat until no longer pink; drain. Remove turkey and keep warm.

Set aside seasoning packet from rice. In the same skillet, saute rice in butter until lightly browned. Stir in the water, cayenne and contents of seasoning packet.

Bring to a boil. Reduce heat; cover and simmer for 15 minutes. Stir in the corn, broccoli, red pepper if desired and turkey. Return to a boil. Reduce heat; cover and simmer for 6-8 minutes or until the rice and vegetables are tender.
Yield: 4-6 servings.

Crumb-Coated Chicken Thighs

Prep: 10 min. | Bake: 35 min.

These spicy roasted chicken thighs don't require a lot of prep time. I often put baking potatoes on the oven rack alongside the chicken. It's a simple and satisfying meal. —Kara de la Vega, Somerset, California

1/4 cup dry bread crumbs
1 teaspoon salt
1 teaspoon ground cumin
1 teaspoon paprika
1 teaspoon chili powder
1 teaspoon curry powder
1/4 teaspoon pepper
8 chicken thighs (5 ounces *each*), skin removed

Preheat oven to 400°.

In a large resealable plastic bag, combine the first seven ingredients. Add chicken, a few pieces at a time, and shake to coat.

Place on a baking sheet coated with nonstick cooking spray. Bake, uncovered, at 400° for 20 minutes. Turn chicken pieces; bake 15-20 minutes longer or until a meat thermometer reads 180°.
Yield: 4 servings.

Golden Glazed Fryer

Prep: 10 min. | Grill: 40 min.

This moist, grilled chicken has a savory coating that's a nice change of pace from tomato-based sauces. This recipe has been passed down in my family for generations.
—Peggy West, Georgetown, Delaware

1 broiler/fryer chicken (3 to 4 pounds), cut up
1/2 cup vegetable oil
1/2 cup cider vinegar
1 egg, lightly beaten
4 teaspoons salt
1-1/2 teaspoon poultry seasoning
1/4 teaspoon pepper

Coat grill rack with nonstick cooking spray before starting the grill. Preheat grill.

Grill chicken skin side down, covered, over medium heat for 15 minutes. Turn; grill 15 minutes longer.

Meanwhile, combine the remaining ingredients; brush over chicken. Grill for 5 minutes. Turn and brush with glaze; grill 5 minutes longer or until meat thermometer reads 170° in the breast pieces and 180° in the dark meat. Discard unused glaze.
Yield: 6 servings.

Lemon Honey Turkey

Prep: 10 min. | Bake: 45 min.

Folks will be smacking their lips when they taste these tender slices of turkey draped in a sweet and tangy sauce. I love cooking with lemon and honey and experimenting with herbs. —Judith Harris, Brainerd, Minnesota

1/3 cup honey
1/4 cup lemon juice
  2 teaspoons dried rosemary, crushed
1/4 teaspoon crushed red pepper flakes
  2 turkey breast tenderloins (12 ounces *each*)
  1 teaspoon cornstarch
  1 teaspoon water
1/8 teaspoon browning sauce, optional

Preheat oven to 350°.

In a small bowl, combine the first four ingredients. Place tenderloins in an 11-in. x 7-in. x 2-in. baking dish coated with nonstick cooking spray. Pour half the sauce over turkey.

Bake, uncovered, at 350° for 40-45 minutes or until a meat thermometer reads 170°, basting occasionally with remaining sauce. Remove turkey to a plate and keep warm.

Transfer drippings to a small saucepan. Combine cornstarch and water until smooth; stir into drippings. Bring to a boil; cook and stir for 1-2 minutes or until thickened. Stir in browning sauce if desired. Serve sauce over turkey.
Yield: 6 servings.

Pecan Chicken

Prep: 10 min. | Bake: 30 min.

A pecan coating adds a pleasant crunch to plain chicken. My family likes dipping the crispy chicken pieces in the easy-to-make sauce.
—Bonnie Jean Lintick, Kathryn, Alberta

- 1/3 cup finely chopped pecans
- 1/3 cup dry bread crumbs
- 1/2 teaspoon dried thyme
- 1/2 teaspoon paprika
- 1/2 teaspoon salt
- 3 tablespoons Dijon mustard
- 4 boneless skinless chicken breast halves (4 ounces *each*)

MAPLE-DIJON SAUCE:
- 1/4 cup maple syrup
- 1 tablespoon Dijon mustard

Preheat oven to 375°.

In a shallow bowl, combine the pecans, bread crumbs, thyme, paprika and salt. Place Dijon mustard in another shallow bowl. Coat chicken with mustard, then roll in pecan mixture.

Place in a greased 13-in. x 9-in. x 2-in. baking dish. Bake, uncovered, at 375° for 30-35 minutes or until juices run clear. In a small bowl, combine sauce ingredients; serve with chicken. **Yield: 4 servings.**

Spinach Turkey Bake

Prep: 20 min. | Bake: 25 min.

Create a new and tasty meal with leftover cooked turkey or chicken and homemade gravy. If you don't have any homemade gravy, use gravy from a jar.
—Emily Chaney, Blue Hill, Maine

- 2 cups uncooked noodles
- 1 package (10 ounces) frozen chopped spinach
- 2 tablespoons butter
- 1-1/2 cups diced cooked turkey
- 1 cup turkey *or* chicken gravy
- 1 carton (8 ounces) sour cream onion dip
- 1/2 teaspoon onion salt
- 2 tablespoons grated Parmesan cheese

Preheat oven to 325°.

Cook noodles and spinach according to their package directions; drain. Stir butter into spinach. Place noodles in a greased 11-in. x 7-in. x 2-in. baking dish; top with spinach.

In a large bowl, combine the turkey, gravy, onion dip and onion salt; spoon over spinach. Sprinkle with Parmesan. Bake, uncovered, at 325° for 25 minutes or until heated through.
Yield: 6 servings.

Chicken and Shells Dinner

Prep: 15 min. | Bake: 20 min.

Like most kids, mine love macaroni and cheese. The addition of chicken and peas makes this a meal-in-one they never refuse.
—LeeAnn McCue, Charlotte, North Carolina

1 package (12 ounces) shells and cheese dinner mix
1/4 cup chopped onion
4 tablespoons butter, *divided*
2 cups cubed cooked chicken
1 package (10 ounces) frozen peas, thawed
2/3 cup mayonnaise
1/3 cup seasoned bread crumbs

Preheat oven to 350°.

Prepare dinner mix according to package directions. Meanwhile, in a small skillet, saute onion in 2 tablespoons butter until tender. Stir the chicken, peas, mayonnaise and sauteed onion into dinner mix.

Transfer to a greased 1-1/2-qt. baking dish. Melt remaining butter; toss with bread crumbs. Sprinkle over top. Bake, uncovered, at 350° for 20-25 minutes or until bubbly.
Yield: 4-6 servings.

Editor's Note: Reduced-fat or fat-free mayonnaise is not recommended for this recipe.

Chicken Tarragon

Prep: 15 min. | Bake: 30 min.

This easy-to-fix entree combines moist chicken breasts with zucchini, carrots and mushrooms. I love tarragon, so I make this dish often.—Ruth Peterson, Jenison, Michigan

4 boneless skinless chicken breast halves
1/2 teaspoon paprika
1/3 cup butter, *divided*
2 medium zucchini, julienned
4 small carrots, julienned
4 large mushrooms, sliced
2 tablespoons minced fresh tarragon *or* 2 teaspoons dried tarragon
1 tablespoon lemon juice
1/2 teaspoon salt
1/8 teaspoon pepper

Preheat oven to 350°.

Sprinkle chicken with paprika. In a skillet, brown chicken in 2 teaspoons butter. Place the vegetables in a greased 13-in. x 9-in. x 2-in. baking dish. Top with chicken.

Melt the remaining butter; stir in the tarragon, lemon juice, salt and pepper. Pour over chicken and vegetables. Cover and bake at 350° for 30-35 minutes or until chicken juices run clear and vegetables are tender.
Yield: 4 servings.

Peanutty Chicken

Prep: 10 min. | Cook: 50 min.

We use peanuts in a variety of dishes. This tender chicken, covered in a tasty gravy and sprinkled with peanuts, has a zip that perks up taste buds.
—Mary Kay Dixson, Decatur, Alabama

1 teaspoon chili powder
1 teaspoon salt
1/4 teaspoon pepper
1 broiler/fryer chicken (3-1/2 to 4 pounds), cut up
5 tablespoons butter
1 cup orange juice
2/3 to 1 cup salted peanuts
Orange slices and minced fresh cilantro *or* parsley, optional

In a small bowl, combine the chili powder, salt and pepper; rub over chicken. In a large skillet, saute chicken in butter until golden brown. Reduce heat; cover and cook for 30 minutes or until juices run clear.

Transfer chicken to a serving platter and keep warm. Add orange juice to skillet, stirring to loosen browned bits from pan; simmer for 5 minutes. Pour over chicken. Sprinkle with peanuts. Garnish with orange slices and cilantro if desired. **Yield: 4 servings.**

30+

One-Dish Chicken with Vegetables

Prep: 15 min. | Bake: 30 min.

I like to cook and try new recipes...my niece and I exchange the good ones. I made this dish and it looked so pretty that I got out my camera and took a picture of it.
—Katherine McKinley, New Albany, Indiana

1 envelope onion soup mix
1/2 teaspoon garlic powder
1/4 cup olive oil
4 boneless skinless chicken breast halves (4 ounces *each*)
4 medium potatoes, cut into chunks
4 medium carrots, cut into 1/4-inch slices

Preheat oven to 425°.

In a small bowl, combine the soup mix, garlic powder and oil. Spoon half into a large resealable plastic bag; add chicken. Seal bag and turn to coat. Spoon the remaining marinade into another large resealable plastic bag; add potatoes and carrots. Seal bag and turn to coat.

Arrange chicken and vegetables in an ungreased 11-in. x 7-in. x 2-in. baking dish. Cover and bake at 425° for 15 minutes. Uncover; bake 15-20 minutes longer or until chicken juices run clear and vegetables are tender.
Yield: 4 servings.

Tangy Turkey Kabobs

Prep: 15 min. | Grill: 20 min.

Unlike traditional kabobs, these call for turkey breast slices, potatoes and apple chunks. The flavorful honey-mustard salad dressing shines through in each delicious bite. —Taste of Home Test Kitchen

- 12 small red potatoes, cut in half
- 1/2 cup honey-mustard salad dressing
- 2 teaspoons dried rosemary, crushed
- 1 pound turkey breast slices, cut into 1-inch strips
- 2 unpeeled green apples, cut into 1-inch pieces

Preheat grill.

Place potatoes in a large saucepan and cover with water. Bring to a boil; cook for 5 minutes or until crisp-tender; drain. Meanwhile, in a small bowl, combine salad dressing and rosemary; set aside.

Fold turkey strips in thirds; thread onto metal or soaked wooden skewers alternately with potatoes and apples.

Spoon half of the dressing over kabobs. Grill, uncovered, over medium-hot heat for 5-7 minutes on each side or until meat juices run clear, basting and turning occasionally with remaining dressing.
Yield: 4 servings.

Southern Fried Chicken

Prep: 10 min. | Cook: 35 min.

This dish was a happy accident. I discovered at the last minute that I didn't have enough all-purpose flour for coating the chicken, so I used pancake mix instead. Everyone adored the change-of-pace flavor. —Patricia Gowen, Amherst, Virginia

- 1 cup pancake mix
- 2 to 3 teaspoons salt
- 1/4 teaspoon pepper
- 1/4 teaspoon paprika
- 1 broiler/fryer chicken (3 to 4 pounds), cut up
- Oil for deep-fat frying

In a large resealable plastic bag, combine the pancake mix, salt, pepper and paprika. Add chicken, a few pieces at a time; shake to coat.

Heat 2 in. of oil in an electric skillet or deep-fat fryer to 375°. Fry chicken, a few pieces at a time for 6 minutes on each side or until golden brown and juices run clear.
Yield: 4-6 servings.

Poultry

Santa Fe Chicken

Prep: 10 min. | Cook: 30 min.

My day is busy from start to finish, so this quick and meaty main dish is one of my menu mainstays. With its lovely golden color, it's pretty enough to serve to company or as a special Sunday dinner.
—Debra Cook, Pampa, Texas

1 large onion, chopped
1 tablespoon butter
1-1/4 cups chicken broth
1 cup salsa
1 cup uncooked long grain rice
1/8 teaspoon garlic powder
4 boneless skinless chicken breast halves (4 ounces *each*)
3/4 cup shredded cheddar cheese
Chopped fresh cilantro, optional

In a large skillet, saute onion in butter until tender. Add broth and salsa; bring to a boil. Stir in rice and garlic powder. Place chicken over rice; cover and simmer for 10 minutes. Turn chicken; cook 10-15 minutes longer or until meat juices run clear. Remove from the heat. Sprinkle with cheese; cover and let stand for 5 minutes. Garnish with cilantro if desired. **Yield: 4 servings.**

Artichoke Chicken

Prep: 10 min. | Bake: 30 min.

A friend agreed to repair some plumbing in exchange for a home-cooked dinner, but he showed up before I could shop for groceries. A can of artichokes in the pantry inspired me to combine a favorite hot dip recipe with a chicken bake with delicious results!
—Lisa Robisch, Cincinnati, Ohio

1 can (14 ounces) water-packed artichoke hearts, rinsed, drained and chopped
3/4 cup grated Parmesan cheese
3/4 cup mayonnaise
Dash garlic powder
4 boneless skinless chicken breast halves (4 ounces *each*)

Preheat oven to 375°.

In a bowl, combine the artichokes, cheese, mayonnaise and garlic powder. Place chicken in a greased 11-in. x 7-in. x 2-in. baking dish. Spread with artichoke mixture. Bake, uncovered, at 375° for 30-35 minutes or until the chicken juices run clear.
Yield: 4 servings.

Editor's Note: Reduced-fat or fat-free mayonnaise is not recommended for this recipe.

The Busy Family Cookbook

Lemon Grilled Chicken

Prep: 5 min. + marinating | Grill: 40 min.

This was one of my mother's standard recipes that she relied on. It's mild lemon taste reminds me of summertime.—Ellen Seidl, Crookston, Nebraska

- 1/2 cup lemon juice
- 1/4 cup vegetable oil
- 3 tablespoons chopped onion
- 1/2 teaspoon salt
- 1/2 teaspoon pepper
- 1/2 teaspoon dried thyme
- 1 garlic clove, minced
- 1 broiler/fryer chicken (3 to 4 pounds), cut up

In a measuring cup, combine the first seven ingredients. Remove 1/4 cup for basting; cover and refrigerate. Pour remaining marinade in a large resealable plastic bag; add chicken. Seal bag and turn to coat; refrigerate for 8 hours or overnight.

Preheat grill.

Drain and discard marinade from chicken. Grill, covered, over medium heat for 20 minutes. Baste with reserved marinade. Grill 20-30 minutes longer or until juices run clear, basting and turning several times.

Yield: 4 servings.

Editor's Note: Marinate chicken the night before or first thing in the morning.

Bacon-Feta Stuffed Chicken

Prep: 15 min. | Cook: 25 min.

My son and I love feta cheese, so we tucked some into quick-cooking chicken breasts to create this dish. I think feta cheese is so underrated. You can buy feta in so many different flavors —basil and tomato is our favorite. —Vicki Smith, Okeechobee, Florida

4 bacon slices, diced
4 boneless skinless chicken breasts (4 ounces *each*)
1/4 cup crumbled feta cheese
1/2 teaspoon salt
1/4 teaspoon pepper
1 tablespoon vegetable oil
2 cans (14-1/2 ounces *each*) diced tomatoes
1 tablespoon dried basil

In a large skillet, cook bacon over medium heat until crisp. While bacon is cooking, carefully cut a slit in the deepest part of each chicken breast. Using a slotted spoon, remove bacon to paper towels; drain, discarding drippings. Fill pocket in chicken with bacon and cheese; secure with toothpicks. Sprinkle with salt and pepper. In a large skillet, brown chicken in oil.

Drain one can of tomatoes; add to skillet. Stir in the remaining tomatoes; sprinkle with basil. Bring to a boil. Reduce heat; cover and simmer for 10 minutes. Simmer, uncovered, for 5 minutes longer or until the chicken is no longer pink and the tomato mixture is thickened.
Yield: 4 servings.

Editor's Note: To save time, use precooked bacon, which is available in the packaged deli meat section of the supermarket.

Honey-Lime Grilled Chicken

Prep: 35 min. | Grill: 15 min.

You won't have to pack a lot of supplies to stir up this easy marinade. It requires only three ingredients and gives a fabulous lime flavor to tender chicken breasts. —Dorothy Smith, El Dorado, Arkansas

1/2 cup honey
1/3 cup soy sauce
1/4 cup lime juice
4 boneless skinless chicken breast halves (4 ounces *each*)

Preheat grill.

In a resealable plastic bag, combine the honey, soy sauce and lime juice; add chicken. Seal and turn to coat. Refrigerate for 30-45 minutes.

Drain and discard marinade. Grill chicken, uncovered, over medium heat for 6-7 minutes on each side or until juices run clear.
Yield: 4 servings.

Seafood

Garlic Lime Shrimp (p. 146)

10

minute recipes

Almond Sole Fillets micro wave

Prep: 10 min.

My husband is a real fish lover. This buttery treatment is his favorite way to prepare sole, perch or halibut. It cooks quickly in the microwave, so it's perfect for a busy weekday. —Erna Farnham, Marengo, Illinois

1/3 cup butter, cubed
1/4 cup slivered almonds
  1 pound sole fillets
  2 tablespoons lemon juice
1/2 teaspoon dill weed
1/4 teaspoon salt
1/4 teaspoon pepper
1/4 teaspoon paprika

In a microwave-safe bowl, combine butter and almonds. Microwave, uncovered, on high for 1-1/2 minutes or until almonds are golden brown.

Place the fillets in a greased microwave-safe 11-in. x 7-in. x 2-in. dish. Top with almond mixture.

In a small bowl, combine the lemon juice, dill, salt and pepper; drizzle over fish. Sprinkle with paprika. Cover and microwave on high for 4-5 minutes or until fish flakes easily with a fork.
Yield: 4 servings.

Editor's Note: This recipe was tested in a 1,100-watt microwave.

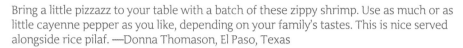

Cajun Shrimp

Prep: 10 min.

Bring a little pizzazz to your table with a batch of these zippy shrimp. Use as much or as little cayenne pepper as you like, depending on your family's tastes. This is nice served alongside rice pilaf. —Donna Thomason, El Paso, Texas

2 teaspoons paprika
1 teaspoon dried thyme
1/2 teaspoon salt
1/4 teaspoon ground nutmeg
1/4 teaspoon garlic powder
1/8 to 1/4 teaspoon cayenne pepper
1 tablespoon olive oil
1 pound uncooked medium shrimp, peeled and deveined

In a large nonstick skillet, saute the paprika, thyme, salt, nutmeg, garlic powder and cayenne in oil for 30 seconds, stirring constantly. Add shrimp; saute for 2-3 minutes or until shrimp turn pink, stirring occasionally.
Yield: 4 servings.

Editor's Note: To save time, purchase shrimp that is already peeled and deveined.

Open-Faced Crab Melts

Prep: 10 min.

Over the years, I've seen these versatile sandwiches please guests at occasions from fancy teas to last-minute suppers. To serve them as appetizers, I add some chili sauce and a little prepared horseradish to the crab mixture.
—Florence McClelland, Fredonia, New York

4 English muffins, split
1 can (6 ounces) crabmeat, drained, flaked and cartilage removed
1/3 cup mayonnaise
1 tablespoon lemon juice
1/2 teaspoon pepper
1/4 teaspoon dried tarragon
1 cup (4 ounces) shredded cheddar cheese

Broil English muffins 4-6 in. from the heat for 2-3 minutes or until golden brown. Meanwhile, in a large bowl, combine the crab, mayonnaise, lemon juice, pepper and tarragon. Spread over each muffin half; sprinkle with cheddar cheese. Broil for 2-3 minutes or until cheese is melted.
Yield: 4 servings.

Seafood

Honeydew Shrimp Salad

Prep: 10 min.

A creamy pickle relish dressing deliciously complements this shrimp and fruit medley. —Lynda Mohan, Scottsdale, Arizona

 1 pound cooked medium shrimp, peeled and deveined
 1/4 cup chopped celery
 1 hard-cooked egg, chopped
 2 tablespoons sunflower kernels
 1/3 cup mayonnaise
 4-1/2 teaspoons Thousand Island salad dressing
 1 tablespoon sweet pickle relish
 1/4 teaspoon salt
 1/8 teaspoon pepper
 1 large honeydew, quartered and seeded

In a large bowl, combine the shrimp, celery, egg and sunflower kernels. In a small bowl, combine the mayonnaise, salad dressing, pickle relish, salt and pepper. Pour over shrimp mixture and toss to coat. Spoon onto honeydew quarters. **Yield: 4 servings.**

Microwave Red Snapper

Prep: 10 min.

We fish a lot, so when I tried this recipe at a microwave cooking class, I knew it was a keeper. My husband requests it several times a month.
—Evelyn Gavin, Cayucos, California

 4 red snapper fillets (6 ounces *each*)
 3/4 cup sour cream
 1/4 cup mayonnaise
 3 tablespoons milk
 1 tablespoon prepared mustard
 1-1/2 teaspoons dill weed
Hot cooked rice

Cut fish into serving-size pieces; place in an ungreased shallow microwave-safe dish. Cover and microwave on high for 3 minutes. Drain liquid.

Meanwhile, combine the sour cream, mayonnaise, milk, mustard and dill; drizzle 1/2 cup over the fish. Microwave, uncovered, on high for 3 minutes or until fish flakes easily with a fork. Serve with rice and remaining sauce. **Yield: 6 servings.**

Editor's Note: This recipe was tested in a 1,100-watt microwave. Reduced-fat or fat-free mayonnaise is not recommended for this recipe.

The Busy Family Cookbook

Salsa Tuna Salad

Prep: 10 min.

A flavorful salsa perks up this fresh-tasting tuna salad. Bright corn and green pepper add pretty color to the mixture. Served on a bed of lettuce, it makes a great light lunch or dinner. —Jennifer Harris, Skellytown, Texas

1/2 cup plain nonfat yogurt
1/4 cup salsa
1/4 teaspoon pepper
2 cans (6 ounces *each*) tuna, drained and flaked
1 cup frozen corn, thawed
1 cup chopped green pepper
Lettuce leaves, optional

In a large bowl, combine the yogurt, salsa and pepper. Stir in the tuna, corn and green pepper. Serve in a lettuce-lined bowl if desired.
Yield: 6 servings.

Open-Faced Tuna Burgers

Prep: 15 min.

This is one of my gang's favorite sandwiches. The zesty salad dressing makes it tastier than just plain mayonnaise. This is also good with canned chicken instead of tuna, or with French dressing instead of the ranch dressing. —Heidi Wilcox, Lapeer, Michigan

  3 slices bread, crusts removed, cubed
1/2 cup evaporated milk
4-1/2 teaspoons ranch salad dressing mix
  2 cans (6 ounces *each*) tuna, drained and flaked
  1 jar (2 ounces) chopped pimientos, drained
  4 hamburger buns, split and toasted

In a large bowl, soak bread cubes in evaporated milk; let stand for 5 minutes. Stir in the salad dressing mix, tuna and pimientos. Spoon about 1/4 cup onto each bun half. Place on a baking sheet. Broil 5-6 in. from the heat for 4 minutes or until golden brown.
Yield: 4 servings.

Breaded Orange Roughy

Prep: 20 min.

My family loves fish, so I serve it often. Seasoned pepper really adds to the flavor of these tender fillets. —Joann Frazier Hensley, McGaheysville, Virginia

  1 cup crushed cornflakes
  2 teaspoons seasoned pepper
1/4 teaspoon salt
  4 egg whites
1/4 cup water
  6 fresh *or* frozen orange roughy fillets (4 ounces *each*)
1/4 cup all-purpose flour

Preheat oven to 425°.

In a shallow dish, combine the cornflakes, seasoned pepper and salt. In another shallow dish, beat egg whites and water. In a third shallow bowl, add flour. Coat fish with flour; dip in egg white mixture, then roll in cornflake mixture.

Place on a baking sheet coated with nonstick cooking spray. Bake at 425° for 9-11 minutes or until fish flakes easily with a fork.
Yield: 6 servings.

Editor's Note: To save time, purchase crushed cornflake crumbs.

Feta Tomato-Basil Fish

Prep: 20 min.

I rely on my husband for the main ingredient in this fuss-free dish. He fills our freezer after his summer fishing trip. —Alicia Szeszol, Lindenhurst, Illinois

1/3	cup chopped onion
1	garlic clove, minced
2	teaspoons olive oil
1	can (14-1/2 ounces) Italian diced tomatoes, drained
1-1/2	teaspoons minced fresh basil *or* 1/2 teaspoon dried basil
1	pound walleye, bass *or* other whitefish fillets
4	ounces crumbled feta cheese

In a saucepan, saute onion and garlic in oil until tender. Add tomatoes and basil. Bring to a boil. Reduce heat; simmer, uncovered, for 5 minutes.

Meanwhile, broil fish 4-6 in. from the heat for 5-6 minutes. Top each fillet with tomato mixture and cheese. Broil 5-7 minutes longer or until fish flakes easily with a fork.
Yield: 4 servings.

Seafood

139

Broiled Orange Roughy

Prep: 20 min.

I'm constantly searching for new ways to prepare healthy meals. This fish dish has long been a favorite at my house—it is so simple to prepare and yet so tasty. Try the same recipe using cod or sole, too. —Dorothy Swanson, Affton, Missouri

1 tablespoon olive oil
1 tablespoon lemon juice
1 teaspoon salt-free seasoning blend
6 orange roughy fillets (about 7 ounces *each*)

ITALIAN SALSA:
2 cups chopped plum tomatoes
1 can (2-1/4 ounces) sliced ripe olives, drained
2 tablespoons lemon juice
2 tablespoons minced fresh parsley
1 teaspoon salt-free seasoning blend
1 teaspoon Italian seasoning

In a small bowl, combine the oil, lemon juice and seasoning blend; spoon over fish. Broil 4-5 in. from the heat for 10-15 minutes or until fish flakes easily with a fork. Meanwhile, in a small bowl, combine the salsa ingredients; serve with fish. **Yield: 6 servings.**

Seafood Fettuccine

Prep: 20 min.

Shrimp gives an elegant touch to this rich and creamy pasta dish. It's a satisfying entree. —Kim Jorgensen, Coulee City, Washington

 1 package (8 ounces) fettuccine
 3/4 pound uncooked medium shrimp, peeled and deveined
 1 can (4 ounces) mushroom stems and pieces, drained
 1/2 teaspoon garlic powder
 1/8 teaspoon salt
 1/8 teaspoon pepper
 1/4 cup butter, cubed
 1/2 cup grated Parmesan cheese
 1/2 cup milk
 1/2 cup sour cream
 Minced fresh parsley, optional

Cook pasta according to package directions. In a large saucepan, saute the shrimp, mushrooms, garlic powder, salt and pepper in butter for 3-5 minutes.

Drain pasta; stir into shrimp mixture along with the Parmesan cheese, milk and sour cream. Cook over medium heat for 3-5 minutes or until heated through (do not boil). Sprinkle with parsley if desired. **Yield: 4 servings.**

Editor's Note: To save time, purchase shrimp that is already peeled and deveined.

Garlic Salmon Linguine

Prep: 20 min.

This garlic-seasoned main dish is a real dinnertime savior. It calls for handy pantry ingredients, including pasta and canned salmon. I serve it with asparagus, rolls and fruit. —Theresa Hagan, Glendale, Arizona

 1 package (16 ounces) linguine
 3 garlic cloves, minced
 1/3 cup olive oil
 1 can (14-3/4 ounces) salmon, drained, bones and skin removed
 3/4 cup chicken broth
 1/4 cup minced fresh parsley
 1/2 teaspoon salt
 1/8 teaspoon cayenne pepper

Cook the linguine according to package directions. Meanwhile, in a large skillet, saute garlic in oil. Stir in the salmon, broth, parsley, salt and cayenne. Cook until heated through. Drain linguine; add to the salmon mixture and toss to coat. **Yield: 6 servings.**

Seafood

Golden Catfish Fillets

Prep: 20 min.

When we visited my grandparents near the Ohio River, my grandmother always made these crisp fillets from Granddad's fresh catch. —Sharon Stevens, Weirton, Virginia

> 3 eggs
> 3/4 cup all-purpose flour
> 3/4 cup cornmeal
> 1 teaspoon garlic powder
> 1/2 teaspoon salt
> 1/2 teaspoon pepper
> 5 catfish fillets (6 ounces *each*)
> Oil for frying

In a shallow bowl, beat eggs until foamy. In another shallow bowl, combine the flour, cornmeal and seasonings. Dip fillets in eggs, then coat with cornmeal mixture.

Heat 1/4 in. of oil in a large skillet; fry fish over medium-high heat for 3-4 minutes on each side or until fish flakes easily with a fork.
Yield: 5 servings.

Creole Tuna

Prep: 15 min.

This speedy recipe has been in my family for as long as I can remember. Because it relies on pantry staples, it's easy to make when you can't decide what to fix for dinner. —Betty Bernat, Bethlehem, New Hampshire

> 1/4 cup chopped green pepper
> 2 tablespoons butter
> 2 tablespoons all-purpose flour
> 1/2 teaspoon sugar
> 1/2 teaspoon salt
> 1/8 teaspoon pepper
> 1/3 cup milk
> 1 can (14-1/2 ounces) stewed tomatoes
> 1 can (6 ounces) tuna, drained and flaked
> 1 teaspoon Creole seasoning
> Hot cooked rice, optional

In a large saucepan, saute green pepper in butter until tender. Stir in the flour, sugar, salt and pepper until blended. Gradually add milk, stirring constantly. Stir in tomatoes. Bring to a boil; cook and stir for 2 minutes. Add tuna and Creole seasoning; heat through. Serve with rice if desired.
Yield: 4 servings.

Editor's Note: The following spices may be substituted for 1 teaspoon Creole seasoning: 1/4 teaspoon *each* salt, garlic powder and paprika; and a pinch *each* of dried thyme, ground cumin and cayenne pepper.

Microwaved Cod

micro wave

Prep: 15 min.

My grandmother handed down the original recipe for this pleasant lemon-and-herb flavored fish. Grandma baked it in the oven, I quickened it up by cooking it in the microwave. —Gloria Warcak, Cedarburg, Wisconsin

1-1/2 pounds cod *or* haddock fillets
1/2 cup white wine *or* chicken broth
2 tablespoons lemon juice
1 tablespoon grated lemon peel
1 tablespoon minced chives
1 tablespoon minced fresh parsley
1/2 teaspoon dried tarragon
Pepper to taste

Place the fillets in an ungreased 11-in. x 7-in. x 2-in. microwave-safe dish. Cover and cook on high for 6 minutes; drain. Add the wine or broth, lemon juice, lemon peel, chives, parsley, tarragon and pepper.

Cover and microwave 4-5 minutes longer or until fish flakes easily with a fork. Let stand for 5 minutes before serving.
Yield: 6 servings.

Editor's Note: This recipe was tested in a 1,100-watt microwave.

Orzo Shrimp Stew

Prep: 20 min.

My husband and I really enjoy seafood, so I don't skimp on shrimp in this mildly seasoned stew. It has other satisfying ingredients, too, like broccoli, tomatoes and pasta. —Lisa Stinger, Hamilton, New Jersey

2-1/2 cups reduced-sodium chicken broth
   5 cups fresh broccoli florets
   1 can (14-1/2 ounces) diced tomatoes, undrained
   1 cup uncooked orzo
   1 pound uncooked medium shrimp, peeled and deveined
 3/4 teaspoon salt
 1/4 teaspoon pepper
   2 teaspoons dried basil
   2 tablespoons butter

In a large nonstick skillet or saucepan, bring broth to a boil. Add the broccoli, tomatoes and orzo. Reduce heat; simmer, uncovered, for 5 minutes, stirring occasionally.

Add the shrimp, salt and pepper. Cover and cook for 4-5 minutes or until shrimp turn pink and orzo is tender. Stir in basil and butter.
Yield: 4 servings.

Editor's Note: To save time, purchase shrimp that is already peeled and deveined.

Angel Hair Tuna

Prep: 20 min.

This recipe came from a dear friend, and it quickly became a favorite standby. Simply toss together a green salad and toast some garlic bread for a complete meal.
—Collette Burch, Edinburg, Texas

   2 packages (5.1 ounces *each*) angel hair pasta with Parmesan cheese dinner mix
   1 can (12 ounces) tuna, drained and flaked
 1/2 teaspoon Italian seasoning
 3/4 cup crushed butter-flavored crackers (about 15)
 1/4 cup butter, melted

Prepare pasta dinner mixes according to package directions. Stir in the tuna and Italian seasoning. Transfer to a large serving bowl; cover and let stand for 5 minutes to thicken. Toss cracker crumbs and butter; sprinkle over the top. Serve immediately.
Yield: 4 servings.

Cajun-Style Catfish
Prep: 20 min.

You'll win a boatload of compliments with these nicely spiced fillets. I got the original recipe from a chef in the culinary arts department of a college where I used to work. —Dolores Barnas, Blasdell, New York

4-1/2 teaspoons paprika
   1 teaspoon onion powder
   1 teaspoon dried oregano
   1 teaspoon pepper
1/2 teaspoon white pepper
1/2 teaspoon dried thyme
1/4 teaspoon cayenne pepper
   4 catfish fillets (6 ounces *each*)
Refrigerated butter-flavored spray

In a shallow bowl, combine the first seven ingredients. Spritz both sides of fish with butter-flavored spray. Dip one side of each fillet in spice mixture.

Place spice side down in a large skillet coated with butter-flavored spray. Cook over medium-high heat for 4-5 minutes on each side or until fish flakes easily with a fork.
Yield: 4 servings.

Editor's Note: This recipe was tested with I Can't Believe It's Not Butter Spray.

Garlic Lime Shrimp

Prep: 20 min.

Our son, a restaurant owner, showed me how to make this quick shrimp and noodle dish zipped up with garlic and cayenne. It's also tasty served over rice.
—Gertraud Casbarro, Summerville, South Carolina

1 pound uncooked large shrimp, peeled and deveined
5 garlic cloves, minced
1/2 teaspoon salt
1/4 to 1/2 teaspoon cayenne pepper
1/2 cup butter
3 tablespoons lime juice
1 tablespoon minced fresh parsley
Hot cooked pasta

In a large skillet, saute the shrimp, garlic, salt and cayenne in butter until the shrimp turn pink, about 5 minutes. Stir in lime juice and parsley. Serve with pasta. **Yield: 4 servings.**

Editor's Note: Start heating the water for the pasta before you begin cooking the shrimp.

Basil Walnut Fish Fillets

Prep: 20 min.

Spreading fish fillets with a seasoned mayonnaise and sour cream mixture keeps the fish moist while baking. For the most flavor, use fresh basil, which is abundant in gardens and grocery stores in summer. —Taste of Home Test Kitchen

1-1/2 pounds fresh *or* frozen cod *or* haddock fillets
3 tablespoons mayonnaise
2 tablespoons sour cream
2 tablespoons grated Parmesan cheese
1 tablespoon minced fresh basil *or* 1 teaspoon dried basil
1/4 cup chopped walnuts

Preheat oven to 425°.

Cut fish into serving-size pieces and place in a greased 13-in. x 9-in. x 2-in. baking dish. In a small bowl, combine the mayonnaise, sour cream, Parmesan cheese and basil; spread over fish.

Sprinkle with walnuts. Bake, uncovered, at 425° for 10-15 minutes or until fish flakes easily with a fork.
Yield: 4 servings.

Editor's Note: Reduced-fat or fat-free mayonnaise is not recommended for this recipe.

Glazed Orange Roughy

Prep: 15 min.

Dijon mustard and apricot fruit spread create a golden glaze for fish fillets in this fast entree. It's hard to believe it calls for only four ingredients. —Jo Baker, Litchfield, Illinois

4 fresh *or* frozen orange roughy fillets (4 ounces *each*)
1/4 cup apricot spreadable fruit *or* orange marmalade
2 teaspoons butter, melted
2 teaspoons Dijon mustard

Place fillets on an ungreased shallow baking pan. Broil 4-6 in. from the heat for 5-6 minutes. Combine the spreadable fruit, butter and mustard; spoon over fillets. Broil 3-4 minutes longer or until fish flakes easily with a fork (do not turn).
Yield: 4 servings.

Seafood

Stir-Fried Shrimp and Mushrooms

Prep: 15 min.

After a tiring but beautiful day of fishing, this is a fast and delicious way to serve our famous Key West pink shrimp. It's always a big hit with guests. —Jeanne Wolfort, Summerland Key, Florida

4 garlic cloves, minced
2 teaspoons vegetable oil
1 pound uncooked medium shrimp, peeled and deveined
3 cups sliced fresh mushrooms
1 cup sliced green onions
1/4 cup chicken broth
Hot cooked rice
Lemon slices

In a large skillet or wok, saute garlic in oil for 1 minute. Add the shrimp, mushrooms and onions; stir-fry for 1 minute. Stir in the broth; cook 2 minutes longer or until shrimp turn pink. Serve with rice; garnish with lemon.
Yield: 4 servings.

Editor's Note: To save time, purchase shrimp that is already peeled and deveined. If serving with rice, start heating the water for boiling before you begin cooking the shrimp, or use instant white or brown rice.

Herbed Orange Roughy

Prep: 20 min.

Family-pleasing fish is never long in the making with this quick-simmering fish dish. My mother created this main dish, which is low in fat and calories. I often use fresh scrod instead of orange roughy. —Carla Weeks, St. Charles, Illinois

4 fresh *or* frozen orange roughy fillets (6 ounces *each*)
1/3 cup lemon juice
1-1/2 teaspoons minced fresh parsley
1-1/2 teaspoons minced fresh basil *or* 1/2 teaspoon dried basil
1/2 teaspoon salt
1/4 teaspoon garlic powder
1/2 cup thinly sliced fresh mushrooms, optional
1/8 teaspoon paprika

Place the fish fillets in a single layer in a large skillet. Sprinkle with the lemon juice, parsley, basil, salt and garlic powder. Place mushrooms over fish if desired. Bring to a boil. Reduce heat; cover and simmer for 6-8 minutes or until fish flakes easily with a fork.
Yield: 4 servings.

Tuna Cheese Melts

Prep: 10 min. | **Cook: 15 min.**

This toasted, cheesy tuna sandwich gets an extra flavor boost from a garlicky sour cream spread. —Bernadine Dirmeyer, Harpster, Ohio

1/2 cup sour cream
1/2 teaspoon garlic salt
8 slices light rye bread
1 can (6 ounces) tuna, drained and flaked
2 tablespoons mayonnaise
4 slices process American cheese
4 tablespoons butter, *divided*

In a small bowl, combine sour cream and garlic salt; spread on one side of each slice of bread. In another small bowl, combine tuna and mayonnaise; spread on four slices of bread. Top with cheese and remaining bread; gently press together.

Melt 2 tablespoons butter in a large skillet over medium heat. Add two sandwiches; toast sandwiches until bread is lightly browned on both sides and cheese is melted. Repeat with remaining butter and sandwiches.
Yield: 4 servings.

Seafood

30 minute recipes

Citrus Garlic Shrimp
Prep: 10 min. | Cook: 20 min.

Garlic is paired with sunny citrus in this special shrimp and linguine combination. It's pretty enough for company. —Diane Jackson, Las Vegas, Nevada

1 package (16 ounces) linguine
1/2 cup olive oil
1/2 cup orange juice
1/3 cup lemon juice
3 to 4 garlic cloves, minced
5 teaspoons grated lemon peel
4 teaspoons grated orange peel
1 teaspoon salt
1/4 teaspoon pepper
1 pound uncooked medium shrimp, peeled and deveined
Shredded Parmesan cheese and minced fresh parsley, optional

Cook linguine according to package directions. Meanwhile, in a blender, combine the oil, juices, garlic, lemon peel, orange peel, salt and pepper; cover and process until blended. Pour into a large skillet; bring to boil. Reduce heat; stir in the shrimp. Simmer, uncovered, for 3-4 minutes or until shrimp turn pink.

Drain linguine; toss with shrimp mixture. Sprinkle with Parmesan cheese and parsley if desired.
Yield: 6 servings.

Editor's Note: To save time, purchase shrimp that is already peeled and deveined.

Pecan-Crusted Salmon

Prep: 20 min. | **Bake: 10 min.**

These delicious salmon fillets are wonderful for company since they take only a few minutes to prepare, yet they taste like you fussed. The nutty coating is a nice complement to the fish.
—Kara Cook, Elk Ridge, Utah

4 salmon fillets (about 6 ounces *each*)
2 cups milk
1 cup finely chopped pecans
1/2 cup all-purpose flour
1/4 cup packed brown sugar
2 teaspoons seasoned salt
2 teaspoons pepper
3 tablespoons vegetable oil

Preheat oven to 400°.

Place salmon fillets in a large resealable plastic bag; add milk. Seal bag and turn to coat. Let stand for 10 minutes.

Meanwhile, in a shallow bowl, combine the pecans, flour, brown sugar, seasoned salt and pepper. Drain fish; coat with pecan mixture, gently pressing into the fish.

In a large skillet, brown salmon over medium-high heat in oil. Transfer to a 15-in. x 10-in. x 1-in. baking pan coated with nonstick cooking spray. Bake at 400° for 8-10 minutes or until fish flakes easily with a fork. **Yield: 4 servings.**

Italian Fish Fillets

Prep: 10 min. | **Cook: 20 min.**

My husband and I resolved to eat healthier, so I was pleased to find this quick recipe for fish fillets. I tried it with cod and added a few twists of my own. Italian salad dressing, diced tomatoes and green pepper give the fish delicious flavor. We can't get enough of it! —Mindy Holliday, Westfield, Indiana

1 medium green *or* sweet yellow pepper, julienned
1 small onion, julienned
1/2 cup fat-free Italian salad dressing
1/2 teaspoon Italian seasoning
2 cans (14-1/2 ounces *each*) diced tomatoes
1-1/2 pounds fresh *or* frozen cod fillets, thawed

In a large nonstick skillet, cook green pepper, onion, salad dressing and Italian seasoning for 5 minutes or until the vegetables are tender. Stir in tomatoes; add fillets. Bring to a boil. Reduce heat; cover and simmer for 10 minutes or until fish flakes easily with a fork. Serve with a slotted spoon.
Yield: 4 servings.

Citrus Cod

Prep: 10 min. | Bake: 20 min.

We enjoy fish frequently, and this baked version has a tempting mild orange flavor. It comes out of the oven flaky and moist.
—Jacquelyn Dixon, La Porte City, Iowa

1 pound frozen cod fillets, thawed
1 tablespoon minced fresh parsley
1/8 teaspoon pepper
1/2 cup chopped onion
1 garlic clove, minced
2 tablespoons butter
1/3 cup orange juice
1 tablespoon lemon juice
1 teaspoon grated orange peel

Preheat oven to 375°.

Cut fillets into serving-size pieces; place in an 11-in. x 7-in. x 2-in. baking dish coated with nonstick cooking spray. Sprinkle with parsley and pepper.

In a small skillet, saute onion and garlic in butter until tender; sprinkle over fish. Combine juices and orange peel; drizzle over fish.

Bake, uncovered, at 375° for 20-25 minutes or until fish flakes easily with a fork.
Yield: 4 servings.

Cajun Shrimp with Potatoes

Prep: 15 min. | Cook: 15 min.

This is a quick-and-easy version of a seafood-stuffed baked potato. Not only does this recipe reduce prep time, it cuts down on cleanup, too. I buy cooked crumbled bacon to speed it along even more. —Angelique Schultz, Denham Springs, Louisiana

1/2 cup chopped onion
2 tablespoons vegetable oil
1/4 cup chopped green onions
1/4 cup chopped celery
6 medium potatoes, peeled and diced
1 teaspoon salt
2 teaspoons Cajun seasoning
1/2 teaspoon pepper
1 pound uncooked medium shrimp, peeled and deveined
1/4 cup crumbled cooked bacon

In a 2-1/2-qt. microwave-safe dish, combine onion and oil. Cover and

microwave on high for 1-3 minutes. Stir in green onions and celery; cover and cook 1-2 minutes longer. Add the potatoes, salt, Cajun seasoning and pepper.

Cover and cook for 7-9 minutes or until potatoes are nearly tender. Stir in shrimp and bacon. Cover and cook on high for 3-1/2 minutes or until shrimp turns pink and potatoes are tender.
Yield: 4 servings.

Editor's Note: This recipe was tested in a 1,100-watt microwave. To save time, purchase shrimp that is already peeled and deveined.

Barbecue Shrimp over Pasta

Prep: 10 min. | Cook: 20 min.

Diced bacon and barbecue sauce really give this shrimp dish a fun kick.
—Michele Field, Sykesville, Maryland

  1 package (16 ounces) linguine
 12 bacon strips, diced
  1 medium onion, chopped
1-1/4 pounds uncooked large shrimp,
      peeled and deveined
1-1/4 cups barbecue sauce
  1/3 cup grated Parmesan cheese

Cook linguine according to package directions. Meanwhile, in a large skillet, cook bacon over medium heat until crisp. Using a slotted spoon, remove to paper towels; drain, reserving 1 tablespoon drippings. Saute onion in the reserved drippings until tender. Add shrimp; cook and stir until no longer pink.

Return bacon to the skillet. Add barbecue sauce; cook and stir over medium heat until heated through. Drain linguine; top with shrimp mixture. Sprinkle with Parmesan cheese.
Yield: 6 servings.

Editor's Note: To save time, purchase shrimp that is already peeled and deveined.

Sunshine Halibut

Prep: 15 min. | **Bake: 15 min.**

Seasoned with garlic, onion and citrus, these fish fillets are moist and tasty, and they look especially pretty on a colorful bed of shredded carrots. This delightful main dish tastes like you fussed, but it can be made in a snap. —Jalayne Luckett, Marion, Illinois

1/3 cup chopped onion
1 garlic clove, minced
2 tablespoons minced fresh parsley
1/2 teaspoon grated orange peel
4 halibut steaks (4 ounces each)
1/4 cup orange juice
1 tablespoon lemon juice
1/4 teaspoon salt
1/4 teaspoon lemon-pepper seasoning

In a nonstick skillet coated with nonstick cooking spray, saute onion and garlic until tender; remove from the heat. Stir in parsley and orange peel.

Place halibut in an 8-in. square baking dish coated with nonstick cooking spray. Top with onion mixture. Combine orange and lemon juices; pour over fish. Sprinkle with salt and lemon-pepper. Cover and bake at 400° for 15-20 minutes or until fish flakes easily with a fork. **Yield: 4 servings.**

Tuna Patties

Prep: 10 min. | **Cook: 20 min.**

My family likes anything involving stuffing mix, so these tuna burgers are a popular request. It takes only minutes to form the moist patties, brown them in a skillet and mix up the sauce, which is served on the side.—Sonya Sherrill, Sioux City, Iowa

2 eggs, lightly beaten
1 can (10-3/4 ounces) condensed cream of mushroom soup, undiluted, *divided*
3/4 cup milk, *divided*
2 cups stuffing mix
1 can (12 ounces) tuna, drained and flaked
2 tablespoons butter

In a large bowl, combine the eggs, a third of the soup and 1/4 cup milk. Stir in stuffing mix and tuna. Shape into eight patties.

In a large skillet, brown patties in butter for 3-4 minutes on each side or until heated through. Meanwhile, in a small saucepan, heat remaining soup and milk. Serve with patties. **Yield: 4 servings.**

Basil Caesar Salmon

Prep: 10 min. | **Bake: 15 min.**

Since I love both salmon and Caesar salad, I created this delish fish dish. It's hard to believe it takes so little effort to prepare such a showy company entree.
—Laurie LaClair, North Richland Hills, Texas

4 salmon fillets (8 ounces *each*)
1/4 cup creamy Caesar salad dressing
Pepper to taste
1 cup Caesar salad croutons, crushed
1/2 cup grated Parmesan cheese
2 teaspoons dried basil
2 tablespoons olive oil

Preheat oven to 350°.

Place salmon in a greased 15-in. x 10-in. x 1-in. baking pan. Spoon the salad dressing over fillets; sprinkle with pepper.

Combine the croutons, Parmesan cheese and basil; sprinkle over fillets and gently press into dressing. Drizzle with oil. Bake, uncovered, at 350° for 15-20 minutes or until fish flakes easily with a fork.
Yield: 4 servings.

Crab-Topped Fish Fillets

Prep: 5 min. | Bake: 25 min.

Elegant but truly no bother, this recipe is perfect for company. Toasting the almonds gives them a little more crunch, which is a delightful way to top the fish fillets.
—Mary Tuthill, Ft. Myers Beach, Florida

4 sole *or* cod fillets *or* fish fillet of your choice (6 ounces *each*)
1 can (6 ounces) crabmeat, drained, flaked and cartilage removed *or* 1 cup imitation crabmeat, chopped
1/2 cup grated Parmesan cheese
1/2 cup mayonnaise
1 teaspoon lemon juice
1/3 cup slivered almonds, toasted
Paprika, optional

Preheat oven to 350°.

Place fillets in a greased 13-in. x 9-in. x 2-in. baking dish. Bake, uncovered, at 350° for 18-22 minutes or until fish flakes easily with a fork. Meanwhile, in a large bowl, combine the crab, Parmesan cheese, mayonnaise and lemon juice.

Drain cooking juices from baking dish; spoon crab mixture over fillets. Broil 4-5 in. from the heat for 5 minutes or until topping is lightly browned. Sprinkle with almonds and paprika if desired.
Yield: 4 servings.

Wild Rice Shrimp Saute

Prep: 15 min. | Cook: 30 min.

Shrimp and wild rice make a delicious combo, and this dish is special enough for company. —Judy Robinette Ommert, Sebring, Florida

2-1/3 cups water
   4 tablespoons butter, *divided*
   1 teaspoon lemon juice
  1/2 teaspoon Worcestershire sauce
  1/2 teaspoon ground mustard
  1/4 teaspoon pepper
   1 package (6 ounces) long grain and wild rice mix
   1 pound uncooked shrimp, peeled and deveined
   2 tablespoons chopped green pepper
   2 tablespoons chopped green onions

In a large saucepan, combine the water, 1 tablespoon butter, lemon juice, Worcestershire sauce, mustard and pepper. Bring to a boil over medium heat. Add rice with seasoning packet; return to a boil. Reduce heat; cover and simmer for 25-30 minutes or until rice is tender and liquid is absorbed.

Meanwhile, in another large skillet, cook the shrimp, green pepper and onions over medium heat in remaining butter. Cook and stir for 7-9 minutes or until shrimp turn pink. Add rice; heat through. **Yield: 4 servings.**

Editor's Note: To save time, purchase shrimp that is already peeled and deveined.

Oven-Fried Catfish

Prep: 10 min. | Bake: 25 min.

These golden baked fillets have the crisp crunch of batter-fried catfish without the extra calories or prep time. I often put the fish and crumb mixture into a plastic bag and shake on the coating without making a mess. —Kay Bell, Palestine, Texas

   1 cup crushed cornflakes
  3/4 teaspoon celery salt
  1/4 teaspoon onion powder
  1/4 teaspoon paprika
  1/8 teaspoon pepper
   6 catfish fillets (6 ounces *each*)
  1/3 cup butter, melted

Preheat oven to 350°.

In a shallow bowl, combine the cornflakes, celery salt, onion powder, paprika and pepper. Brush the fish fillets with butter; coat with crumb mixture.

Place in a greased 13-in. x 9-in. x 2-in. baking dish. Bake, uncovered, at 350° for 25 minutes or until fish flakes easily with a fork. **Yield: 6 servings.**

Editor's Note: To save time, purchase crushed cornflake crumbs.

Seafood

157

Italian Orange Roughy

Prep: 10 min. | Bake: 30 min.

This dish is delicious, foolproof and very low in fat. I prepare it on weeknights when I need a quick supper, but I've also used it for company meals. The Italian tomatoes and lemon-pepper seasoning give the mild fillets a little zest.—Michelle Haerr, Eureka, Illinois

4 orange roughy fillets (6 ounces *each*)
1/4 teaspoon lemon-pepper seasoning
1/4 teaspoon salt
1/4 cup finely chopped onion
1/4 cup finely chopped celery
1 can (14-1/2 ounces) Italian diced tomatoes, undrained

Preheat oven to 350°.

Arrange fish fillets in an ungreased 13-in. x 9-in. x 2-in. baking dish. Sprinkle with lemon-pepper and salt. Cover with onion and celery. Top with tomatoes. Bake at 350° for 30-40 minutes or until fish flakes easily with a fork.

Yield: 4 servings.

Swiss Tuna Bake

Prep: 20 min. | Bake: 20 min.

My husband enjoys cooking just as much as I do. One night he tossed together this comforting casserole from meager ingredients we had in our cupboard. It turned out to be the best-tasting tuna casserole I have ever had! Swiss cheese flavors the noodles nicely. —Joanne Callahan, Far Hills, New Jersey

4 cups medium egg noodles
1-1/2 cups (6 ounces) shredded Swiss cheese
1 cup mayonnaise
1 can (6 ounces) tuna, drained and flaked
1 cup seasoned bread crumbs, *divided*

Preheat oven to 350°.

Cook noodles according to package directions; drain. In a large bowl, combine the noodles, cheese, mayonnaise and tuna. Sprinkle 1/2 cup bread crumbs into a greased 9-in. square baking dish. Spread the noodle mixture over crumbs. Sprinkle with remaining crumbs. Bake, uncovered, at 350° for 20 minutes or until heated through.

Yield: 4 servings.

Editor's Note: Reduced-fat or fat-free mayonnaise is not recommended for this recipe.

The Busy Family Cookbook

Stuffed Walleye

Prep: 20 min. | **Bake: 20 min.**

Walleye is the No. 1 game fish in the Midwest. It's a thrill to catch and tastes great, too. This recipe, created by my husband, is a favorite of my family.
—Kim Leonard, Kalamazoo, Michigan

4 bacon strips, halved
1/4 cup chopped onion
2 celery ribs, finely chopped
1 can (6 ounces) crabmeat, drained, flaked and cartilage removed *or* 1 cup imitation crabmeat, flaked
1/4 cup butter, cubed
4 cups crushed seasoned stuffing
1-1/2 cups boiling water
1/2 teaspoon salt
1/8 teaspoon pepper
1/8 teaspoon cayenne pepper
4 walleye fillets (about 8 ounces each)

Preheat oven to 425°.

In a large skillet, cook bacon over medium heat until crisp; remove to paper towels; drain. In the same skillet, saute the onion, celery and crab in butter until vegetables are tender. Transfer to a large bowl; add the stuffing, water, salt, pepper and cayenne; toss to moisten.

Place fillets in a greased 15-in. x 10-in. x 1-in. baking pan. Spoon stuffing mixture over fillets; top each with two pieces of bacon. Bake, uncovered, at 425° for 20-25 minutes or until fish flakes easily with a fork.
Yield: 4 servings.

Seafood

30+

Herbed Salmon Steaks

Prep: 10 min. | **Bake: 30 min.**

This is one of my husband's favorites. We prepare these delightful yet simple steaks with salmon that we catch ourselves. —Karyn Schlamp, Vanderhoof, British Columbia

1/4 cup butter, melted
2/3 cup crushed saltines (about 20 crackers)
1/4 cup grated Parmesan cheese
1/2 teaspoon salt
1/2 teaspoon dried basil
1/2 teaspoon dried oregano
1/4 teaspoon garlic powder
4 salmon steaks (6 to 8 ounces *each*)

Preheat oven to 350°.

Place butter in a shallow dish. In another shallow dish, combine the cracker crumbs, Parmesan cheese, salt, basil, oregano and garlic powder. Dip salmon into butter, then coat both sides with crumb mixture.

Place in a greased 13-in. x 9-in. x 2-in. baking dish. Bake, uncovered, at 350° for 30-35 minutes or until fish flakes easily with a fork.
Yield: 4 servings.

Angler's Delight

Prep: 20 min. | Cook: 25 min.

Cayenne pepper, taco seasoning and cumin give this fried fish a colorful coating and fantastic southwestern flavor. The slightly crispy fillets are accented by a splash of lime. Prepare the recipe with haddock, cod or any firm fish you prefer.
—Taste of Home Test Kitchen

6 frozen haddock *or* cod fillet (6 ounces *each*), thawed
1/2 cup lime juice
1/2 cup all-purpose flour
2 tablespoons taco seasoning
1/2 teaspoon ground cumin
1/4 teaspoon cayenne pepper
3 tablespoons vegetable oil

In a 13-in. x 9-in. x 2-in. baking dish, arrange fish in a single layer. Pour lime juice over fish. Let stand for 15 minutes.

Meanwhile, in a shallow dish, combine the flour, taco seasoning, cumin and cayenne. Remove fillets from juice and pat dry with paper towels; discard lime juice. Coat fillets with flour mixture.

In a large skillet, cook fillets, in batches, over medium-high heat in oil for 6-8 minutes on each side or until fish flakes easily with a fork.
Yield: 6 servings.

___

Editor's Note: To save time, cook in two large skillets.

Baked Halibut

Prep: 10 min. | Bake: 30 min.

I got this easy delicious recipe from Sandy Schroth of the Puffin Bed & Breakfast in Gustavus, Alaska. It's so simple to make. While the fish is baking, make a salad or vegetable to go with it. —Sandy Schroth, Gustavus, Alaska

3 pounds halibut steaks (1 inch thick)
1 cup (8 ounces) sour cream
1/2 cup grated Parmesan cheese
1/4 cup butter, softened
1/2 teaspoon dill weed
1/2 teaspoon salt
1/4 teaspoon pepper
Paprika

Preheat oven to 375°.

Place halibut in a greased 13-in. x 9-in. x 2-in. baking dish. Combine the sour cream, Parmesan cheese, butter, dill, salt and pepper; spoon over halibut.

Cover and bake at 375° for 20 minutes. Uncover; sprinkle with paprika. Bake 10-15 minutes longer or until fish flakes easily with a fork.
Yield: 6 servings.

Seafood

30+ Oven Fish 'n' Chips

Prep: 20 min. | Bake: 25 min.

Enjoy moist, flavorful fish with a coating that's as crunchy and golden as the deep-fried variety...plus crisp, irresistible "fries!"
—Janice Mitchell, Aurora, Colorado

2 tablespoons olive oil
1/4 teaspoon pepper
4 medium baking potatoes
  (1 pound), peeled

FISH:

1/3 cup all-purpose flour
1/4 teaspoon pepper
1/4 cup egg substitute
2 tablespoons water
2/3 cup crushed cornflakes
1 tablespoons grated
  Parmesan cheese
1/8 teaspoon cayenne
  pepper
1 pound frozen haddock
  fillets, thawed

Tartar sauce, optional

Preheat oven to 425°.

In a large bowl, combine oil and pepper. Cut potatoes lengthwise into 1/2-in. strips. Add to oil mixture; toss to coat. Place on a 15-in. x 10-in. x 1-in. baking pan that has been coated with nonstick cooking spray. Bake, uncovered, at 425° for 25-30 minutes or until golden brown and crisp.

Meanwhile, combine flour and pepper in a shallow dish. In a second dish, beat egg substitute and water. In a third dish, combine the cornflakes, cheese and cayenne. Dredge fish in flour, then dip in egg mixture and roll in crumb mixture.

Place on a baking sheet that has been coated with nonstick cooking spray. Bake at 425° for 10-15 minutes or until fish flakes easily with a fork. Serve with chips and tartar sauce if desired. **Yield: 4 servings.**

Editor's Note: To save time, place the fish in the oven after the potatoes have baked for 15 minutes.

Meatless

Ravioli Primavera (p. 166)

Fluffy Scrambled Eggs

Prep: 10 min.

I started fixing these eggs years ago when we raised chickens and had fresh ingredients every morning. They're hard to beat when it comes to taste and texture. You can add zip and substance to the eggs by mixing in bits of red or green pepper and diced sausage. —Marjorie Carey, Freeport, Florida

8 eggs
1 can (5 ounces) evaporated milk
2 tablespoons butter
Salt and pepper to taste

In a bowl, whisk the eggs and milk. In a large skillet, heat butter until hot. Add egg mixture; cook and stir over medium heat until eggs are completely set. Season with salt and pepper.
Yield: 4 servings.

Black Bean Burritos

Prep: 10 min.

My neighbor and I discovered these delicious, low-fat burritos a few years ago. On nights my husband or I have a meeting, we can have a satisfying supper on the table in minutes. —Angela Studebaker, Goshen, Indiana

3 tablespoons chopped onion
3 tablespoons chopped green pepper
1 can (15 ounces) black beans, rinsed and drained
4 flour tortillas (8 inches), warmed
1 cup (4 ounces) shredded Mexican cheese blend
1 medium tomato, chopped
1 cup shredded lettuce
Salsa, optional

In a nonstick skillet coated with nonstick cooking spray, saute onion and green pepper until tender. Stir in beans; heat through.

Spoon about 1/2 cupful off center of each tortilla. Sprinkle with the cheese, tomato and lettuce. Fold sides and ends over filling and roll up. Serve with salsa if desired.
Yield: 4 servings.

Tomato Spiral Toss

Prep: 20 min.

When my husband and I don't have a lot of time, we fix this pleasing pasta dish. It's easy to prepare, and easy on the pocketbook. We like to use homegrown tomatoes from our garden. —Nichole Lynch, Powell River, British Columbia

8 ounces uncooked spiral pasta
2-1/2 cups diced fresh tomatoes
1 tablespoon dried basil
1/4 to 1/2 cup vegetable oil
2 tablespoons cider vinegar
2 garlic cloves, minced
1/4 teaspoon salt
1/8 teaspoon pepper
3 tablespoons grated Parmesan cheese

Cook the pasta according to package directions. Meanwhile, combine tomatoes and basil in a serving bowl; set aside.

In a small bowl, combine the oil, vinegar, garlic, salt and pepper. Drain pasta; add to tomato mixture. Drizzle with oil mixture; toss to coat. Sprinkle with Parmesan cheese. Serve immediately.
Yield: 6 servings.

Meatless

Ravioli Primavera

Prep: 20 min.

Frozen vegetables and ravioli are used to hurry along this colorful main dish. It's pleasantly seasoned with minced garlic and fresh parsley. —Lois McAtee, Oceanside, California

4 cups frozen cheese ravioli
1 package (16 ounces) frozen Italian vegetables, thawed
1/4 cup olive oil
2 garlic cloves, minced
1/4 cup vegetable *or* chicken broth
2 tablespoons minced fresh parsley
1/4 teaspoon salt
1/4 teaspoon pepper

Prepare ravioli according to package directions. Meanwhile, in a skillet, saute vegetables in oil for 3 minutes or until tender. Add garlic, saute for 1 minute or until garlic is tender.

Stir in broth. Simmer, uncovered, for 2 minutes. Stir in the parsley, salt and pepper; cook 2 minutes longer or until vegetables are tender. Drain pasta. Add to vegetable mixture; toss to coat. **Yield: 4 servings.**

Spinach Pancake Quesadillas

Prep: 15 min.

You can give a savory twist to pancakes with this no-fuss treatment. Folded over a spinach filling, leftover pancakes become a special lunch or simple dinner when garnished with sour cream and tomatoes. —Anna Free, Loudonville, Ohio

1 package (10 ounces) fresh spinach
3 tablespoons water
1 package (3 ounces) cream cheese, softened
1/8 teaspoon ground nutmeg
4 large pancakes
1/4 cup shredded Swiss cheese
1/4 cup shredded part-skim mozzarella cheese
Sour cream and chopped tomato, optional

In a large saucepan, bring spinach and water to a boil. Reduce heat; cover and cook for 3-4 minutes or until spinach is wilted. Drain well and chop.

Meanwhile, in a large mixing bowl, beat cream cheese and nutmeg. Stir in the spinach. Spread over pancakes; sprinkle with cheeses. Place each on a microwave-safe plate.

Microwave, uncovered, on high for 30-60 seconds or until cheese is melted. Fold in half; top with sour cream and tomato if desired.
Yield: 4 servings.

Editor's Note: This recipe was tested in a 1,100-watt microwave. To save time, use frozen cooked pancakes. Heat according to package directions.

Hot 'n' Spicy Omelet

Prep: 15 min.

Red pepper flakes add plenty of fiery zip to this omelet. It's a favorite at our house—for breakfast, brunch or supper—with sausage or bacon, home fries and hot biscuits. —Dixie Terry, Marion, Illinois

1 tablespoon vegetable oil
1 tablespoon butter
8 eggs
2 tablespoons water
4 garlic cloves, minced
1/2 teaspoon salt
1/4 teaspoon pepper
1/4 teaspoon crushed red pepper flakes

In a large nonstick skillet, melt butter and oil over medium-high heat. Whisk the eggs, water, garlic, salt and pepper. Add egg mixture to skillet (mixture should set immediately at edges).

As eggs set, push cooked edges toward the center, letting the uncooked portion flow underneath. When the eggs are set; fold in half. Invert omelet onto a plate to serve. Sprinkle with red pepper flakes.
Yield: 4 servings.

Microwaved Italian Eggplant micro wave

Prep: 20 min.

If you're trying to cut back on meat, you'll appreciate this main dish. The microwave makes it fast to fix these crumb-topped eggplant slices.
—Joan Donahue, Bensalem, Pennsylvania

2 small eggplants, peeled
1/4 cup dried bread crumbs
1/2 teaspoon dried oregano
1 tablespoon mayonnaise
1 cup spaghetti sauce
1 cup (4 ounces) shredded part-skim mozzarella cheese
2 tablespoons grated Parmesan cheese

Cut eggplant into 3/4-in. slices. In a shallow bowl, combine the bread crumbs and oregano. Brush one side of each eggplant slice with mayonnaise. Dip

mayonnaise side into crumb mixture; place crumb side up in a shallow 2-qt. microwave-safe dish.

Cover and microwave on high for 6-8 minutes or until tender. Drizzle with spaghetti sauce and sprinkle with cheeses. Cook, uncovered, for 2 to 2-1/2 minutes longer or until cheese is melted.
Yield: 4 servings.

Editor's Note: This recipe was tested in a 1,100-watt microwave. Reduced-fat or fat-free mayonnaise is not recommended for this recipe.

Meatless

Scrambled Egg Sandwich
Prep: 20 min.

This savory sub is ideal for brunch, lunch or dinner—it's like eating an omelet sandwich. For variety, use different cheese, such as provolone, or French or Italian bread.
—Kim Dunbar, Willow Springs, Illinois

1 loaf (16 ounces) frozen garlic bread, thawed
1/2 cup finely chopped onion
1/2 cup finely chopped green pepper
3 tablespoons butter
10 eggs
1/4 cup milk
Salt and pepper to taste
6 to 8 slices part-skim mozzarella cheese

Bake garlic bread according to package directions. Meanwhile, in a large skillet, saute onion and green pepper in butter until crisp-tender. In a bowl, whisk the eggs, milk, salt and pepper. Pour into skillet; cook and stir over medium heat until eggs are completely set. Remove from the heat and keep warm.

Arrange cheese slices on bottom half of bread; spoon eggs over cheese. Replace bread top. Slice and serve immediately.
Yield: 6 servings.

Pasta and Veggies in Garlic Sauce
Prep: 20 min.

Big garlic flavor and a little heat from red pepper flakes help perk up this fresh-tasting pasta dish. It's great on it's own or as a side dish with chicken and beef entrees.
—Doris Heath, Franklin, North Carolina

12 ounces uncooked penne pasta
6 garlic cloves, minced
1/4 teaspoon crushed red pepper flakes, optional
2 tablespoons olive oil
1 can (15 ounces) garbanzo beans *or* chickpeas, rinsed and drained
2 medium tomatoes, seeded and cut into 1/2-inch pieces
1 package (9 ounces) fresh baby spinach
1/4 teaspoon salt
1/4 cup grated Parmesan cheese

Cook the pasta according to package directions. Meanwhile, in a large skillet, saute garlic and pepper flakes in oil for 1 minute. Add garbanzo beans and tomatoes; cook and stir for 2 minutes. Add spinach and salt; cook and stir until spinach is wilted.

Drain pasta; add to vegetable mixture. Sprinkle with Parmesan cheese; toss to coat.
Yield: 6 servings.

Asparagus Frittata

Prep: 20 min.

You would never guess that egg substitute takes the place of eggs in this fun variation on a traditional frittata. Chock-full of fresh asparagus, this dish is perfect for a light dinner or lunch. —James Bates, Hermiston, Oregon

1 cup water
2/3 pound fresh asparagus, trimmed and cut into 1-inch pieces
1 medium onion, chopped
2 teaspoons olive oil
2 tablespoons minced fresh parsley
1-1/2 cups egg substitute
5 tablespoons shredded Parmesan cheese, *divided*
1/4 teaspoon salt
1/8 teaspoon pepper
1/4 cup shredded reduced-fat cheddar cheese

In a small saucepan, bring water to a boil. Add asparagus; cover and boil for 3 minutes. Drain and immediately place asparagus in ice water; drain and pat dry. In a 10-in. ovenproof skillet, saute onion in oil until tender. Add parsley and asparagus; toss to coat.

In a small bowl, combine egg substitute, 3 tablespoons Parmesan cheese, salt and pepper. Pour over the asparagus mixture; cover and cook over medium heat for 8-10 minutes or until eggs are nearly set. Sprinkle with remaining Parmesan. Place uncovered skillet in the broiler, 6 in. from the heat, for 2 minutes or until eggs are set. Sprinkle with cheddar cheese. Cut into quarters. Serve immediately.
Yield: 4 servings.

Meatless

Veggie Burgers

Prep: 20 min.

We created these quick vegetable patties to use up some of our garden bounty. To suit your family's tastes, include more of the vegetables you like and leave out the ones you don't for a specialty sandwich that's all your own.
—Mary James, Port Orchard, Washington

1 small zucchini, grated
1 medium uncooked potato, peeled and grated
1 medium carrot, grated
1/4 cup grated onion
3/4 cup egg substitute
Pepper to taste
12 slices whole wheat bread, toasted
Sliced red onion and lettuce leaves, optional

In a large bowl, combine the first six ingredients. For each burger, pour about 1/2 cup batter onto a hot griddle lightly coated with nonstick cooking spray. Cook for 2-3 minutes on each side or until golden brown. Serve on toasted bread with onion and lettuce if desired.
Yield: 6 burgers.

Walnut Cream Pasta

Prep: 20 min.

I take advantage of the local walnut supply by fixing this change-of-pace pasta. —Kim Gilliland, Simi Valley, California

1 package (12 ounces) fettuccine
2 garlic cloves, minced
3 tablespoons butter
1/2 cup chicken broth
1/4 cup sour cream
1/4 cup heavy whipping cream
1/4 teaspoon salt
1/8 teaspoon pepper
1 cup grated Parmesan cheese
1 cup finely chopped walnuts

Cook the fettuccine according to the package directions. Meanwhile, in a small saucepan, saute garlic in butter for 1 minute or until tender. Gradually stir in broth.

In a large bowl, combine the sour cream, whipping cream, salt and pepper; stir into broth mixture (do not boil). Drain fettuccine and transfer to a large serving bowl. Add the cream sauce, Parmesan cheese and walnuts; toss to coat. **Yield: 6 servings.**

Jelly Pancake Sandwiches

Prep: 20 min.

I made up this recipe for friends who are like me and don't like syrup on their pancakes. It's great to eat on the go. Use any jelly or peanut butter or both to make peanut butter and jelly sandwiches. —Laura Muskopf, Wooster, Ohio

2 cups biscuit/baking mix
1 teaspoon ground cinnamon
1/4 teaspoon salt
1 cup milk
2 eggs, lightly beaten
Strawberry preserves *or* seedless strawberry jam

In a large bowl, combine the biscuit mix, cinnamon and salt. Stir in milk and eggs until blended.

Pour batter by 1/4 cupfuls onto a greased hot griddle; turn when bubbles form on top. Cook until the second side is golden brown. Spread half of the pancakes with jelly; top with remaining pancakes. **Yield: 5 servings.**

Meatless

Spinach Tomato Linguine

Prep: 10 min. | Cook: 20 min.

Chock-full of garden freshness, this colorful toss makes an excellent meatless entree or side dish. Sometimes I substitute penne pasta and add cooked chicken for a heartier main meal. Using garlic-flavored feta cheese is a great touch.
—Rosemary Averkamp, Genoa, Wisconsin

8 ounces uncooked linguine

3 cups chopped seeded plum tomatoes

1 package (10 ounces) frozen chopped spinach, thawed and squeezed dry

1/2 cup chopped green onions

1 teaspoon olive oil

1/4 teaspoon salt

1/4 teaspoon garlic salt

4 ounces crumbled feta cheese

Cook linguine according to package directions. Meanwhile, in a large nonstick skillet, saute the tomatoes, spinach and onions in oil until tomatoes are softened. Sprinkle with salt and garlic salt. Reduce heat. Stir in the cheese; until heated through.

Drain linguine; transfer to a serving bowl. Add tomato mixture; toss to coat.
Yield: 4 servings.

Microwave Mac 'n' Cheese

micro
wave

Prep: 15 min. | **Cook: 15 min.**

My family prefers homemade macaroni and cheese over the kind you get out of the box. This recipe is an easy way to keep them happy. Whenever we have a family get-together, I bring this comforting dish. Its "from-scratch" taste can't be beat.
—Linda Gingrich, Freeburg, Pennsylvania

2 cups uncooked elbow macaroni
2 cups hot water
1/3 cup butter, cubed
1/4 cup chopped onion
3/4 teaspoon salt
1/4 teaspoon pepper
1/4 teaspoon ground mustard
1/3 cup all-purpose flour
1-1/4 cups milk
8 ounces process cheese (Velveeta), cubed

In a 2-qt. microwave-safe dish, combine first seven ingredients. Cover and microwave on high for 3 minutes; stir. Cover and cook at 50% power 3 minutes longer or until mixture comes to a boil.

Combine flour and milk until smooth; gradually stir into macaroni mixture. Add cheese. Cover and cook on high for 6-8 minutes or until the macaroni is tender and sauce is bubbly, stirring every 3 minutes.
Yield: 4 servings.

Editor's Note: This recipe was tested in a 1,100-watt microwave.

Easy Pasta Alfredo

Prep: 5 min. | **Cook: 20 min.**

Who would believe that five simple ingredients could taste so rich and delicious? This creamy, comforting sauce can be made in a matter of minutes.
—Karin De Carlo, Milford, Pennsylvania

1 package (19 ounces) frozen cheese tortellini
1 cup heavy whipping cream
1/2 cup butter, cubed
1/8 teaspoon ground nutmeg
1 cup shredded Parmesan cheese

Cook tortellini according to package directions. Meanwhile in a small saucepan, combine cream, butter and nutmeg. Cook, uncovered, over medium-low heat until heated through (do not boil). Reduce heat; add Parmesan cheese, stirring until cheese is melted.

Drain pasta; transfer to a large serving bowl. Add cheese sauce; toss to coat.
Yield: 4 servings.

Meatless

Three-Cheese Rice Lasagna micro wave

Prep: 10 min. | Cook: 15 min.

Fans of traditional lasagna are sure to be intrigued by this tasty twist—a rice-based version. I discovered this recipe in a weight-loss class, and my family loves it. It has all the flavor of classic lasagna made with noodles yet only a fraction of the fat.
—Gwen Cantwell, Sharon, Wisconsin

1 jar (14 ounces) meatless spaghetti sauce
1 jar (4-1/2 ounces) sliced mushrooms, drained
1 cup (8 ounces) 1% cottage cheese
1 cup (4 ounces) shredded part-skim mozzarella cheese
1 egg white
3 cups cooked long grain rice
2 tablespoons grated Parmesan cheese

In a small bowl, combine spaghetti sauce and mushrooms; set aside. In another bowl, combine the cottage cheese, mozzarella cheese and egg white.

In a microwave-safe 8-in. square baking dish coated with nonstick cooking spray, layer a third of the sauce, half of the rice and half of the cottage cheese mixture; repeat layers. Top with the remaining sauce.

Microwave at 50% power for 7-12 minutes or until heated through. Sprinkle with Parmesan cheese. Let stand for 5 minutes before serving.
Yield: 6 servings.

Editor's Note: This recipe was tested in a 1,100-watt microwave. When cooking rice, make extra to have on hand. Cooked rice can be refrigerated for up to 7 days and frozen for up to 6 months. For convenience, package a cup or two of rice in refrigerator/freezer bags. Flatten rice out in the bags before freezing. This way it will defrost more quickly.

Pasta with Marinara Sauce

Prep: 10 min. | Cook: 20 min.

You don't have to settle for prepared sauce when this homemade marinara is so simple and tasty. Add Italian sausage links for a more robust flavor.
—Diane Hixon, Niceville, Florida

2 garlic cloves, sliced
1/3 cup olive oil
1 can (28 ounces) diced tomatoes, undrained
3 tablespoons minced fresh parsley
2 tablespoons minced onion
2 bay leaves
Salt and pepper to taste
1 tablespoon chopped fresh basil
Hot cooked pasta

In a large saucepan, cook garlic in oil over medium heat for 3 minutes or until golden. Add the tomatoes, parsley, onion, bay leaves, salt and pepper; bring to a boil. Reduce heat; cover and simmer for 15 minutes. Discard bay leaves. Stir in basil. Serve over pasta.
Yield: 4 servings.

Editor's Note: Start heating the water for the pasta before you begin cooking the garlic.

Fruit-Filled Puff Pancake

Prep: 15 min. | **Bake: 10 min.**

My husband and I often make a meal of this fruity puff pancake. The combination of cinnamon, blueberries and bananas is wonderful.
—LeAnne Senger, Oregon City, Oregon

1 tablespoon butter
1/3 cup all-purpose flour
3 tablespoons sugar, *divided*
1/4 teaspoon salt
3 eggs, lightly beaten
1/2 cup milk
1-1/2 cups fresh *or* frozen blueberries
1 medium ripe banana, sliced
1/4 teaspoon ground cinnamon

Preheat oven to 400°.

Place butter in a 9-in. pie plate. Bake at 400° for 4-5 minutes or until melted. Meanwhile, in a large bowl, combine the flour, 1 tablespoon sugar and salt. Add eggs and milk; whisk until smooth.

Pour into hot pie plate. Bake at 400° for 10-12 minutes or until edges are puffed and golden brown. Meanwhile, combine blueberries and banana.

In a small bowl, combine cinnamon and remaining sugar. Spoon fruit mixture onto pancake; sprinkle with cinnamon-sugar. Cut into wedges.
Yield: 4 servings.

Picante Omelet Pie

Prep: 10 min. | Bake: 20 min.

This zippy egg bake is a favorite of one of my daughters. I like to serve it for brunch when my daughter stops by before church on Sunday, but it also makes a tasty dinner.
—Phyllis Carlson, Gardner, Kansas

1/2 cup picante sauce
1 cup (4 ounces) shredded Monterey Jack cheese
1 cup (4 ounces) shredded cheddar cheese
6 eggs
1 cup (8 ounces) sour cream
Tomato slices and minced fresh cilantro, optional

Preheat oven to 375°.

Pour the picante sauce into a lightly greased 9-in. pie plate. Sprinkle with cheeses; set aside. In a blender, combine eggs and sour cream; cover and process until smooth. Pour over cheese.

Bake at 375° for 20-25 minutes or until a knife inserted near the center comes out clean. Let stand for 5 minutes before cutting. Garnish with tomato and cilantro if desired.
Yield: 6 servings.

Carrot Burgers

Prep: 20 min. | Cook: 10 min.

These carrot patties were a big hit with my children when they were growing up. Cornflakes provide the taste that kids find so appealing.
—Phyllis Moody, King William, Virginia

1-1/2 cups diced carrots
2 cups crushed cornflakes
2 eggs, lightly beaten
1/4 cup finely chopped celery
1 tablespoon finely chopped onion
1/2 teaspoon salt
1/4 teaspoon sugar
1/8 teaspoon pepper
2 tablespoons vegetable oil
Hamburger buns, optional

Place 1 in. of water and carrots in a large skillet; bring to a boil. Reduce heat; cover and simmer for 5-10 minutes or until crisp-tender; drain.

In a large bowl, combine the carrots, cornflakes, eggs, celery, onion, salt, sugar and pepper. Form into six patties. Heat oil in a skillet over medium heat; cook patties for 3 minutes on each side or until browned. Serve on buns if desired.
Yield: 6 servings.

Blintz Pancakes

Prep: 10 min. | Cook: 20 min.

Blending sour cream and cottage cheese—ingredients traditionally associated with blintzes—into the batter of these pancakes provides them with their old-fashioned flavor. Top the family favorites with berry syrup to turn an ordinary morning into an extraordinary day. —Dianna Digoy, San Diego, California

- 1 cup all-purpose flour
- 1 tablespoon sugar
- 1/2 teaspoon salt
- 1 cup (8 ounces) sour cream
- 1 cup (8 ounces) 4% cottage cheese
- 4 eggs, lightly beaten

Strawberry *or* blueberry syrup

Sliced fresh strawberries, optional

In a large bowl, combine the flour, sugar and salt. Stir in the sour cream, cottage cheese and eggs until blended.

Pour batter by 1/4 cupful onto a greased hot griddle in batches; turn when bubbles form on top. Cook until the second side is golden brown. Serve with syrup and strawberries if desired. **Yield: 12 pancakes.**

Spinach Feta Turnovers

Prep: 20 min. | Bake: 10 min.

My wife really enjoys these quick and easy turnovers. She says they are delicious and melt in your mouth. —David Baruch, Weston, Florida

- 2 eggs *or* 1/2 cup egg substitute
- 1 package (10 ounces) frozen leaf spinach, thawed, squeezed dry and chopped
- 3/4 cup crumbled feta cheese
- 2 garlic cloves, minced
- 1/4 teaspoon pepper
- 1 tube (10 ounces) refrigerated pizza crust

Preheat oven to 425°.

In a small bowl, whisk eggs; reserving 1 tablespoon egg and set aside. In a large bowl, combine the spinach, feta cheese, garlic, pepper and remaining eggs.

Unroll pizza dough; roll into a 12-in. square. Cut into four 3-in. squares. Top each square with about 1/3 cup spinach mixture. Fold into a triangle and pinch edges to seal. Cut slits in top; brush with reserved egg.

Place on a greased baking sheet. Bake at 425° for 8-10 minutes or until golden brown. **Yield: 4 servings.**

Meatless

Fluffy Harvest Omelet

Prep: 35 min. | **Bake: 15 min.**

With its mushrooms, zucchini and tomato sauce, this hearty omelet isn't just for breakfast. Your family will savor it as a change-of-pace lunch or dinner. And you can alter the ingredients to include whatever vegetables you have on hand.
—Taste of Home Test Kitchen

6 eggs, *separated*
1/4 teaspoon salt
1/4 cup half-and-half cream
1/4 cup grated Parmesan cheese
1/4 teaspoon pepper
2 tablespoons butter
1 can (15 ounces) chunky Italian tomato sauce
1 cup cubed fresh zucchini
3/4 cup sliced fresh mushrooms
1 cup (4 ounces) shredded part-skim mozzarella cheese

Preheat oven to 350°.

In a large mixing bowl, beat egg whites until soft peaks form. Add salt; continue beating until stiff peaks form. In a small mixing bowl, beat the egg yolks, cream, Parmesan cheese and pepper until foamy. Gently fold in the egg whites.

Melt butter in a 10-in. ovenproof skillet; pour egg mixture into skillet; cover and cook over medium-low heat for 8-10 minutes or until eggs are nearly set.

Uncover; bake in a 350° oven for 5-8 minutes or until top is golden brown and eggs are set. Meanwhile, in a small saucepan, combine the tomato sauce, zucchini and mushrooms. Cook, uncovered, for 10 minutes or until zucchini is tender.

Sprinkle mozzarella cheese over omelet; fold in half and top with tomato sauce. Cut into wedges. Serve immediately. **Yield: 4 servings.**

Spinach Burritos

Prep: 20 min. | **Bake: 20 min.**

I made up this recipe a couple years ago after trying a similar dish in a restaurant. My son tells me these burritos are awesome!
—Dolores Zornow, Poynette, Wisconsin

1/2 cup chopped onion
2 garlic cloves, minced
2 teaspoons butter
1 package (10 ounces) frozen chopped spinach, thawed and squeezed dry
1/8 teaspoon pepper
6 fat-free flour tortillas (10 inches), warmed
3/4 cup picante sauce, *divided*
2 cups (8 ounces) shredded reduced-fat cheddar cheese, *divided*

Preheat oven to 350°.

In a skillet, saute onion and garlic in butter. Add spinach and pepper; cook for 2-3 minutes or until heated through.

Place about 3 tablespoonfuls of spinach mixture off center on each tortilla; top with 1 tablespoon picante sauce and 2 tablespoons cheese. Fold sides and ends over filling and roll up.

Place seam side down in a 13-in. x 9-in. x 2-in. baking dish coated with nonstick cooking spray. Top with remaining picante sauce and cheese. Bake, uncovered, at 350° for 20-25 minutes or until heated through and cheese is melted.
Yield: 6 servings.

Scrumptious Spaghetti

Prep: 15 min. | **Cook: 25 min.**

This quick entree is one of my favorites. Start the chunky spaghetti sauce first, so it simmers while you make the rest of your meal.—Sherry Horton, Sioux Falls, South Dakota

1 medium green pepper, chopped
1 medium onion, chopped
1 garlic clove, minced
1 tablespoon olive oil
1 can (15 ounces) tomato sauce
2 tablespoons sugar
1/2 to 1 teaspoon dried oregano
1 package (16 ounces) spaghetti
1/4 cup grated Parmesan cheese, optional

In a large skillet, saute the green pepper, onion and garlic in oil until tender. Stir in the tomato sauce, sugar and oregano. Cover and simmer for 20 minutes, stirring occasionally.

Meanwhile, cook spaghetti according to package directions. Drain; transfer to a serving dish. Serve with sauce. Sprinkle with Parmesan cheese if desired.
Yield: 4-6 servings.

Meatless

Meatless Chili Bake

Prep: 20 min. | Bake: 25 min.

My husband is a farmer, and this delicious dish is easy and quick to fix whenever he decides to come in and eat. Our children all like it, too. —Lisa Flamme, Willis Point, Texas

2-1/2 cups uncooked spiral pasta
1 can (15 ounces) vegetarian chili with beans
1 jar (12 ounces) chunky salsa
1 can (11 ounces) whole kernel corn, drained
1/2 cup shredded cheddar cheese

Preheat oven to 400°.

Cook pasta according to package directions; drain. In a large bowl, combine the chili, salsa and corn. Add pasta; toss to coat.

Transfer to a greased shallow 2-qt. baking dish; sprinkle with cheese. Bake, uncovered, at 400° for 25-30 minutes or until heated through.
Yield: 4-6 servings.

Black Bean Nacho Bake

Prep: 20 min. | Bake: 30 min.

Pasta, black beans and nacho cheese soup combine in this speedy six-ingredient supper. Top servings of this zippy casserole with cheddar cheese and crunchy tortilla chips. —Melodie Gay, Salt Lake City, Utah

1 package (7 ounces) small pasta shells
1 can (15 ounces) black beans, rinsed and drained
1 can (11 ounces) condensed nacho cheese soup, undiluted
1/3 cup milk
1/2 cup crushed tortilla chips
1/2 cup shredded cheddar cheese

Preheat oven to 350°.

Cook the pasta according to package directions; drain. In a large bowl, combine macaroni and beans. In a small bowl, combine soup and milk; stir into macaroni mixture.

Transfer to a greased 8-in. square baking dish. Cover and bake at 350° for 25 minutes. Uncover; sprinkle with tortilla chips and cheese. Bake 5-10 minutes longer or until pasta is tender and cheese is melted.
Yield: 4 servings.

Creamy Asparagus on Toast

Prep: 20 min. | Bake: 15 min.

If you have hard-cooked eggs left over from Easter, here's a way to use some of them. It's delicious for a luncheon or light supper. —Laura Nelson, Geneseo, Illinois

1 pound fresh asparagus, trimmed
2 hard-cooked eggs, sliced
1/4 cup butter plus 3 tablespoons butter, *divided*
1/4 cup all-purpose flour
1/4 teaspoon salt
Dash pepper
2 cups milk
1 cup (4 ounces) shredded cheddar cheese
1/2 cup soft bread crumbs
4 slices bread, toasted and halved

Preheat oven to 375°.

In a large skillet, bring 1/2 in. of water to a boil. Add asparagus; cover and boil for 3 minutes or until crisp-tender. Drain. Transfer to a greased 11-in. x 7-in. x 2-in. baking dish. Arrange eggs over the top.

In a large saucepan, melt 1/4 cup butter; gradually stir in the flour, salt and pepper until smooth. Gradually add milk. Bring to a boil; cook and stir for 2 minutes or until thickened. Reduce heat; add cheese and stir until melted. Pour over eggs.

In a small skillet, melt the remaining butter; toss with bread crumbs. Sprinkle over top of casserole. Bake, uncovered, at 375° for 15 minutes or until lightly browned. Serve with toast.
Yield: 4 servings.

Meatless

Spinach Lasagna Roll-Ups

Prep: 30 min. | Bake: 20 min.

One night I was having friends stop by who were on a tight schedule. I wanted them to stay for dinner, but I need to fix something in short order. So, I created these savory spirals, which feature a creamy three-cheese filling. These roll-ups taste like lasagna, but bake in a fraction of the time. —Julia Trachsel, Victoria, British Columbia

12 lasagna noodles
2 eggs, lightly beaten
2-1/2 cups ricotta cheese
2-1/2 cups (10 ounces) shredded part-skim mozzarella cheese
1/2 cup grated Parmesan cheese
1 package (10 ounces) frozen chopped spinach, thawed and squeezed dry
1/4 teaspoon salt
1/4 teaspoon pepper
1/4 teaspoon ground nutmeg
1 jar (26 ounces) meatless spaghetti sauce

Preheat oven to 375°.

Cook lasagna noodles according to package directions. Meanwhile, in a large bowl, combine the eggs, cheeses, spinach, salt, pepper and nutmeg. Drain noodles. Spread 1/3 cup cheese mixture over each noodle; carefully roll up.

Pour 1 cup spaghetti sauce into an ungreased 13-in. x 9-in. x 2-in. baking dish. Place roll-ups seam side down over sauce. Top with remaining sauce. Bake, uncovered, at 375° for 20-25 minutes or until heated through.
Yield: 6 servings.

Zucchini Pie

Prep: 25 min. | Bake: 25 min.

For a light lunch or brunch, fix this quiche-like zucchini pie.
—Melissa Collins, South Daytona, Florida

- 1 tube (8 ounces) refrigerated crescent rolls
- 3 medium zucchini, thinly sliced
- 1 garlic clove, minced
- 2 tablespoons butter
- 2 teaspoons minced fresh parsley
- 1 teaspoon snipped fresh dill
- 1/4 teaspoon salt
- 1/4 teaspoon pepper
- 1 cup (4 ounces) shredded Monterey Jack cheese, *divided*
- 2 eggs, lightly beaten

Preheat oven to 375°.

Separate crescent dough into eight triangles; place in a greased 9-in. pie plate with points toward center. Press onto bottom and up sides of plate to form a crust; seal perforations.

In a skillet, saute zucchini and garlic in butter until crisp-tender. Add the parsley, dill, salt, pepper and 1/2 cup cheese. Spoon into crust. Pour eggs over top; top with remaining cheese.

Cover edges loosely with foil. Bake at 375° for 25-30 minutes or until a knife inserted near the center comes out clean. Let stand for 5 minutes before cutting. **Yield: 6 servings.**

Veggie Cheese Squares

Prep: 20 min. | Bake: 30 min.

One busy afternoon when my fridge was almost bare, I created this recipe. Now this nice and easy dish is a suppertime standby. —Dixie Terry, Goreville, Illinois

- 1-1/2 cups fresh broccoli florets
- 1 medium sweet red pepper, julienned
- 2 garlic cloves, minced
- 2 tablespoons olive oil
- 4 eggs
- 1 cup milk
- 1 cup (4 ounces) shredded cheddar cheese, *divided*
- 1/2 teaspoon dried thyme
- 1/4 teaspoon salt

Preheat oven to 350°.

In a large skillet, saute the broccoli, red pepper and garlic in oil. Spoon into a greased 9-in. square baking dish. In another large bowl, combine the eggs, milk, 3/4 cup cheese, thyme and salt.

Pour over the broccoli mixture. Bake, uncovered, at 350° for 25-30 minutes. Sprinkle with remaining cheese. Bake for 5 minutes or until cheese is melted. Let stand for 5 minutes before cutting. **Yield: 4-6 servings.**

Meatless

Picante Biscuit Bake

Prep: 5 min. | **Bake: 30 min.**

This tasty Mexican-flavored casserole calls for just six convenient ingredients, so it's a breeze to put together. If you're a meat lover, you can add a pound of browned ground beef. Or try a pizza variation using pizza sauce, pepperoni and mozzarella cheese. —Lanita Anderson, Jacksonville, North Carolina

2 tubes (12 ounces *each*) refrigerated buttermilk biscuits

1 jar (16 ounces) picante sauce *or* salsa

1 medium green pepper, chopped

1 medium onion, chopped

1 can (2-1/4 ounces) sliced ripe olives, drained

2 cups (8 ounces) shredded Monterey Jack cheese

Quarter the biscuits; place in a greased 13-in. x 9-in. x 2-in. baking dish. Top with picante sauce, green pepper, onion and olives.

Bake, uncovered, at 350° for 20 minutes. Sprinkle with cheese. Bake 10 minutes longer or until the cheese is melted. **Yield: 6 servings.**

Chili Casserole

Prep: 10 min. | **Bake: 30 min.**

I threw together this main dish when my husband unexpectedly invited his hunting buddies for dinner. It was on the table by the time they'd unpacked their gear and washed up. —Karen Bruggman, Edmonds, Washington

3 cans (15 ounces *each*) vegetarian chili with beans

1 can (4 ounces) chopped green chilies

1 can (2-1/4 ounces) sliced ripe olives, drained

2 cups (8 ounces) shredded cheddar cheese

2 cups ranch-flavored tortilla chips, crushed

In a bowl, combine all ingredients. Transfer to a greased 2-1/2-qt. baking dish. Bake, uncovered, at 350° for 30-35 minutes or until bubbly. **Yield: 6 servings.**

Sides & Salads

Penne from Heaven (p. 213)

10

minute recipes

Baby Corn Romaine Salad

Prep: 10 min.

My kids really enjoy this green salad, which is made with romaine lettuce, broccoli, corn and crumbled bacon. It uses bottled dressing, so it's quick to fix, too.
—Kathryn Maxson, Mountlake Terrace, Washington

6 cups torn romaine

2 cups fresh broccoli florets

1 can (15 ounces) whole baby corn, rinsed, drained and cut into 1/2-inch pieces

3 tablespoons crumbled cooked bacon

1/2 cup fat-free Caesar *or* Italian salad dressing

In a large salad bowl, combine the romaine, broccoli, corn and bacon. Drizzle with dressing; toss to coat.
Yield: 6 servings.

Colorful Bean Salad

Prep: 10 min.

My bean salad is a mainstay, both for meals and neighborhood potlucks. People rave about the cumin dressing with its zesty flavor. The salad tastes even better when made ahead and marinated in the fridge overnight. —Beth Brown, Naples, Florida

- 3 tablespoons olive oil
- 3 tablespoons red wine vinegar
- 1/2 teaspoon garlic powder
- 1/2 teaspoon ground cumin
- 1/4 teaspoon salt
- 1/4 teaspoon pepper
- 1 can (16 ounces) kidney beans, rinsed and drained
- 1 can (15 ounces) black beans, rinsed and drained
- 1 can (11 ounces) Mexicorn, drained
- 1/4 cup thinly sliced green onions

In a large bowl, combine the first six ingredients. Add the beans, corn and onions; stir to coat. Cover and refrigerate until serving. Serve with a slotted spoon.
Yield: 6 servings.

French-Style Green Beans

Prep: 10 min.

These green beans go nicely with chicken or fish. I like to serve them for our church steak dinner. If you like, a smattering of onions can be used to pep up the mild flavor of the beans. —Hope Meece, Ambia, Indiana

- 1/3 cup slivered almonds
- 3 tablespoons butter
- 1 package (10 ounces) frozen French-style green beans, thawed
- 1/4 teaspoon salt

In a large skillet, saute almonds in butter for 1-2 minutes or until lightly browned. Add beans and salt; cook and stir for 1-2 minutes or until heated through.
Yield: 4 servings.

Sides & Salads

Basil Cherry Tomatoes

Prep: 10 min.

These tomatoes are a delicious side dish to add Italian flair to any dinner. Basil and olive oil are simple additions to sweet cherry tomatoes, but the flavors are wonderful together.
—Melissa Stevens, Elk River, Minnesota

3 pints cherry tomatoes, halved
1/2 cup chopped fresh basil
1-1/2 teaspoons olive oil
Salt and pepper to taste
Lettuce leaves, optional

In a large bowl, combine the tomatoes, basil, oil, salt and pepper. Cover and refrigerate until serving. Serve on lettuce if desired.
Yield: 4-6 servings.

Chili-Cheese Mashed Potatoes

Prep: 10 min.

Instant mashed potatoes are jazzed up with garlic, green chilies and cheese to create this speedy side dish. It's really tasty. —Peter Halferty, Corpus Christi, Texas

2-3/4 cups water
1 cup milk
1-1/2 teaspoons salt
1 tablespoon butter
3 garlic cloves, minced
3 cups instant mashed potato flakes
2 cans (4 ounces *each*) chopped green chilies
1 cup (4 ounces) shredded Mexican cheese blend

In a large saucepan, bring water, milk and salt to a boil. Add the butter, garlic, potato flakes and chilies; stir until thickened. Sprinkle with cheese.
Yield: 6 servings.

Melon with Sweet Lime Dressing

Prep: 10 min.

A simple lime dressing coats cubed cantaloupe and honeydew for a refreshing treat.
—Taste of Home Test Kitchen

3 cups cubed cantaloupe
3 cups cubed honeydew
2 tablespoons orange marmalade
2 tablespoons lime juice
1 tablespoon honey
1 teaspoon chopped fresh mint

In a large bowl, combine cantaloupe and honeydew. In a small bowl, combine remaining ingredients. Pour over fruit; toss gently to coat.
Yield: 6 servings.

Sides & Salads

Crispy 'n' Crunchy Salad

Prep: 10 min.

I always have the easy ingredients for this fun combination on hand. Plus, kids don't mind eating their fruits and veggies when they're glazed with sweet honey. —Lorri Speer, Centralia, Washington

1 medium Golden Delicious apple, chopped
1 medium red apple, chopped
2 celery ribs, thinly sliced
1/2 cup chopped walnuts
1/2 cup golden raisins
1/4 cup honey

In a large bowl, combine the apples, celery, walnuts and raisins. Add the honey; toss to coat. Serve immediately. **Yield: 6 servings.**

Stir-Fried Asparagus

Prep: 10 min.

Tender, garden-fresh asparagus goes with so many entrees. The flavor of the asparagus comes through in this nicely seasoned side. —Jeanette Lawrence, Vacaville, California

3 tablespoons butter
1 teaspoon chicken bouillon granules
1/8 teaspoon celery salt
1/8 teaspoon pepper
1-1/2 pounds fresh asparagus, trimmed and cut into 2-inch pieces (about 4 cups)
1 teaspoon soy sauce

In a large skillet, melt butter, combine bouillon, celery salt and pepper. Add asparagus and toss to coat. Cover and cook for over medium-high heat for 2 minutes or until asparagus is crisp-tender, stirring occasionally. Stir in soy sauce; serve immediately. **Yield: 4 servings.**

Mock Caesar Salad

Prep: 10 min.

This salad has the flavor of an authentic Caesar salad but without the fuss. You can keep the dressing on hand to quickly and deliciously top a variety of greens and vegetables.
—Taste of Home Test Kitchen

   3 tablespoons mayonnaise
   2 teaspoons grated
     Parmesan cheese
1-1/2 teaspoons red wine
     vinegar
   1/2 teaspoon garlic powder
   1/2 teaspoon lemon juice
   4 cups torn romaine
     lettuce
   1/4 cup Caesar salad
     croutons
   2 tablespoons shredded
     Parmesan cheese

In a jar with a tight-fitting lid, combine first five ingredients; shake well. Place lettuce in a large bowl; drizzle with dressing and toss to coat. Sprinkle with croutons and shredded cheese. **Yield: 4 servings.**

Apple Salad

Prep: 10 min.

With only six ingredients, this simple, little salad is easy to assemble. A creamy dressy coasts the crunchy apples, celery and chewy dates. —Beverly Little, Marietta, Georgia

   3 celery ribs, finely chopped
   4 medium apples, peeled and
     chopped
   1 cup fat-free whipped topping
1/4 cup chopped dates *or* raisins
   2 tablespoons chopped pecans
   4 teaspoons reduced-fat mayonnaise

In a bowl, combine all the ingredients. Cover and refrigerate until serving. **Yield: 6 servings.**

Sides & Salads

Southwest Skillet Corn

Prep: 10 min.

This colorful stir-fried side nicely complements any Mexican menu.
—Marilyn Smudzinski, Peru, Illinois

1 medium sweet red pepper, chopped
1 tablespoon finely chopped seeded jalapeno pepper
1 tablespoon butter
1-1/2 teaspoons ground cumin
1 package (16 ounces) frozen corn, thawed
1/3 cup minced fresh cilantro

In a large nonstick skillet, saute red pepper and jalapeno in butter until tender. Add cumin; cook for 30 seconds. Add corn and cilantro; saute 2 minutes longer or until heated through.
Yield: 4 servings.

Editor's Note: When cutting or seeding hot peppers, use rubber or plastic gloves to protect your hands. Avoid touching your face.

Artichoke Tossed Salad

Prep: 10 min.

I used to care for an elderly woman who loved artichokes, so I created this salad especially for her. Not only is it convenient to make, but you can make it fancy by adding shrimp too.
—Melissa Mosness, Loveland, Colorado

2 cups *each* torn romaine, leaf and iceberg lettuce

1 jar (6-1/2 ounces) marinated artichoke hearts, drained and chopped

1 cup sliced fresh mushrooms

1 can (2-1/4 ounces) sliced ripe olives, drained

1/2 cup Italian salad dressing

In a salad bowl, combine the lettuce, artichokes, mushrooms and olives. Drizzle with salad dressing; toss to coat. Serve immediately.
Yield: 6 servings.

Seasoned Broccoli Spears micro wave

Prep: 10 min.

Dressing up broccoli is a snap with this recipe. Fresh broccoli spears are flavored with lemon-pepper, garlic salt and thyme.
—Taste of Home Test Kitchen

1-1/2 pounds fresh broccoli, cut into spears

1/4 cup water

2 tablespoons butter

1 teaspoon lemon-pepper seasoning

1/2 teaspoon garlic salt

1/2 teaspoon dried thyme

Place the broccoli in a microwave-safe bowl; add water. Cover and microwave on high for 4-5 minutes or until tender; drain. Stir in the remaining ingredients.
Yield: 6 servings.

Editor's Note: This recipe was tested in a 1,100-watt microwave.

Sides & Salads

Broccoli Coleslaw

Prep: 10 min.

Folks will be pleasantly surprised when they taste this unique coleslaw made with broccoli instead of cabbage. The light vinegar dressing isn't overpowering. —Taste of Home Test Kitchen

6 cups broccoli coleslaw mix
1/2 cup chopped green onions
1/3 cup vegetable oil
1/4 cup cider vinegar
2 tablespoons sugar
1 teaspoon seasoned salt
1/2 teaspoon dill weed
1/4 teaspoon celery seed
1/4 teaspoon pepper

In a large bowl, combine coleslaw mix and onions. In a jar with a tight-fitting lid, combine the remaining ingredients; shake well. Drizzle over coleslaw; toss to coat.
Yield: 6 servings.

Editor's Note: Broccoli coleslaw mix may be found in the produce section of most grocery stores.

Swiss Spinach Salad

Prep: 10 min.

When I toss my spinach with Swiss cheese and bacon, the salad tastes like quiche lorraine...without the effort. Plus, it's special enough to serve at patio parties with family and friends. —Nella Parker, Hersey, Michigan

1 package (6 ounces) fresh baby spinach
1 cup (4 ounces) shredded Swiss cheese
3 tablespoons crumbled cooked bacon
1/2 cup Caesar salad dressing
Salad croutons

In a large bowl, combine the spinach, cheese and bacon. Drizzle with dressing and toss to coat. Top with croutons. Serve immediately.
Yield: 4-6 servings.

The Busy Family Cookbook

Greek Tossed Salad

Prep: 10 min.

The prep of this salad takes just minutes due to the convenience of packaged greens and bottled dressing. The pretty medley gets its great Greek flavor from feta cheese, sliced cucumber and ripe olives. You can also use kalamata olives.
—Vicki Smith, Okeechobee, Florida

5 cups ready-to-serve salad greens
3/4 cup sliced cucumber
1 medium tomato, cut into wedges
2 tablespoons crumbled feta cheese
2 tablespoons sliced ripe olives
2/3 cup Greek vinaigrette *or* salad dressing of your choice

In a salad bowl, combine the greens, cucumber, tomato, cheese and olives. Drizzle with dressing; toss to coat. **Yield: 4 servings.**

Spicy Creamed Corn

Prep: 10 min.

One of my family's favorite vegetables is corn. It tastes delicious and goes very well with turkey and chicken. It's a simple way to add a touch of spice to your meal.
—Nancy McDonald, Burns, Wyoming

1 package (3 ounces) cream cheese, cubed

1 can (15-1/4 ounces) whole kernel corn, drained

1 can (4 ounces) chopped green chilies

1/4 cup sliced green onions

1/4 cup chopped sweet red pepper

In a large saucepan, combine all the ingredients. Cook over medium heat until cream cheese is melted and mixture is blended, stirring often.
Yield: 4 servings.

Italian Rice

Prep: 20 min.

Bring a bit of Italy to the table without the usual pasta and sauce. This colorful side dish blends fluffy rice, fresh spinach and roasted red peppers. The amount of garlic can be adjusted to fit your personal taste. For me, the more garlic, the better!
—Michelle Armistead, Marlboro, New Jersey

2/3 cup uncooked rice
2 garlic cloves, minced
2 teaspoons olive oil
8 cups fresh spinach (about 10 ounces), chopped
1 tablespoon balsamic vinegar
1/2 teaspoon salt
1/8 teaspoon pepper
1/2 cup chopped roasted sweet red peppers

Cook rice according to package directions. Meanwhile, in a large nonstick skillet, saute garlic in oil for 1 minute. Stir in spinach. Cover and cook for 3-4 minutes or until tender; drain well. Add the vinegar, salt and pepper. Stir in the rice and red peppers until combined. Cook and stir until heated through.
Yield: 4 servings.

Editor's Note: When minutes count, use instant white or brown rice.

Tomato Pea Couscous

Prep: 20 min.

I modified a recipe I saw in a magazine to create this healthier version. With just a hint of cumin, this dish is an ideal accompaniment for fish, chicken or pork.
—Sondra Ostheimer, Boscobel, Wisconsin

1/2 cup chopped onion
2 garlic cloves, minced
1 tablespoon olive oil
1/2 cup ground cumin
1 cup reduced-sodium chicken broth *or* vegetable broth
1 cup frozen peas
1/2 cup coarsely chopped seeded tomato
3/4 cup uncooked couscous

In a large saucepan, saute onion and garlic in oil until tender. Stir in cumin; cook and stir for 30 seconds. Stir in the broth, peas and tomato. Cook for 1-2 minutes or until peas are almost tender. Stir in couscous; cover. Remove from the heat; let stand for 5 minutes. Fluff with a fork.
Yield: 4 servings.

Sides & Salads

Orange Broccoli

Prep: 20 min.

My broccoli side dish is an appealing partner for any entree. A buttery hint of citrus comes through deliciously in the sauce, and almonds add taste and texture.
—Tricia Moore, Somersworth, New Hampshire

2 pounds fresh broccoli florets
5 tablespoons butter, cubed
1/4 cup orange juice
1 teaspoon grated orange peel
1/2 teaspoon salt
1/3 cup slivered almonds

Place 1 in. of water in a saucepan; add broccoli. Bring to a boil. Reduce heat; cover and simmer for 5-8 minutes or until crisp-tender. Drain and keep warm.

In the same pan, combine the butter, orange juice, orange peel and salt; heat until butter is melted. Return the broccoli to the saucepan; toss to coat. Transfer to a serving bowl; sprinkle with almonds. **Yield: 6 servings.**

Buttery Peas and Carrots

Prep: 20 min.

This simple side dish is one you'll rely on often to serve with a variety of main courses.
—Taste of Home Test Kitchen

2-1/2 cups baby carrots, halved
lengthwise
2 tablespoons butter
1-1/2 cups frozen peas
2 tablespoons water
1 teaspoon sugar
Salt and pepper to taste

In a skillet, saute carrots in butter for 5 minutes. Stir in the remaining ingredients. Cover and simmer for 10-12 minutes or until the vegetables are tender. **Yield: 4 servings.**

Tarragon-Almond Green Beans

Prep: 20 min.

A hint of balsamic vinegar gives a unique taste to this simple side. Sliced almonds dress up green beans tastefully when company's coming. I can't think of an entree this dish doesn't complement. —Glenda Malan, Lake Forest, California

1-1/2 pounds fresh green beans, trimmed
1/3 cup sliced green onions
1 garlic clove, minced
2 teaspoons olive oil
1/4 cup balsamic vinegar
4 teaspoons sugar
1-1/2 teaspoons minced fresh tarragon *or* 1/2 teaspoon dried tarragon
1/8 teaspoon salt
1/4 cup sliced almonds, toasted

Place beans in a large saucepan and cover with water. Bring to a boil. Cook, uncovered, for 8-10 minutes or until crisp-tender; drain.

Meanwhile, in a nonstick skillet, saute onions and garlic in oil until onions are tender. Add the vinegar, sugar, tarragon and salt. Bring to a boil; cook until liquid is reduced by half. Drain beans; add to onion mixture. Cook and stir until heated through. Sprinkle with almonds.
Yield: 6 servings.

minute recipes

Pecan Brussels Sprouts
micro
wave

Prep: 15 min.

Your family will eagerly eat their vegetables when you serve this dish. Crunchy pecans are a nice contrast to the tender brussels sprouts. —Taste of Home Test Kitchen

12 ounces fresh *or* frozen brussels sprouts (about 3 cups)
3 tablespoons water
1 cup pecan halves
2 tablespoons butter, melted
1/4 teaspoon salt
1/8 teaspoon pepper
1/8 teaspoon ground nutmeg

If using fresh Brussels sprouts, trim ends and cut an x in the core of each. In a microwave-safe dish, combine the brussels sprouts and water. Cover and microwave on high for 3-4 minutes or until tender; drain. Add the pecans, butter, salt, pepper and nutmeg; toss to coat. **Yield: 4 servings.**

Editor's Note: This recipe was tested in a 1,100-watt microwave.

Spanish Rice

Prep: 15 min.

Instant rice and convenient canned goods simplify the stovetop preparation of this tangy side dish. Its traditional taste makes it a perfect accompaniment to the Mexican-style entree. —Flo Burtnett, Gage, Oklahoma

1 cup chopped onion
1/2 cup chopped green pepper
1 tablespoon vegetable oil
1 cup uncooked instant rice
1 can (14-1/2 ounces) stewed tomatoes
3/4 cup tomato juice
1/2 teaspoon prepared mustard

In a large skillet, saute onion and green pepper in oil until tender. Stir in the remaining ingredients. Bring to a boil; reduce heat. Simmer, uncovered, for 5 minutes or until rice is tender and liquid is absorbed.
Yield: 6 servings.

The Busy Family Cookbook

Zucchini Corn Saute

Prep: 20 min.

I enjoy ethnic cooking. So I usually serve this quick side dish with baked chiles rellenos and diced fresh tomatoes. It's also good with a Moroccan-type meal.
—Barbara Lundgren, New Brighton, Minnesota

4-1/2 cups sliced zucchini
  (1/4-inch slices)
1/4 cup diced onion
1 tablespoon olive oil
1-1/2 cups fresh *or* frozen corn,
  thawed
1/2 teaspoon salt
1/4 teaspoon ground cumin
1/8 teaspoon pepper

In a nonstick skillet, saute zucchini and onion in oil for 4-5 minutes. Stir in corn; saute for 2 minutes or until vegetables are tender. Sprinkle with the salt, cumin and pepper. **Yield: 4 servings.**

Pasta Veggie Medley

Prep: 20 min.

You won't waste a second making this speedy veggie dish. Cook the pasta while you're sauting the vegetables, and they'll be done at the same time.
—Edith Ruth Muldoon, Baldwin, New York

1 package (8 ounces) medium tube
  pasta
1 medium onion, chopped
2 tablespoons vegetable oil
2 small zucchini, julienned
2 medium carrots, julienned
2 tablespoons grated Parmesan
  cheese

Cook the pasta according to package directions. Meanwhile, in a skillet, saute onion in oil until tender. Add zucchini and carrots; stir-fry until carrots are tender. Drain pasta; place in a serving bowl. Add vegetables and toss gently. Sprinkle with Parmesan cheese. **Yield: 4-6 servings.**

Sides & Salads

20
minute recipes

Pepperoni Angel Hair

Prep: 20 min.

This noodle side dish is so versatile that it can accompany steak, pork chops, chicken or even hamburgers. Chill leftovers to serve as a cool main-dish salad on a warm summer night. When time allows, I like to replace the pepperoni with sliced cooked chicken.
—Julie Mosher, Coldwater, Michigan

8 ounces uncooked angel hair pasta, broken into thirds

1 small cucumber, peeled and chopped

1 medium green pepper, chopped

1 package (8 ounces) sliced pepperoni, quartered

2 cans (2-1/4 ounces *each*) sliced ripe olives, drained

1/2 cup Italian salad dressing

1-1/4 cups shredded Parmesan cheese

Cook the pasta according to package directions. Meanwhile, combine the cucumber, green pepper, pepperoni and olives in a large bowl. Drain pasta and rinse in cold water; add to pepperoni mixture. Drizzle with salad dressing and sprinkle with Parmesan cheese; toss to coat.
Yield: 4-6 servings.

Taco Salad

Prep: 15 min.

I find this fresh-tasting salad is the perfect accompaniment to zippy burritos. Plus, it's really quick to toss together.
—Kathy Ybarra, Rock Springs, Wyoming

- 6 cups chopped iceberg lettuce
- 1/2 cup finely chopped onion
- 3/4 to 1 cup kidney beans, rinsed and drained
- 1-1/2 cups (6 ounces) shredded cheddar cheese
- 1 medium tomato, chopped
- 4 cups taco-flavored tortilla chips
- 1/2 cup Thousand Island salad dressing

In a large bowl, layer the first five ingredients in order listed. Just before serving, add chips and salad dressing; toss to coat. **Yield: 4-6 servings.**

Sesame Asparagus

Prep: 20 min.

In this fast and easy recipe, garlic, butter and chicken broth enhance the delicate flavor of fresh young asparagus. And sesame seeds add just the right amount of crunch.
—Taste of Home Test Kitchen

- 1 pound fresh asparagus, cut in half
- 1 garlic clove, minced
- 2 tablespoons butter
- 1/2 cup chicken broth
- 1 tablespoon sesame seeds, toasted

In a large skillet, saute the asparagus and garlic in butter for 2 minutes. Stir in broth; bring to a boil. Reduce heat; cover and simmer for 5-6 minutes or until asparagus is crisp-tender. Transfer to a serving dish with a slotted spoon; sprinkle with sesame seeds. **Yield: 4 servings.**

Herbed Egg Noodles

Prep: 20 min.

A seasoned butter sauce pleasantly coats tender noodles, making this perfect alongside any meaty entree.
—Taste of Home Test Kitchen

8 ounces uncooked wide egg noodles
3 tablespoons butter
1 garlic clove, minced
1/4 teaspoon salt
1/4 teaspoon dill weed
1/4 teaspoon dried thyme

Cook noodles according to package directions. Meanwhile, in a skillet, melt butter. Stir in the garlic, salt, dill and thyme. Drain noodles and add to butter mixture; toss to coat.
Yield: 4 servings.

Savory Rice Pilaf

Prep: 20 min.

Carrots, asparagus and water chestnuts are combined to make a savory blend of flavors and textures. —Grady Walker, Tulsa, Oklahoma

2 cups uncooked instant rice
2 celery ribs, chopped
2 tablespoons butter
1/4 cup chopped walnuts
5 green onions, thinly sliced
1 can (8 ounces) sliced water chestnuts, drained, optional
1 teaspoon salt
1/8 teaspoon pepper
1/8 teaspoon curry powder
1/8 teaspoon rubbed sage

Cook the rice according to the package directions. Meanwhile, in a small skillet, saute celery in butter for 2 minutes. Add the walnuts, onions, water chestnuts if desired and seasonings; saute 2 minutes longer. Stir into the rice.
Yield: 4 servings.

The Busy Family Cookbook

Cheese Sauce over Cauliflower

Prep: 20 min.

This versatile side dish goes well with all kinds of meat—pork, baked ham, chicken or turkey. The cheesy sauce dresses up the cauliflower deliciously!
—Ruby Zein, Monona, Wisconsin

1 large head cauliflower
1-1/2 teaspoons salt
3 tablespoons butter
3 tablespoons all-purpose flour
1/2 teaspoon dried thyme
1-1/2 cups milk
1-1/2 cups (6 ounces) shredded cheddar cheese
Paprika
Minced fresh parsley

In a large saucepan, bring 1 in. of water, cauliflower and salt to a boil. Reduce heat; cover and cook for 5-15 minutes or until cauliflower is crisp-tender.

Meanwhile, in a small saucepan, melt butter; stir in flour and thyme until blended. Gradually add milk. Bring to a boil; cook and stir for 2 minutes or until thickened. Reduce heat; add cheese, stirring cheese is until melted.

Drain and pat cauliflower dry; place on a serving platter. Top with cheese sauce; sprinkle with paprika and parsley. Cut into wedges.
Yield: 6 servings.

Sides & Salads

Creamed Sweet Peas

Prep: 20 min.

Mom's garden in the '40s provided us with many delicious vegetables, but her sweet peas were the best. She would pick them fresh, shell them and fix the best creamed sweet peas ever on her huge wood stove. —Jean Patten, Pineville, Louisiana

　1　tablespoon all-purpose flour
　1/4　cup sugar
　2/3　cup milk
　2　cups fresh sweet peas *or* 1 package (10 ounces) frozen peas, thawed
　1/4　teaspoon pepper

In a medium saucepan, combine flour, sugar and milk. Stir in peas and pepper; bring to a boil. Reduce heat; simmer for 10-12 minutes or until peas are heated through and sauce has thickened. **Yield: 4 servings.**

Lemon Angel Hair

Prep: 20 min.

Angel hair pasta gets loads of flavor from lemon and Parmesan cheese. A hint of garlic and flecks of fresh parsley add interest, too. This simple side goes well with chicken, fish, seafood or pork.
—Meg Mongell, Plainfield, Indiana

- 8 ounces uncooked angel hair pasta
- 1/4 cup minced fresh parsley
- 3 teaspoons grated lemon peel
- 2 teaspoons minced garlic
- 6 tablespoons olive oil
- 3 tablespoons lemon juice
- 1/2 teaspoon salt
- 1/4 teaspoon pepper
- 1/3 cup grated Parmesan cheese

Cook pasta according to package directions. Meanwhile, in a large skillet, saute the parsley, lemon peel and garlic in oil until garlic is tender. Drain pasta; add to the skillet. Sprinkle with lemon juice, salt and pepper; toss to coat. Top with Parmesan cheese.
Yield: 4 servings.

Seasoned French Fries

Prep: 5 min. | Bake: 15 min.

These fuss-free spuds come together quickly with frozen crinkle-cut fries and just a few other ingredients. They're perfect with a sandwich, hamburger or hot dog.
—Sharon Crider, Stoughton, Wisconsin

- 5 cups frozen crinkle-cut french fries
- 1 teaspoon onion salt
- 1/4 teaspoon paprika
- 1/3 cup grated Parmesan cheese

Preheat oven to 450°.

Arrange french fries in a greased 15-in. x 10-in. x 1-in. baking pan. Sprinkle with onion salt and paprika; toss to coat. Bake at 450° for 15-20 minutes or until lightly browned. Sprinkle with Parmesan cheese; toss to coat.
Yield: 4 servings.

Sides & Salads

Tangy Carrot Coins
Prep: 20 min.

This colorful side dish is as easy to fix as plain carrots, but the light, creamy coating makes them extra yummy.
—Lois Stephen, Mt. Morris, Michigan

1 pound carrots, sliced
3 tablespoons butter
1 tablespoon brown sugar
1 tablespoon Dijon mustard
1/8 teaspoon salt

Place 1 in. of water in a large saucepan; add carrots. Bring to a boil. Reduce heat; cover and simmer for 7-9 minutes or until carrots are crisp-tender. Drain.

Add remaining ingredients; cook and stir over medium heat for 1-2 minutes or until sauce is thickened and carrots are coated.
Yield: 4 servings.

Maple Baked Beans
micro wave

Prep: 20 min.

Canned beans are jazzed up with maple syrup and just a dash of cinnamon for a unique taste twist. This sweet, saucy side dish is a snap to fix in the microwave, so it's handy to add to summertime menus. —Susan Baxter, Morgantown, Indiana

2 cans (15-3/4 ounces *each*) pork and beans
1/2 cup ketchup
1/2 cup maple syrup
Dash ground cinnamon

In a large microwave-safe bowl, combine all ingredients. Microwave, uncovered, on high for 11-15 minutes or until mixture reaches desired thickness, stirring every 5 minutes. Let stand for 5 minutes before serving.
Yield: 4-6 servings.

Editor's Note: This recipe was tested in a 1,100-watt microwave.

Alfredo Potatoes

Prep: 15 min. | **Cook: 10 min.**

These cheesy stuffed potatoes are great for a meal or as a side dish. Cut the recipe in half and use a small potato for an after-school snack. —Peter Barry, Norrisville, Maryland

- 2 large baking potatoes
- 1 cup prepared Alfredo sauce
- 1 teaspoon garlic powder
- 1/2 teaspoon pepper
- 1/8 teaspoon dried thyme
- 1 cup (4 ounces) shredded cheddar cheese, *divided*
- 1/2 cup shredded part-skim mozzarella cheese

Pierce potatoes several times with a fork and place on a microwave-safe plate. Microwave on high for 4-1/2 to 7 minutes or until tender. Allow potatoes to cool slightly.

Meanwhile, in a bowl, combine the Alfredo sauce, garlic powder, pepper and thyme. Stir in 1/2 cup cheddar cheese and mozzarella cheese. Cut potatoes in half lengthwise. Scoop out the pulp and add to the sauce mixture; mix well. Spoon into potato shells. Sprinkle with remaining cheddar cheese. Microwave on high for 45 seconds or until cheese is melted.

Yield: 4 servings.

Editor's Note: This recipe was tested in a 1,100-watt microwave.

Baked Sweet Potato Chips

Prep: 10 min. | **Bake: 20 min.**

The next time you have the hungries, don't reach for high-fat junk food. Instead, spend a few minutes preparing these oven-baked sweet potato slices. —Taste of Home Test Kitchen

- 2 medium sweet potatoes (about 7 ounces *each*)
- 1 teaspoon dried rosemary, crushed
- 1 teaspoon dried parsley flakes
- 3/4 teaspoon garlic salt
- 1/2 teaspoon paprika
- 1/4 teaspoon ground mustard

Dash white pepper

Preheat oven to 400°.

Cut potatoes into 1/8-in. slices; spray both sides of slices with nonstick cooking spray. In a bowl, combine seasonings. Add the potatoes; toss gently to coat. Arrange in a single layer in two 15-in. x 10-in. x 1-in. baking pans coated with nonstick cooking spray.

Bake, uncovered, at 400° for 20-25 minutes or until potatoes are golden brown and tender, turning several times.

Yield: 5 dozen chips.

Sides & Salads

Hearty Baked Potatoes

micro
wave

Prep: 5 min. | Cook: 15 min.

Adding ham to these veggie-topped potatoes makes them a complete meal-in-one. With plenty of cheese and a tasty sauce, too, they're sure to satisfy even the biggest appetites at dinnertime. —Barbara Schindler, Napoleon, Ohio

4 large baking potatoes (about 3 pounds)
2-1/2 cups California-blend vegetables
2 cups cubed fully cooked ham
1 can (10-3/4 ounces) condensed cream of broccoli soup, undiluted
1/2 cup shredded cheddar cheese
1/4 teaspoon garlic powder
1/4 teaspoon pepper

Scrub and pierce potatoes; place on a microwave-safe plate. Microwave, uncovered, on high for 12-14 minutes or until tender, turning once. Meanwhile, in a small saucepan, combine the remaining ingredients. Cook and stir over medium-low heat until cheese is melted.

Cut an X in the top of each potato; fluff pulp with a fork. Top with vegetable mixture.
Yield: 4 servings.

Editor's Note: This recipe was tested in a 1,100-watt microwave.

Italian Pasta and Peas

Prep: 10 min. | **Cook: 20 min.**

If your family doesn't care for peas, substitute frozen green beans or broccoli. By stirring in cubed cooked chicken or ham, this becomes a mouth-watering main dish with little effort.
—Taste of Home Test Kitchen

1-1/2 cups water
1/2 cup milk
1 tablespoon butter
1 package (4.1 ounces) quick-cooking bow tie pasta and Parmesan/Romano sauce mix
1 cup frozen peas
1 can (4 ounces) mushroom stems and pieces, drained
1/2 teaspoon dried oregano

In a large saucepan, combine the water, milk and butter; bring to a boil. Stir in pasta and sauce mix. Cook over medium heat for 8 minutes, stirring occasionally.

Stir in the peas, mushrooms and oregano; cook 3-4 minutes longer or until pasta is tender. Remove from the heat. Sauce will thicken upon standing. **Yield: 4 servings.**

Editor's Note: This recipe was tested with Lipton's Bow Tie Pasta in a Creamy Parmesan and Romano Cheese Sauce Mix.

Creamed Spinach

Prep: 5 min. | **Bake: 25 min.**

This delicious recipe is a lifesaver during the holidays, when time is short. With only three ingredients, it's also easy to double. —Sherri Hoover, Perth Road, Ontario

2 packages (10 ounces *each*) frozen chopped spinach, thawed and well drained
2 cups (16 ounces) sour cream
1 envelope onion soup mix

Preheat oven to 350°.

In a large bowl, combine all ingredients. Spoon into a greased 1-qt. baking dish. Cover and bake at 350° for 25-30 minutes or until heated through. **Yield: 4 servings.**

Sides & Salads

Paprika Potatoes 'n' Beans

Prep: 10 min. | **Cook: 15 min.**

The skins of red potatoes are very thin and tender, so cooks often choose to leave them on not only for the color but for the extra vitamins. This side dish cooks basically unattended, allowing you to focus on the rest of dinner. —Taste of Home Test Kitchen

1/2 pounds medium red potatoes, cut into 3/4-inch pieces

2 cups frozen cut green beans

3 tablespoons butter, melted

1/2 teaspoon salt *or* garlic salt

1/4 teaspoon pepper

1/4 teaspoon paprika

Place potatoes in a large saucepan and cover with water. Bring to a boil. Reduce heat; cover and cook for 7-12 minutes. Add beans; cover and cook 3-5 minutes longer or until potatoes and beans are tender. Drain.

Meanwhile, in a small bowl, combine the butter, salt, pepper and paprika; drizzle over potatoes and gently stir to coat. **Yield: 4 servings.**

Microwave Acorn Squash

Prep: 15 min. | **Cook: 10 min.**

micro
wave

Acorn squash is my favorite fall vegetable—and it cooks quickly when you microwave it. —Rita McPherson, Nashua, New Hampshire

2 medium acorn squash

2/3 cup crushed butter-flavored crackers

1/3 cup butter, melted

3 tablespoons brown sugar

1/8 teaspoon ground nutmeg

Place squash on a microwave-safe plate, microwave on high for 3-4 minutes. Cut in half; remove seeds and strings. Cut a thin slice from bottom of squash with a sharp knife to allow it to sit flat. Place squash cut side down on in a microwave-safe dish. Cover and microwave for 4-1/2 minutes.

Meanwhile, combine the crackers, butter, brown sugar and nutmeg. Turn squash over; fill with cracker mixture. Microwave for 1-2 minutes or until squash is tender. **Yield: 4 servings.**

Editor's Note: This recipe was tested in a 1,100-watt microwave.

Penne from Heaven

Prep: 10 min. | Cook: 20 min.

This fast, fresh-tasting side dish comes very close to a delicious treatment for pasta I enjoyed while in Italy. You can also serve it with a green salad and toasted garlic bread for a light meal. —Dorothy Roche, Menomonee Falls, Wisconsin

6 ounces uncooked penne pasta
1/2 pound fresh mushrooms, sliced
1 tablespoon olive oil
1 can (14-1/2 ounces) diced tomatoes, undrained
1 tablespoon minced fresh basil *or* 1 teaspoon dried basil
1/4 teaspoon salt
1/3 cup crumbled feta cheese

Cook the pasta according to package directions. Meanwhile, in a large skillet, saute mushrooms in oil for 5 minutes. Add the tomatoes, basil and salt; cook and stir for 5 minutes. Drain pasta and add to the skillet. Stir in the cheese; heat through.
Yield: 5 servings.

Sides & Salads

Lemon-Glazed Carrots

Prep: 10 min. | Cook: 15 min.

These make a super side dish. The lovely sweet-sour carrots are a special treat.
—Ruby Williams, Bogalusa, Louisiana

1-1/2 pounds medium carrots, cut into
    1/2-inch diagonal slices
3 tablespoons butter
3 tablespoons brown sugar
3 tablespoons lemon juice
1/4 teaspoon salt
Grated lemon peel, optional

In a large skillet, place 1 in. of water; add carrots. Bring to a boil. Reduce heat; cover and simmer for 10-12 minutes or until crisp-tender.

Meanwhile, in a small saucepan, melt butter. Add the brown sugar, lemon juice and salt; bring to a boil, stirring constantly. Drain carrots; add butter mixture and toss gently. Garnish with lemon peel if desired.
Yield: 6 servings.

Potatoes O'Brien

Prep: 10 min. | **Cook: 20 min.**

I usually serve these colorful potatoes for breakfast, but they're great as a tasty potato side dish for just about any meal. My family often asks me to prepare them instead of regular fried potatoes.
—Nila Towler, Baird, Texas

1/2 cup chopped onion
1/2 cup chopped green pepper
1/2 cup chopped sweet red pepper
4 medium red potatoes, cubed
3 tablespoons vegetable oil
1/4 cup beef broth
1/2 teaspoon Worcestershire sauce
1 teaspoon salt

In a large skillet, saute the onion, peppers and potatoes in oil for 4 minutes or until the vegetables are crisp-tender. Meanwhile in a small bowl, combine broth, Worcestershire sauce and salt; pour over vegetables.

Cover and cook for 10 minutes or until potatoes are tender, stirring occasionally. Uncover and cook for 3-4 minutes or until liquid is absorbed.
Yield: 4 servings.

Artichoke Orzo Pilaf

Prep: 10 min. | **Cook: 20 min.**

Canned artichoke hearts bring a tangy taste to orzo pasta in this side dish. This saute is quick, easy and tasty, too. —Stacy Crochet, Watertown, Connecticut

1 medium leek (white portion only), chopped
1 cup uncooked orzo pasta
2 tablespoons olive oil
1 can (14-1/2 ounces) reduced-sodium chicken broth *or* vegetable broth
1 cup water
2 teaspoons Italian seasoning
1 can (14 ounces) water-packed artichoke hearts, rinsed, drained and chopped
2 tablespoons grated Parmesan cheese

In a large nonstick skillet, saute leek and orzo in oil for 3 minutes or until leek is tender. Add the broth, water and Italian seasoning; bring to a boil. Reduce heat; simmer, uncovered, for 15 minutes or until liquid is absorbed. Stir in artichoke hearts and Parmesan cheese. Serve immediately.
Yield: 6 servings.

Sides & Salads

Sauteed Summer Squash

Prep: 15 min. | Cook: 10 min.

I take advantage of my garden's bounty with this simple side. Since we like squash best when it still has a little crunch, it takes only a few minutes to cook. —Mrs. Gloria Warczak, Cedarburg, Wisconsin

2 small zucchini, julienned
2 small yellow summer squash, julienned
1 small sweet red pepper, julienned
1 small onion, julienned
2 tablespoons vegetable oil
1-1/2 teaspoons seasoned salt
1/2 teaspoon pepper

In a large skillet, saute the zucchini, summer squash, red pepper and onion in oil for 8 minutes or until crisp-tender. Sprinkle with seasoned salt and pepper.
Yield: 6 servings.

Cheesy Rice with Peas

Prep: 10 min. | Bake: 20 min.

Before I work on the rest of the meal, I assemble this rice dish. That way it's baking while I prepare the rest of the meal. I usually have leftover cooked rice in the refrigerator, so this side dish goes together quickly. —Yvonne Bellomo, Ebensburg, Pennsylvania

2-1/4 cups cooked long grain rice
1 package (10 ounces) frozen peas, thawed
1 jar (6 ounces) sliced mushrooms, drained
6 ounces process cheese (Velveeta), cubed

Preheat oven to 350°.

In a bowl, combine all the ingredients. Transfer to a greased 1-1/2-qt. baking dish. Cover and bake at 350° for 20 minutes or until heated through. Stir before serving.
Yield: 6 servings.

Editor's Note: When cooking rice, make extra to have on hand. Cooked rice can be refrigerated for up to 7 days and frozen for up to 6 months. For convenience, package a cup or two of rice in refrigerator/freezer bags. Flatten rice out in the bags before freezing. That way it will defrost more quickly.

Creamed New Potatoes

Prep: 10 min. | Cook: 20 min.

My mother always made this dish with sour cream, but I substituted buttermilk and added more herbs. Thyme and tarragon give these saucy potatoes a fresh taste I really enjoy.
—Lillian Julow, Gainesville, Florida

2-1/2 pounds unpeeled small red potatoes, cut into 1-inch slices
1 teaspoon salt
1 package (8 ounces) cream cheese, cubed
1 cup buttermilk
6 green onions, chopped
1 teaspoon dried thyme
1 teaspoon dried tarragon
1/4 teaspoon pepper
3 tablespoons minced fresh parsley

Place potatoes in a large saucepan and cover with water; add salt. Bring to a boil. Reduce heat; cover and cook for 15-20 minutes or until tender.

Meanwhile, in another saucepan, combine the cream cheese and buttermilk; cook and stir over medium heat until cheese is melted and mixture is smooth. Remove from the heat; add the onions, thyme, tarragon and pepper. Drain potatoes and place in a serving bowl; add cream sauce and toss to coat. Sprinkle with parsley.
Yield: 6 servings.

Garlic Mashed Potatoes

Prep: 10 min. | Cook: 20 min.

Mashed potatoes and garlic are both foods I love, so this seemed like the perfect recipe for me. People say these potatoes rival varieties some restaurants are now serving.
—Myra Innes, Auburn, Kansas

6 medium potatoes, peeled and quartered
4 to 5 garlic cloves
5 cups water
2 tablespoons olive oil
1/2 to 1 teaspoon salt
Pinch pepper

Place potatoes and garlic in a large saucepan and cover with water. Bring to a boil. Reduce heat; cover and cook for 15-20 minutes or until tender.

Drain, reserving 2/3 cup cooking liquid. Mash potato mixture. Add the oil, salt, pepper and reserved liquid; stir until smooth.
Yield: 4-6 servings.

Sides & Salads

Cheesy Broccoli Macaroni

Prep: 5 min. | **Cook: 20 min.**

You'll need just four ingredients to fix this macaroni and cheese, which gets extra flavor from broccoli and bacon. It makes a nice lunch or side dish for supper. —Dorothy Pritchett, Wills Point, Texas

2-1/2 cups uncooked elbow macaroni
1 cup frozen chopped broccoli
8 ounces process cheese (Velveeta), cubed
3 bacon strips, cooked and crumbled

Cook macaroni according to package directions. Meanwhile, in a large saucepan, cook broccoli according to package directions until crisp-tender; drain. Add the cheese; cook and stir over medium-low heat until cheese is melted.

Drain macaroni; transfer to a large bowl. Stir in the cheese mixture. Sprinkle with bacon. **Yield: 4 servings.**

Editor's Note: Cook the bacon while the macaroni is cooking or to save time, use precooked bacon, which is available in the packaged deli meat section of the supermarket.

Easy au Gratin Potatoes

Prep: 25 min. | **Bake: 5 min.**

One taste of this comforting dish and you'll never reach for a store-bought box of au gratin potatoes again! The thinly sliced spuds cook up tender in no time. Your family will request this recipe many times over. —Taste of Home Test Kitchen

3/4 cup half-and-half cream
1/2 cup milk
1/2 teaspoon salt
1/4 teaspoon garlic powder
3 medium potatoes, peeled and thinly sliced
1 cup seasoned salad croutons, *divided*
1/8 teaspoon pepper
1/2 cup shredded cheddar cheese

Preheat oven to 400°.

In a large saucepan, bring cream, milk, salt and garlic powder to a boil. Add potatoes; reduce heat. Cover and simmer for 10-15 minutes or until the potatoes are tender. Coarsely crush 1/4 cup of croutons. Remove potatoes from the heat. Gently stir in crushed croutons and pepper.

Pour into a greased 1-1/2-qt. baking dish. Sprinkle with cheese and remaining croutons. Bake, uncovered, at 400° for 5-6 minutes or until the cheese is melted. **Yield: 4 servings.**

Noodle Rice Pilaf

Prep: 5 min. | Cook: 30 min.

By adding a few fine egg noodles to a rice pilaf, you can have a deliciously different side dish. Terrific with fish, this dish also goes well with meat or poultry.
—Kathy Schrecengost, Oswego, New York

1/4 cup butter, cubed
1 cup uncooked long grain rice
1/2 cup uncooked fine egg noodles *or* vermicelli
2-3/4 cups chicken broth
2 tablespoons minced fresh parsley

In a large saucepan, cook and stir the rice and noodles in butter for 3-4 minutes or until lightly browned. Stir in broth; bring to a boil. Reduce heat; cover and simmer for 20-25 minutes or until broth is absorbed and rice is tender. Stir in parsley. **Yield: 4 servings.**

Oven-Roasted Root Vegetables

Prep: 20 min. | Bake: 40 min.

All kinds of root vegetables star in this colorful medley. Fresh thyme and sage season the mix of rutabaga, parsnips and butternut squash. This side dish is satisfying any time of year. Besides being delicious, it's very easy to prepare.
—Mitzi Sentiff, Alexandria, Virginia

2 cups cubed peeled rutabaga
2 cups cubed peeled parsnips
2 cups cubed peeled butternut squash
2 medium onions, chopped
1 tablespoon olive oil
1/2 teaspoon salt
1/8 teaspoon pepper
1 tablespoon minced fresh thyme *or* 1 teaspoon dried thyme
1 tablespoon minced fresh sage *or* 1 teaspoon rubbed sage

Preheat oven to 400°.

In a large bowl, combine the rutabaga, parsnips, squash and onions. Add the oil, salt and pepper; toss to coat. Arrange in a single layer in a 15-in. x 10-in. x 1-in. baking pan coated with nonstick cooking spray.

Bake, uncovered, at 400° for 40-50 minutes, stirring occasionally. Sprinkle with herbs; toss to coat.
Yield: 4 servings.

30+
minute recipes

Broccoli Brown Rice Pilaf

Prep: 5 min. | **Cook: 50 min.**

This is one of my favorite low-fat dishes—it's fabulous! Rosemary, garlic, almonds and sunflower kernels flavor the broccoli and rice. Sometimes I add cooked cubed chicken for a complete meal. —Mari Condit, Brooklyn Center, Minnesota

1 cup uncooked brown rice	In a large nonstick skillet coated with nonstick cooking spray, saute rice until lightly browned. Add the broth, rosemary and garlic; bring to a boil. Reduce heat; cover and simmer for 40 minutes or until rice is almost tender.
2-1/4 cups reduced-sodium chicken broth *or* vegetable broth	
2 tablespoons minced fresh rosemary *or* 2 teaspoons dried rosemary, crushed	
2 garlic cloves, minced	
2 cups chopped fresh broccoli	Stir in the broccoli, almonds, sunflower kernels, salt and pepper. Cover and cook 3-5 minutes longer or until rice is tender and broccoli is crisp-tender. Fluff with a fork. **Yield: 6 servings.**
1/4 cup slivered almonds	
1/4 cup unsalted sunflower kernels	
1/2 teaspoon salt	
1/8 teaspoon pepper	

Scalloped Basil Tomatoes

Prep: 20 min. | **Bake: 35 min.**

If your garden is flooded with tomatoes, be sure to try this scrumptious baked side dish. It goes over big at family, church and club dinners. Cubes of French bread are combined with mildly seasoned tomatoes, then sprinkled with Parmesan cheese and baked. —Edna Apostol, Savannah, Missouri

16 plum tomatoes	Peel tomatoes and cut into 1/2-in. cubes; drain. In a large nonstick skillet, cook bread in oil over medium heat for 5-7 minutes or until lightly browned. Add the tomatoes, sugar and garlic; cook and stir for 5 minutes. Stir in the salt, pepper and basil.
2 cups cubed crustless French bread (1/2-inch cubes)	
1 tablespoon olive oil	
1 tablespoon sugar	
3 garlic cloves, minced	
1/2 teaspoon salt	
1/8 teaspoon pepper	Pour into a 1-1/2-qt. baking dish. Sprinkle with cheese. Bake, uncovered, at 350° for 35-40 minutes or until bubbly. **Yield: 6 servings.**
1/4 cup thinly sliced fresh basil leaves	
3 tablespoons shredded Parmesan cheese	

Sides & Salads

Mixed Vegetable Casserole

Prep: 10 min. | **Bake: 30 min.**

While vacationing in France, I learned the importance of serving foods that look as good as they taste. This colorful side dish is pleasing to the eye as well as the palate, and has guests asking for seconds. —Sarah Burks, Wathena, Kansas

1 package (16 ounces) frozen mixed vegetables, thawed
1 large onion, chopped
3 celery ribs, chopped
1 cup (4 ounces) shredded cheddar cheese
1 cup mayonnaise
3/4 cup crushed butter-flavored crackers
1/4 cup butter, melted

Preheat oven to 350°.

In a large bowl, combine the first five ingredients. Spoon into a greased 1-1/2-qt. baking dish. Combine the cracker crumbs and butter until crumbly; sprinkle over the top. Bake, uncovered, at 350° for 30-35 minutes or until heated through.
Yield: 6 servings.

Editor's Note: Reduced-fat or fat-free mayonnaise may not be substituted for regular mayonnaise in this recipe.

Broccoli Corn Bake

Prep: 10 min. | **Bake: 30 min.**

Everyone who eats this casserole raves about it. I love it when something so good is so easy to make. —Breta Soldat, Johnston, Iowa

1-1/2 cups crushed butter-flavored crackers
3 tablespoons butter, melted
2-1/2 cups frozen broccoli cuts, thawed
1 can (15-1/4 ounces) whole kernel corn, drained
1 can (14-3/4 ounces) cream-style corn

Preheat oven to 350°.

In a large bowl, combine cracker crumbs and butter; set aside 1/2 cup for topping. Stir vegetables into the remaining crumb mixture.

Transfer to a greased 1-1/2-qt. baking dish. Sprinkle with reserved crumb topping. Bake, uncovered, at 350° for 30-35 minutes or until bubbly and top is golden brown.
Yield: 6 servings.

The Busy Family Cookbook

Parmesan Potato Rounds

Prep: 10 min. | **Bake: 25 min.**

These pretty, cheese-coated potato slices go so well with lamb chops, and are easy to prepare. It's the first recipe I turn to when I have potatoes and onions ready in the garden. —Sandra McKenzie, Braham, Minnesota

4 medium red potatoes, thinly sliced
1 small onion, thinly sliced and
   separated into rings
3 tablespoons butter, melted
1/3 cup grated Parmesan cheese
1/4 teaspoon salt
1/8 teaspoon pepper
1/8 teaspoon garlic powder

Preheat oven to 450°.

Place half of the potatoes in a greased 2-qt. baking dish. Top with onion and remaining potatoes; drizzle with butter. Sprinkle with Parmesan cheese, salt, pepper and garlic powder. Bake, uncovered, at 450° for 25-30 minutes or until the potatoes are golden brown and tender.
Yield: 4 servings.

Sides & Salads

Acorn Squash Slices

Prep: 15 min. | **Bake: 40 min.**

Acorn squash is a favorite with my family. This recipe gets sweet maple flavor from syrup and an appealing crunch from pecans. It's easy, too, because you don't have to peel the squash.
—Mrs. Richard Lamb, Williamsburg, Indiana

2 medium acorn squash (about 1-1/2 pounds each)
1/2 teaspoon salt
3/4 cup maple syrup
2 tablespoons butter, melted
1/3 cup chopped pecans, optional

Preheat oven to 350°.

Cut squash in half lengthwise; remove and discard seeds and membrane. Cut each half crosswise into 1/2-in. slices; discard ends.

Place slices in a greased 13-in. x 9-in. x 2-in. baking dish. Sprinkle with salt. Combine syrup and butter; pour over squash. Sprinkle with pecans if desired.

Cover and bake at 350° for 40-45 minutes or until tender. **Yield: 6 servings.**

Balsamic Roasted Red Potatoes

Prep: 15 min. | **Bake: 30 min.**

My family loves potatoes, and I fix them many different ways. This tasty version is one of our favorites. Well-seasoned with garlic, thyme, nutmeg and rosemary, plus balsamic vinegar, these potatoes are sure to stand out at any meal.
—Bev Bosveld, Waupun, Wisconsin

2 pounds small red potatoes, quartered
1 tablespoon finely chopped green onion
6 garlic cloves, minced
2 tablespoons olive oil
1 teaspoon dried thyme
1 teaspoon dried rosemary, crushed
1/8 teaspoon ground nutmeg
1/4 cup balsamic vinegar
3/4 teaspoon salt
1/4 teaspoon pepper

Preheat oven to 400°.

In a large nonstick skillet, cook the potatoes, onion and garlic in oil over medium-high heat for 2-3 minutes or until heated through. Stir in the thyme, rosemary and nutmeg. Cook and stir 2-3 minutes longer or until heated through.

Transfer to a 15-in. x 10-in. x 1-in. baking pan coated with nonstick cooking spray. Bake at 400° for 25-30 minutes or until potatoes are golden and almost tender. Add the vinegar, salt and pepper; toss well. Bake 5-8 minutes longer or until potatoes are tender.
Yield: 6 servings.

Desserts

Chocolate Cookie Cake (p. 244)

Cheesecake Waffle Cups

Prep: 10 min.

I've found a fun way to serve cheesecake. The crunchy store-bought bowls hold a smooth cream cheese filling that's layered with cherry pie filling. They're a snap to prepare and are attractive, too. Blueberry pie filling would be a nice alternative.
—Janice Greenhaigh, Florence, Kentucky

1 package (8 ounces) cream cheese, softened
1 can (14 ounces) sweetened condensed milk
1/3 cup lemon juice
1 teaspoon vanilla extract
4 waffle bowls
1 cup cherry pie filling

In a small mixing bowl, beat cream cheese until smooth. Gradually beat in milk until smooth. Stir in lemon juice and vanilla. Spoon about 1/3 cup into each waffle bowl; top with 2 tablespoons pie filling. Repeat layers.
Yield: 4 servings.

Brownie Sundaes

Prep: 10 min.

With prepared brownies, I can fix this sweet treat in a flash. For extra flair, I roll the ice cream in pecans before placing the scoops on top of the brownies. It's a perfect finish to a mouth-watering meal.
—Mrs. Ruth Lee, Troy, Ontario

3/4 cup semisweet chocolate chips
1/2 cup evaporated milk
2 tablespoons brown sugar
2 teaspoons butter
1/2 teaspoon vanilla extract
6 prepared brownies (3 inches square)
6 scoops vanilla *or* chocolate fudge ice cream
1/2 cup chopped pecans

In a large saucepan, combine the chocolate chips, milk and brown sugar. Cook and stir over medium heat for 5 minutes or until chocolate is melted and sugar is dissolved. Remove from the heat; stir in butter and vanilla until smooth.

Spoon about 2 tablespoons warm chocolate sauce onto each dessert plate. Top with a brownie and a scoop of ice cream. Drizzle with additional chocolate sauce if desired. Sprinkle with pecans. **Yield: 6 servings.**

Raspberry Cupcake Dessert

Prep: 10 min.

Kids of all ages will love this dessert. While I prefer homemade whipped cream, purchased whipped topping is an easy option for this rich dessert.
—Edith Ruth Muldoon, Baldwin, New York

2 cream-filled chocolate cupcakes, cut in half
1 to 2 cups heavy whipping cream
3 tablespoons confectioners' sugar
1/2 teaspoon vanilla extract
1 to 1-1/2 cups fresh *or* frozen raspberries, thawed and drained
Additional raspberries, optional

Place one cupcake half each in four dessert dishes. In a large mixing bowl, beat cream until soft peaks form. Beat in sugar and vanilla until stiff peaks form. Fold in raspberries. Spoon over cupcakes. Garnish with additional berries if desired. Chill until serving.
Yield: 4 servings.

Editor's Note: This recipe was prepared with Hostess brand cupcakes.

Desserts

Citrus Shortcake

Prep: 10 min.

When it comes to dessert, it doesn't get much simpler that this. I like to mix the whipped topping with the lemon yogurt early in the day, then store it in the refrigerator until we're ready for dessert. I sometimes use scones instead of the shortcakes and raspberries for the strawberries. —Eileen Warren, Windsor, Ontario

1 cup (8 ounces) lemon yogurt
1 cup whipped topping
4 individual round sponge cakes
1/4 cup orange juice
2-2/3 cups sliced fresh strawberries

In a small bowl, combine the yogurt and whipped topping. Place sponge cakes on dessert plates; drizzle with orange juice. Spread with half of the yogurt mixture. Top with strawberries and remaining yogurt mixture. **Yield: 4 servings.**

Chocolate Fudge Mousse

Prep: 10 min.

Instant pudding is the secret ingredient that makes this mousse such a breeze to prepare. It's so much quicker and easier to whip up than a traditional mousse. But it's equally fluffy and luscious, so it even satisfies my husband's rather large sweet tooth. —Carly Carter, Nashville, Tennessee

2 cups cold milk
1 package (3.9 ounces) instant chocolate pudding mix
1/4 cup hot fudge ice cream topping
3 cups whipped topping

In a bowl, whisk milk and pudding mix for 2 minutes. Let stand for 2 minutes or until soft-set. Stir in fudge topping. Fold in whipped topping. Spoon into dessert dishes. Chill until serving. **Yield: 6 servings.**

Butterscotch Parfaits

Prep: 10 min.

These yummy parfaits are impossible to turn down. You can also change the pudding flavor to suit your taste.
—Judi Klee, Nebraska City, Nebraska

- 2 cups cold milk
- 1 package (3.4 ounces) instant butterscotch pudding mix
- 18 vanilla wafers, coarsely crushed
- 1 carton (8 ounces) frozen whipped topping, thawed
- 6 maraschino cherries, optional

In a large mixing bowl, whisk milk and pudding mix for 2 minutes. Let stand for 2 minutes or until soft-set.

In six parfait glasses, alternate layers of pudding, wafer crumbs and whipped topping. Garnish with cherry if desired. Refrigerate until serving.
Yield: 6 servings.

Editor's Note: While the pudding is standing, crush the vanilla wafers. Place them in a resealable plastic bag and crush them with a meat mallet.

Ambrosia Tarts

Prep: 10 min.

I created this dessert for my niece who loves the tangy combination of fruit and marshmallows. —Marilou Robinson, Portland, Oregon

- 1 can (11 ounces) mandarin oranges, drained
- 1 can (8 ounces) crushed pineapple, drained
- 1/2 cup miniature marshmallows
- 1/4 cup flaked coconut
- 1 cup whipped topping
- 4 individual graham cracker shells

In a large bowl, combine the oranges, pineapple, marshmallows and coconut. Fold in whipped topping. Spoon into shells. Chill until serving.
Yield: 4 servings.

Desserts

Frosty Peanut Butter Pie

plan ahead

Prep: 10 min. + freezing

With only a handful of ingredients, this pie promises to deliver well-deserved compliments. Whenever I bring this creamy, make-ahead dessert to get-togethers, I'm asked for the recipe. —Christi Gillentine, Tulsa, Oklahoma

   4 ounces cream cheese, softened
1/4 cup peanut butter
1/4 cup sugar
   1 teaspoon vanilla extract
   1 package (8 ounces) frozen whipped topping, thawed
   1 chocolate crumb crust (8 inches)
   2 teaspoons chocolate syrup

In a large mixing bowl, beat the cream cheese, peanut butter, sugar and vanilla until smooth. Fold in the whipped topping. Spoon into the crust. Drizzle with chocolate syrup. Cover and freeze for 4 hours or until set. Remove from the freezer 30 minutes before serving.
Yield: 6 servings.

Editor's Note: Make this recipe the night before you plan to serve. Just before you sit down for dinner, remove the pie from the freezer.

Raspberry Almond Rounds

Prep: 20 min.

Folks will find these nutty raspberry rounds so enticing you may not want to divulge that they begin with refrigerated biscuit dough! These sweet treats bake up in a hurry. —Taste of Home Test Kitchen

- 2 tablespoons butter, melted
- 1 tube (7-1/2 ounces) refrigerated buttermilk biscuits, separated into 10 biscuits
- 2 tablespoons sugar
- 1/4 cup raspberry preserves
- 2 tablespoons slivered almonds

Preheat oven to 425°.

Brush butter on both sides of biscuits. Place biscuits on a greased baking sheet or in a greased 9-in. round baking pan; sprinkle with sugar.

Using the end of a wooden spoon handle, make a 3/8-in. to 1/2-in. deep indentation in the center of each biscuit; fill with a rounded teaspoon of preserves.

Sprinkle with almonds. Bake at 425° for 9-11 minutes or until golden brown.
Yield: 4-6 servings.

Frosty Blueberry Dessert

plan ahead

Prep: 15 min. + freezing

If you're looking for a different way to showcase blueberries, try this quick-to-assemble recipe. The sweet squares make a refreshing dessert.
—Evelyn Pedersen, Shoreview, Minnesota

- 1 can (21 ounces) blueberry pie filling
- 1 can (12 ounces) evaporated milk
- 1/4 cup lemon juice
- 1/4 teaspoon almond extract
- 1 carton (8 ounces) frozen whipped topping, thawed

Additional whipped topping, optional

In a large bowl, combine the pie filling, milk, lemon juice and extract. Fold in whipped topping. Spread in a greased 11-in. x 7-in. x 2-in. dish. Cover and freeze for up to 2 months.

Remove from the freezer 20 minutes before serving. Cut into squares. Garnish with additional whipped topping if desired.
Yield: 12-15 servings.

Editor's Note: Make this recipe the night before you plan to serve. Just before you sit down for dinner, remove the dessert from the freezer.

Desserts

20
minute recipes

Microwave Cherry Crisp micro wave

Prep: 20 min.

I use the microwave oven to produce a treat with old-fashioned flavor. It tastes just like an old-time crisp with half the fuss and mess. —Debra Morello, Edwards, California

1 can (21 ounces) cherry
   pie filling
3/4 cup packed brown sugar
2/3 cup quick-cooking oats
1/3 cup all-purpose flour
1/4 cup butter, cubed
Vanilla ice cream, optional

Spoon filling into a greased 9-in. pie plate. In a small bowl, combine the brown sugar, oats and flour; cut in butter until crumbly. Sprinkle over filling. Microwave on high for 7-9 minutes. Serve warm with ice cream if desired.
Yield: 4-6 servings.

Editor's Note: This recipe was tested in a 1,100-watt microwave.

Lemon Berry Trifle

Prep: 15 min.

If fresh berries are not available, use the quick-frozen varieties, or peaches or nectarines. It's a simple-to-make sweet—perfect for summer. But we enjoy it so much, I make it all year. —Nanci Keatley, Salem, Oregon

5 cups cubed angel food cake
1 carton (8 ounces) lemon yogurt
1 cup whipping topping, *divided*
3 cups mixed fresh berries
Lemon peel, optional

Place cake cubes in a 2-qt. serving bowl or individual dishes. Combine yogurt and 3/4 cup whipped topping; spoon over cake. Top with berries. Top with remaining whipped topping and lemon peel if desired.
Yield: 4-6 servings.

The Busy Family Cookbook

No-Bake Chocolate Torte

plan ahead →

Prep: 20 min. + chilling

Here's a delightful dessert that only looks like you fussed all day. With its attractive appearance and wonderful taste, no one will know that you saved time by spreading an easy-to-prepare frosting on a store-bought pound cake. —Taste of Home Test Kitchen

- 1 frozen pound cake (10-3/4 ounces), thawed
- 2 cups heavy whipping cream
- 6 tablespoons confectioners' sugar
- 6 tablespoons baking cocoa
- 1/2 teaspoon almond extract
- 1/2 cup sliced almonds, toasted, optional

Slice pound cake lengthwise into three layers and set aside. In a large mixing bowl, beat cream until soft peaks form. Gradually add sugar and cocoa; beat until stiff peaks form. Stir in extract.

Place one layer of cake on a serving platter; top with 1 cup frosting. Repeat layers. Frost top and sides with remaining frosting. Garnish with almonds if desired. Chill for at least 15 minutes. Refrigerate any leftovers. **Yield: 4-6 servings.**

Editor's Note: Make this before you prepare the entree. That way it can chill, while you prepare the rest of the meal.

Banana Butterfinger Pudding
Prep: 15 min.

This is such a versatile dessert. You can substitute other kinds of candy bars to suit your preference. The pudding flavor can be changed as well—perhaps to vanilla or butterscotch.
—LaVerna Mjones, Moorhead, Minnesota

1 cup cold milk
1 package (3.4 ounces) instant banana pudding mix
3 Butterfinger candy bars (2.1 ounces *each*), crushed
1 carton (8 ounces) frozen whipped topping, thawed
3 medium firm bananas, sliced

In a large bowl, whisk milk and pudding mix for 2 minutes. Let stand for 2 minutes or until soft-set. Set aside 1/3 cup crushed candy for topping. Fold the whipped topping, bananas and remaining candy into pudding.

Spoon into serving dishes; Chill until serving. Sprinkle with the reserved candy just before serving.
Yield: 4-6 servings.

No-Bake Cheesecake
Prep: 15 min.

Cooking and collecting new recipes are my favorite hobbies. Since I discovered this one around 5 years ago, my family's requested it often. It's so creamy and rich, you won't believe it has only five ingredients. —Michelle Overton, Oak Ridge, Tennessee

1-1/2 cups semisweet chocolate chips
2 packages (one 8 ounces, one 3 ounces) cream cheese, softened
1/4 cup sugar
1 carton (8 ounces) frozen whipped topping, thawed
1 chocolate crumb crust (9 inches)

In a microwave or heavy saucepan, melt the chocolate chips; stir until smooth and set aside. In a large mixing bowl, beat cream cheese and sugar until smooth. Beat in melted chocolate and whipped topping at low speed. Pour into the crust. Cover and refrigerate for at least 4 hours.
Yield: 6-8 servings.

Editor's Note: Make this recipe the night before you plan to serve it.

20 minute recipes

Pineapple Angel Dessert

Prep: 20 min.

Sprinkling slices of angel food cake with confectioners' sugar gives each bite a sweet and crunchy texture. Be sure to watch closely so the sugar doesn't burn. —Taste of Home Test Kitchen

2 cans (8 ounces *each*) crushed pineapple, drained
2 tablespoons sugar
2 tablespoons heavy whipping cream
1/8 teaspoon ground cinnamon
Dash ground ginger
4 slices prepared angel food cake (1 inch thick)
Confectioners' sugar
Toasted coconut

In a small saucepan, combine the pineapple, sugar, cream, cinnamon and ginger. Cook and stir over medium heat for 5 minutes.

Meanwhile, place the cake on a baking sheet and sprinkle with confectioners' sugar. Broil 5-6 in. from the heat for 3-4 minutes or until golden brown. Drizzle sauce over the cake; sprinkle with coconut.
Yield: 4 servings.

Melon Ambrosia plan ahead

Prep: 20 min. + chilling

Each time I serve this refreshing dessert, it gets rave reviews. With three kinds of melon, it's lovely and colorful but so simple to prepare. —Edie DeSpain, Logan, Utah

1 cup watermelon balls *or* cubes
1 cup cantaloupe balls *or* cubes
1 cup honeydew balls *or* cubes
1/3 cup lime juice
2 tablespoons sugar
2 tablespoons honey
1/4 cup flaked coconut, toasted
Fresh mint, optional

In a large bowl, combine the melon balls. In another bowl, combine the lime juice, sugar and honey; pour over melon and toss to coat. Cover and refrigerate for at least 1 hour. Sprinkle with coconut. Garnish with mint if desired.
Yield: 4 servings.

Editor's Note: Make this before you prepare the entree. That way it can chill, while you prepare the rest of the meal.

Desserts

235

20

Cookie Ice Cream Sandwiches

Prep: 15 min.

These tempting treats take advantage of store-bought oatmeal cookies, ice cream and peanut butter. You can roll them in crushed candy bars or nuts for an even fancier look. Just pop them in the freezer when you're eating. —Melissa Stevens, Elk River, Minnesota

Peanut butter
   12 oatmeal raisin cookies
    1 pint vanilla ice cream *or* flavor of
      your choice
Miniature chocolate chips

Spread peanut butter over the bottom of six cookies. Top with a scoop of ice cream. Top with another cookie; press down gently. Roll sides of ice cream sandwich in chocolate chips. Serve immediately or wrap in plastic wrap and freeze.
Yield: 6 servings.

Pears with Raspberry Sauce

Prep: 20 min.

The yummy recipe came about when I was expecting company and wanted to make a light, pretty dessert with items that I already had on hand. My guests really enjoyed it. I now make it as often as I can—new audience, same dessert, everybody loves it!
—Constance Rak, Westlake, Ohio

  4 medium firm pears
  2 cups white grape juice
  1 cup sugar
  2 tablespoons lemon juice
  1 package (10 ounces) frozen sweetened raspberries, thawed
Whipped cream

Core pears from bottom, leaving stems intact. Peel pears; set aside. In a large saucepan, bring the grape juice, sugar and lemon juice to a boil; add pears. Reduce heat; cover and simmer for 5-7 minutes or until tender; drain.

While pears are poaching, place raspberries in a blender; cover and process until pureed. Strain, reserving juice; set aside. Discard seeds.

For each serving, spoon raspberry sauce on plate, then top with a pear. Garnish with whipped cream.
Yield: 4 servings.

Chocolate Marshmallow Squares

Prep: 15 min.

You don't need to sit around the campfire to capture the popular taste of s'mores. Everyone will have fun covering the crackers with marshmallows, chocolate chips and ice cream topping. —Taste of Home Test Kitchen

  8 whole graham crackers
  1 cup miniature marshmallows
1/2 cup semisweet chocolate chips
  2 tablespoons caramel *or* butterscotch ice cream topping

Place whole graham crackers 1 in. apart on a baking sheet. Top each cracker with marshmallows and chocolate chips. Drizzle with ice cream topping.

Bake at 350° for 5-7 minutes or until the marshmallows are puffed and the chips are slightly melted. Cool for 2-3 minutes before serving.
Yield: 4 servings.

Crunchy Fudge Drops

Prep: 25 min.

Both semisweet chocolate and butterscotch chips make these no-bake bites luscious. I take them everywhere—our church coffee hour, my card group, you name it. Nobody can eat just one. —Loraine Meyer, Bend, Oregon

1/2 cup semisweet chocolate chips
1/2 cup butterscotch chips
1/2 cup plus 2 tablespoons granola without raisins
1/2 cup chopped pecans

In a microwave or heavy saucepan, melt chocolate and butterscotch chips; stir until smooth. Stir in granola and pecans. Drop by rounded teaspoonfuls onto waxed paper-lined baking sheets. Refrigerate until firm. Store in an airtight container.
Yield: 2 dozen.

Chocolate Caramel Pie plan ahead

Prep: 30 min. + chilling

This deliciously rich pie recipe came from a local restaurant. I think it is one of the most wonderful desserts I've ever eaten. —Joan Gocking, Moundsville, West Virginia

1 cups (6 ounces) semisweet chocolate chips, *divided*
1/4 cup chopped pecans
1 pastry shell (9 inches), baked
1/4 cup caramel ice cream topping
2 packages (8 ounces *each*) cream cheese, softened
3/4 cup confectioners' sugar
2 tablespoons heavy whipping cream
Whipped cream and additional chocolate chips, pecans and caramel topping for garnish, optional

Sprinkle 1/4 cup of chocolate chips and pecans into pastry shell. Pour caramel topping over chip and pecans; set aside.

In a large mixing bowl, beat cream cheese and sugar until smooth. Meanwhile, in a small saucepan, combine cream and remaining chips; cook and stir over low heat until smooth.

Gradually beat into cream cheese mixture. Carefully spread into pastry shell. Chill until set. Garnish as desired.
Yield: 8 servings.

Editor's Note: Make this recipe the night before you plan to serve.

Cranberry Peach Crisp

Prep: 10 min. | Bake: 20 min.

Have a taste for a fruit crisp but don't have time to make it from scratch? This clever recipe simply combines canned peaches and cranberry sauce with a cookie crumb topping for a sweet, crunchy treat. —Taste of Home Test Kitchen

1 can (15-1/4 ounces) sliced peaches, drained
1 can (16 ounces) whole-berry cranberry sauce
1/2 cup packed brown sugar
1/2 cup all-purpose flour
1/2 cup crumbled oatmeal *or* sugar cookies
1/4 cup chopped walnuts
1/4 cup butter, melted

Preheat oven to 400°.

Arrange peaches in a greased shallow 2-qt. baking dish. Stir cranberry sauce and pour over peaches. In a small bowl, combine the brown sugar, flour, cookie crumbs and nuts; sprinkle over fruit. Drizzle with butter. Bake, uncovered, at 400° for 18-20 minutes or until bubbly.
Yield: 4-6 servings.

Editor's Note: Pop this into the oven right before you sit down for dinner.

Chocolate Cream Cheese Pie

Prep: 25 min.

This dessert makes a cool and creamy finish to any meal. Since the pudding needs time to set, I usually start this first, then make the rest of the meal. —Rhonda Hogan, Eugene, Oregon

1 package (3 ounces) cream cheese, softened
2 tablespoons sugar
1-3/4 cups cold milk, *divided*
2 cups whipped topping, *divided*
1 graham cracker crust (9 inches)
1 package (3.9 ounces) instant chocolate pudding mix
Miniature semisweet chocolate chips, optional

In a small mixing bowl, beat the cream cheese, sugar and 1 tablespoon milk until smooth. Fold in 1 cup whipped topping. Spread evenly into crust.

In a large mixing bowl, whisk the remaining milk with the pudding mix for 2 minutes. Let stand for 2 minutes or until soft-set. Pour over cream cheese mixture. Chill until set.

Just before serving, garnish with remaining whipped topping and chocolate chips if desired. **Yield: 6 servings.**

Baked Ginger Pears

Prep: 10 min. | **Bake: 20 min.**

These dressed-up canned pears are a nice alternative to baked apples. Sweetened with a little brown sugar and sprinkled with pecans and ginger, they're wonderful served warm or cold. —Shirley Glaab, Hattiesburg, Mississippi

2 cans (15 ounces *each*) reduced-sugar pear halves
1/3 cup packed brown sugar
1/4 cup chopped pecans
1 teaspoon lemon juice
1/2 teaspoon ground ginger
4 gingersnap cookies, crumbled

Preheat oven to 350°.

Drain pears, reserving juice; set aside eight pear halves and 1/4 cup juice (save remaining pears and juice for another use).

Arrange pear halves cut side up in an ungreased 5-cup baking dish. Combine the brown sugar, pecans, lemon juice and ginger; sprinkle over pears.

Spoon reserved pear juice around pears. Bake, uncovered, at 350° for 20-25 minutes or until bubbly. Garnish with cookie crumbs.
Yield: 4 servings.

Editor's Note: Pop this into the oven right before you sit down for dinner.

Cinnamon Baked Apples

Prep: 10 min. | **Bake: 20 min.**

The heavenly aroma of these baked apples is sure to bring your family to the table without you even asking. Served with a scoop of vanilla ice cream or whipped cream, it's an old-fashioned ending to any comforting meal. —Margaret McNeil, Germantown, Tennessee

- 3 large tart apples, peeled, cored and cut into wedges
- 2 tablespoons lemon juice
- 2/3 cup apple juice
- 2/3 cup packed brown sugar
- 2 tablespoons butter
- 1/4 teaspoon ground cinnamon
- 4 cinnamon sticks (3 inches), optional

Whipped topping, optional

Preheat oven to 375°.

Place apples in an ungreased 11-in. x 7-in. x 2-in. baking dish. Drizzle with lemon juice; toss to coat. Set aside.

In a small saucepan, combine the apple juice, brown sugar, butter and ground cinnamon. Cook and stir over medium heat until sugar is dissolved and butter is melted. Pour over apples. Add cinnamon sticks if desired.

Bake, uncovered, at 375° for 20 minutes or until apples are tender. Discard cinnamon. Serve warm with whipped topping if desired.
Yield: 4 servings.

Editor's Note: To save time, peel the apples, then use an apple corer/wedger to core and cut the fruit into pieces.

Chocolate Ice Cream Syrup

Prep: 25 min.

When our four children were growing up, we served this sweet chocolate sauce over homemade ice cream. Now when we have friends over for cards, we finish the evening with sundaes made with this syrup. —Dorothy Mekemson, Humboldt, Iowa

- 6 squares (1 ounce *each*) unsweetened chocolate
- 3 tablespoons butter, cubed
- 2 cups sugar
- 1 can (12 ounces) evaporated milk

Ice cream

In a microwave, melt chocolate and butter; stir until smooth. Transfer to a small saucepan. Add the sugar alternately with milk, stirring constantly. Cook for 15 minutes, stirring often. Serve warm over ice cream. Refrigerate leftovers.
Yield: 2-1/2 cups.

Desserts

30+
minute recipes

Raspberry Chocolate Puffs

Prep: 25 min. | Bake: 20 min. + cooling

This is my "show-off" dessert because it makes a spectacular presentation. Every time I serve it, my friends rave about this fancy and fun treat. Although it looks like you fussed, the recipe is actually quick and easy. —Anneliese Deising, Plymouth, Michigan

1 cup vanilla *or* white chips
1 cup raspberry *or* milk chocolate chips
1 cup chopped pecans
1 package (17.3 ounces) frozen puff pastry, thawed
1 package (12 ounces) frozen unsweetened raspberries, thawed
1 cup confectioners' sugar
Fresh raspberries, additional vanilla and raspberry chips and confectioners' sugar, optional

Preheat oven to 425°.

In a large bowl, combine chips and pecans; set aside. On a lightly floured surface, roll each pastry sheet into a 12-in. square. Cut each in half lengthwise and widthwise, making eight 6-in. squares. Spoon the chip mixture in the center of each square. Pull all corners together below the tips of the corners, forming a pouch. Fold the corner tips down. Place on an ungreased baking sheet. Bake at 425° for 18-20 minutes or until golden brown. Remove to a wire rack to cool.

While puffs are baking, in a food processor, puree raspberries and confectioners' sugar. Strain and discard seeds. Spoon raspberry sauce onto dessert plates; top with pastry pouches. If desired, garnish with raspberries and chips; dust with confectioners' sugar.
Yield: 8 servings.

Caramel Pear Crumble

Prep: 25 min. | **Bake: 30 min.**

This is the first recipe I turn to after my mother shares juicy pears from her orchard. The down-home flavor of the not-too-sweet dessert is a welcomed alternative to apple crisp. Its crumbly topping and hint of caramel keep friends asking for more.
—Karen Ann Bland, Gove, Kansas

1-1/4 cups all-purpose flour
1 cup quick-cooking oats
1 cup packed brown sugar
1 teaspoon ground cinnamon
1/2 cup butter, melted
20 caramels
1 tablespoon milk
3 medium pears, peeled and sliced
Whipped topping and additional cinnamon, optional

In a small bowl, combine the flour, oats, brown sugar and cinnamon. Stir in butter (mixture will be crumbly); set aside 1 cup.

Press the remaining mixture into an ungreased 8-in. square baking dish.

In a small saucepan over low heat, cook and stir caramels and milk until caramels are melted and mixture is smooth. Remove from the heat. Arrange pears over crust; spoon caramel mixture over pears. Sprinkle with the reserved crumb mixture.

Bake at 350° for 30-35 minutes or until the pears are tender and top is golden brown. Serve warm. Garnish with whipped topping and cinnamon if desired.
Yield: 6 servings.

Candy Bar Cookie Squares

Prep: 10 min. | **Bake: 25 min. + cooling**

Be prepared—the squares disappear fast! These sweets feature chunks of Snickers bars and use a yellow cake mix. Also try it with a chocolate mix. —Amy Voights, Brodhead, Wisconsin

1 package (18-1/4 ounces) yellow cake mix
1/2 cup packed brown sugar
2 eggs
1/2 cup butter, melted
3 Snickers candy bars (2.07 ounces each) , chopped

Preheat oven to 350°.

In a large mixing bowl, combine the dry cake mix, brown sugar, eggs and butter. Beat on low speed for 2 minutes, scraping bowl occasionally. Stir in chopped candy.

Spread into an ungreased 13-in. x 9-in. x 2-in. baking pan. Bake at 350° for 25-30 minutes or until a toothpick comes out clean. Cool on a wire rack. Cut into squares.
Yield: 2 dozen.

Desserts

30+ Chocolate Cookie Cake

minute recipes

Prep: 20 min. | Bake: 35 min. + cooling

This cake is a showstopper that tastes as good as it looks. It's a quicker version of a favorite scratch cake.
—Renee Zimmer, Gig Harbor, Washington

1 package (18-1/4 ounces) white cake mix
16 cream-filled chocolate sandwich cookies, coarsely crushed
1 package (3 ounces) cream cheese, softened
2 tablespoons milk
2 cups heavy whipping cream
3/4 cup confectioners' sugar
Additional cream-filled chocolate sandwich cookies

Prepare cake batter according to package directions; stir in crushed cookies. Spoon into a greased and floured 10-in. fluted tube pan. Bake at 350° for 33-38 minutes or until a toothpick inserted near the center comes out clean. Cool for 10 minutes before removing from pan to a wire rack to cool completely.

In a small mixing bowl, beat cream cheese and milk until smooth. Beat in cream until mixture begins to thicken. Add confectioners' sugar; beat until stiff peaks form. Frost cake. Garnish with additional cookies. Refrigerate leftovers.
Yield: 12-16 servings.

Rich Cheesecake Bars

Prep: 10 min. | Bake: 30 min. + cooling

I take turns with some of the ladies at church to provide coffee time snacks for adult Bible class and Sunday school. These gooey bars, a traditional St. Louis dessert, are a favorite. —Tammy Helle, St. Louis, Missouri

1 package (9 ounces) yellow cake mix
3 tablespoons butter, softened
1 egg

TOPPING:
1 package (3 ounces) cream cheese, softened
2 cups confectioners' sugar
1 egg

Preheat oven to 350°.

In a large mixing bowl, combine the dry cake mix, butter and egg. Spread into a greased 9-in. square baking pan. In a small mixing bowl, combine the cream cheese, confectioners' sugar and egg; spread evenly over batter.

Bake at 350° for 30-35 minutes or until a toothpick inserted near the center comes out clean. Cool on a wire rack. Store in the refrigerator.
Yield: 2 dozen.

Editor's Note: Make this before you prepare the entree. That way it can cool, while dinner is being eaten.

The Busy Family Cookbook

Boston Cream Pie

Prep: 20 min. | Bake: 30 min. + cooling

Convenient cake and pudding mixes help create this delectable dessert in no time.
—Edwina Olson, Enid, Oklahoma

1 package (18-1/4 ounces) yellow cake mix
1-1/2 cups cold milk
1 package (3.4 ounces) instant vanilla pudding mix
2 squares (1 ounce *each*) unsweetened chocolate
2 tablespoons butter
1 cup confectioners' sugar
1/2 teaspoon vanilla extract
2 to 3 tablespoons hot water

Preheat oven to 350°.

Prepare cake batter according to package directions. Divide between two greased and floured 9-in. round baking pans.

Bake at 350° for 28-33 minutes or until the cake springs back when lightly touched.

Cool for 10 minutes before removing cake from pans to wire racks to cool completely.

In a bowl, whisk milk and pudding mix for 2 minutes. Let stand for 2 minutes or until soft-set. Cover and refrigerate. In a microwave or heavy saucepan, melt chocolate and butter; stir until smooth. Stir in confectioners' sugar, vanilla and enough water to achieve a thick glaze; set aside.

To assemble, place one cake layer on a serving plate; spread with pudding. Top with the second cake layer. Spoon chocolate glaze over the top, allowing it to drip down sides of cake. Refrigerate until serving.
Yield: 6-8 servings.

Editor's Note: Prepare pudding mix and glaze while cake is cooling.

Bonnie Blue-Barb Pie

Prep: 15 min. | **Bake: 45 min.**

We are fortunate to have a healthy rhubarb patch in our garden. It keeps us supplied with rhubarb from spring until well into fall.
—Andrea Holcomb, Torrington, Connecticut

1-1/2 cups fresh *or* frozen
    rhubarb, cut into 1/2-inch
    pieces
1-1/2 cups fresh *or* frozen
    blueberries
  1 cup sugar
  1/4 cup all-purpose flour
  1/4 teaspoon salt
Pastry for double-crust pie
  (9 inches)
    2 tablespoons butter

Preheat oven to 450°.

In a bowl, combine rhubarb and blueberries. Combine sugar, flour and salt. Sprinkle over fruit; toss lightly. Line a 9-in. pie plate with pastry; add filling. Dot with butter. Top with remaining pastry or make a lattice crust.

Bake at 450° for 10 minutes. Reduce heat to 350°; bake for 35 minutes or until golden brown. **Yield: 8 servings.**

Editor's Note: If using frozen blueberries, do not thaw before adding to batter. If using frozen rhubarb, measure rhubarb while still frozen, then thaw completely. Drain in a colander, but do not press liquid out.

Walnut-Rippled Coffee Cake

Prep: 15 min. | **Bake: 40 min. + cooling**

This moist cake offers a delightful surprise of cinnamon, nuts and brown sugar in every bite and it's so easy because it uses a boxed mix. —Nanetta Larson, Canton, South Dakota

  1 package (18-1/4 ounces) yellow
    cake mix
  2 tablespoons sugar
  4 eggs
  1 cup (8 ounces) sour cream
1/3 cup vegetable oil
1/4 cup water
  1 cup chopped walnuts
  2 tablespoons brown sugar
  2 teaspoons ground cinnamon

Preheat oven to 350°.

Set aside 2 tablespoons cake mix. Place the remaining cake mix in a large mixing bowl.

Add the sugar, eggs, sour cream, oil and water; beat on low speed for 2 minutes.

Pour half into a greased fluted 10-in. tube pan. Combine the walnuts, brown sugar, cinnamon and reserved dry cake mix; sprinkle over batter. Top with the remaining batter. Bake at 350° for 40-45 minutes or until a toothpick inserted near the center comes out clean. Cool for 10 minutes before removing from pan to wire rack. **Yield: 12-14 servings.**

Editor's Note: Make this before you prepare the entree. That way it can cool, while dinner is being eaten.

Peach Cake Dessert

Prep: 20 min. | Bake: 40 min.

You can name just about any fruit except citrus, and it's grown here in northwestern Pennsylvania. Serve this cake with whipped cream or ice cream. —Virginia Slater, West Sunbury, Pennsylvania

- 1 cup sugar
- 1 tablespoon all-purpose flour
- 1 to 2 teaspoons ground cinnamon
- 5 medium fresh peaches, peeled and sliced

CAKE:
- 1/4 cup butter, softened
- 1/2 cup sugar
- 1 egg
- 1 cup all-purpose flour
- 2 teaspoons baking powder
- 1/4 teaspoon salt
- 1/4 cup milk

Preheat oven to 350°.

In a large bowl, combine the sugar, flour and cinnamon. Add peaches; toss to coat. Transfer to a greased 8-in. square baking dish.

In a large mixing bowl, cream butter and sugar until light and fluffy. Beat in egg. Combine the flour, baking powder and salt; add to the creamed mixture alternately with milk.

Drop by spoonfuls onto peaches; spread evenly. Bake at 350° for 40-45 minutes or until a toothpick inserted near the center comes out clean. Serve warm. **Yield: 6 servings.**

Tart Cherry Crisp

Prep: 10 min. | Bake: 30 min.

Our family first made this dessert after an outing to a cherry orchard. We used the fresh fruit we picked to make this crisp. —Mrs. Chaya Grossman, Brooklyn, New York

- 4 cups pitted fresh *or* frozen tart cherries *or* 2 cans (14-1/2 ounces) pitted tart cherries, drained
- 2 tablespoons sugar
- 1/2 cup all-purpose flour
- 1/2 cup packed brown sugar
- 1 teaspoon ground cinnamon
- 1/4 teaspoon salt
- 1/4 cup cold butter

Preheat oven to 375°.

Place cherries in an ungreased 9-in. pie plate. Sprinkle with sugar. In a bowl, combine the flour, brown sugar, cinnamon and salt. Cut in butter until mixture resembles coarse crumbs. Sprinkle over cherries.

Bake, uncovered, at 375° for 30-40 minutes or until top is bubbly. Serve warm. **Yield: 6 servings.**

Editor's Note: Pop this into the oven right before you sit down for dinner.

Desserts

Mocha Pie

plan ahead

Prep: 20 min. + chilling | Bake: 15 min. + cooling

A friend gave me this divine recipe after I asked how she managed to put together such an elegant pie after a long day at work. Prepared cookie dough, marshmallow creme and a little instant coffee make it a breeze to assemble.
—Barbara Keller, Highlands Ranch, Colorado

1 tube (18 ounces) refrigerated chocolate chip cookie dough

1 package (3 ounces) cream cheese, softened

2 tablespoons milk

1 jar (7 ounces) marshmallow creme

1 tablespoon instant coffee granules

1 tablespoon hot water

1 carton (8 ounces) frozen whipped topping, thawed

2 tablespoons chocolate syrup, *divided*

3 tablespoons chopped walnuts

Preheat oven to 375°.

Cut cookie dough in half width-wise; let one half stand at room temperature for 5-10 minutes to soften (save the other half for another use).

Press dough onto the bottom and up the sides of an ungreased 9-in. pie plate. Bake, uncovered, at 375° for 11-12 minutes or until lightly browned. Cool on a wire rack.

In a large mixing bowl, beat cream cheese and milk until smooth. Add the marshmallow creme; beat until blended. Dissolve coffee granules in water. Fold the coffee, whipped topping and 1 tablespoon chocolate syrup into the cream cheese mixture. Pour into cooled crust. Chill for 1 hour.

Just before serving, sprinkle with nuts and drizzle with remaining chocolate syrup.
Yield: 6-8 servings.

Editor's Note: Make this the day before you plan to serve it.

Alphabetical Index

Acorn Squash Slices, 224
Alfredo Potatoes, 209
Almond Sole Fillets, 134
Almost Stuffed Peppers, 28
Aloha Chicken, 99
Ambrosia Tarts, 229
Angel Hair Tuna, 144
Angler's Delight, 161
Apple Salad, 191
Apricot Ham Steaks, 48
Apricot Salsa Chicken, 113
Artichoke Beef Steaks, 33
Artichoke Chicken, 130
Artichoke Orzo Pilaf, 215
Artichoke Tossed Salad, 193
Asian Beef Noodles, 32
Asian Turkey Burgers, 94
Asparagus Frittata, 169
Au Gratin Taters 'n' Chops, 76

Baby Corn Romaine Salad, 186
Bacon Cheddar Quiche, 53
Bacon Cheese Frittata, 72
Bacon Cheeseburger Pasta, 21
Bacon-Feta Stuffed Chicken, 132
Bacon-Wrapped Chicken, 118
Baked Garlic Chicken, 104
Baked Ginger Pears, 240
Baked Halibut, 161
Baked Sweet Potato Chips, 209
Balsamic Roasted Red
    Potatoes, 224
Banana Butterfinger Pudding, 234
Barbecue Kielbasa, 55
Barbecue Macaroni Beef, 14
Barbecue Shrimp over Pasta, 153
Barbecued Chicken Pizza, 97
Barbecued Ham Buns, 49
Barbecued Onion Meat Loaves, 30
Basil Caesar Salmon, 155
Basil Cherry Tomatoes, 188
Basil Orange Chops, 69
Basil Walnut Fish Fillets, 147
Bean and Ham Pasta, 67
Beef and Pepper Linguine, 34
Beef Fried Rice, 15
Black Bean Burritos, 164
Black Bean Nacho Bake, 180
Blintz Pancakes, 177
Bonnie Blue-Barb Pie, 246
Boston Cream Pie, 245
Bow Tie Turkey Bake, 102
Breaded Orange Roughy, 138
Breaded Pork Roll-Ups, 66
Breaded Turkey Breasts, 90
Broccoli Brown Rice Pilaf, 221
Broccoli Coleslaw, 194

Broccoli Corn Bake, 222
Broiled Chicken Cordon Bleu, 86
Broiled Orange Roughy, 140
Brownie Sundaes, 227
Butterscotch Parfaits, 229
Buttery Peas and Carrots, 198

Cajun Chicken Club, 96
Cajun Chops, 59
Cajun Shrimp, 135
Cajun Shrimp with Potatoes, 152
Cajun-Style Catfish, 145
Candy Bar Cookie Squares, 243
Caramel Pear Crumble, 243
Carrot Burgers, 176
Cashew Chicken, 116
Cheddar Chicken Spirals, 103
Cheese Sauce over
    Cauliflower, 205
Cheeseburger Chowder, 31
Cheesecake Waffle Cups, 226
Cheesy Broccoli Macaroni, 218
Cheesy Rice with Peas, 216
Chicken a la King, 93
Chicken Amandine, 108
Chicken 'n' Chips, 117
Chicken and Shells Dinner, 126
Chicken Chili, 102
Chicken Mushroom Fettuccine, 90
Chicken Parmigiana, 119
Chicken Salad Clubs, 85
Chicken Salsa Pizza, 93
Chicken Stir-Fry Bake, 105
Chicken Stroganoff, 94
Chicken Tarragon, 126
Chicken Veggie Casserole, 100
Chicken with Apple Cream
    Sauce, 109
Chicken with Mushroom
    Sauce, 120
Chicken with Peach Stuffing, 104
Chili Bow Tie Bake, 33
Chili Burgers, 11
Chili Casserole, 184
Chili-Cheese Mashed Potatoes, 188
Chipped Beef on Toast, 8
Chocolate Caramel Pie, 238
Chocolate Cookie Cake, 244
Chocolate Cream Cheese Pie, 240
Chocolate Fudge Mousse, 228
Chocolate Ice Cream Syrup, 241
Chocolate Marshmallow
    Squares, 237
Cinnamon Baked Apples, 241
Citrus Cod, 152
Citrus Garlic Shrimp, 150
Citrus Shortcake, 228

Cold Day Chili, 24
Colorful Bean Salad, 187
Colorful Chicken Croissants, 88
Cookie Ice Cream Sandwiches, 236
Corn Bread Hamburger Pie, 28
Corn Bread Taco Bake, 43
Corned Beef and Cabbage
    Sandwiches, 9
Corned Beef Stir-Fry, 30
Corny Chicken Wraps, 84
Crab-Topped Fish Fillets, 156
Cranberry-Orange Turkey
    Cutlets, 97
Cranberry Peach Crisp, 239
Creamed New Potatoes, 217
Creamed Spinach, 211
Creamed Sweet Peas, 206
Creamy Asparagus on Toast, 181
Creamy Herbed Meatballs, 38
Creole Tuna, 142
Crispy 'n' Crunchy Salad, 190
Crispy Chicken, 114
Crumb-Coated Chicken
    Thighs, 122
Crunchy Fudge Drops, 238
Cube Steak Diane, 21
Curried Chicken 'n' Broccoli, 101

Dilly Pork Chops, 51

Easy au Gratin Potatoes, 218
Easy Italian Chicken, 106
Easy Pasta Alfredo, 173

Fabulous Beef Fajitas, 45
Family-Favorite Chicken Salad, 85
Festive Pork, 58
Feta Tomato-Basil Fish, 139
Fiesta Chicken 'n' Stuffing, 87
Flavorful Mac and Cheese, 52
Fluffy Harvest Omelet, 178
Fluffy Scrambled Eggs, 164
French-Style Green Beans, 187
Frosty Blueberry Dessert, 231
Frosty Peanut Butter Pie, 230
Fruit-Filled Puff Pancake, 175

Garlic Lime Shrimp, 146
Garlic Mashed Potatoes, 217
Garlic Salmon Linguine, 141
Gingered Pepper Steak, 17
Glazed Orange Roughy, 147
Golden Burger Spirals, 40
Golden Catfish Fillets, 142
Golden Chicken and Autumn
    Vegetables, 118
Golden Glazed Fryer, 123

Golden Pork Chops, 80
Greek Ham Wraps, 57
Greek Tossed Salad, 195
Grilled Roast Beef Sandwiches, 16

Hearty Baked Potatoes, 210
Herbed Egg Noodles, 204
Herbed Orange Roughy, 148
Herbed Pork Medallions, 60
Herbed Salmon Steaks, 160
Honey Chicken Stir-Fry, 115
Honey Garlic Chicken, 107
Honey-Lime Grilled Chicken, 132
Honey-Mustard Chicken, 98
Honey-Mustard Pork Scallopini, 54
Honeydew Shrimp Salad, 136
Hot 'n' Spicy Omelet, 167
Hurry-Up Ham 'n' Noodles, 68

Italian Beef Sandwiches, 12
Italian Fish Fillets, 151
Italian Flank Steak, 15
Italian Orange Roughy, 158
Italian Pasta and Peas, 211
Italian Rice, 197
Italian Sausage Skillet, 64
Italian Subs, 50
Italian Turkey Burgers, 114

Jalapeno Swiss Burgers, 24
Jelly Pancake Sandwiches, 171

Lemon Angel Hair, 207
Lemon Berry Trifle, 232
Lemon-Glazed Carrots, 214
Lemon Grilled Chicken, 131
Lemon Honey Turkey, 124

Maple Baked Beans, 208
Maple-Glazed Kabobs, 73
Marinated Pork Loin, 76
Meat Loaf Pie, 38
Meatballs Monte Carlo, 44
Meatless Chili Bake, 180
Melon Ambrosia, 235
Melon with Sweet Lime
    Dressing, 189
Mexican Pork and Pasta, 75
Mexicana Skillet Stew, 43
Microwave Acorn Squash, 212
Microwave Cherry Crisp, 232
Microwave Mac 'n' Cheese, 173
Microwave Red Snapper, 136
Microwaved Cod, 143
Microwaved Italian Eggplant, 167
Minestrone Macaroni, 26
Mini Italian Meat Loaves, 40
Mixed Vegetable Casserole, 222
Mocha Pie, 248
Mock Caesar Salad, 191

Mozzarella Beef Sandwiches, 8
Mushroom Beef Tenderloin, 20
Mushroom Cheeseburgers, 12
Mustard Chicken Breasts, 92

No-Bake Cheesecake, 234
No-Bake Chocolate Torte, 233
No-Fuss Ham Patties, 53
Noodle Rice Pilaf, 219

One-Dish Chicken with
    Vegetables, 128
One-Dish Spaghetti, 29
One-for-All Marinated Beef, 22
Onion Salisbury Steak, 27
Onion Turkey Meatballs, 117
Open-Faced Crab Melts, 135
Open-Faced Tuna Burgers, 138
Orange Broccoli, 198
Oriental Pork Cabbage Stir-Fry, 62
Orzo Shrimp Stew, 144
Oven Fish 'n' Chips, 162
Oven-Fried Catfish, 157
Oven-Roasted Root
    Vegetables, 220

Paprika Potatoes 'n' Beans, 212
Parmesan Chicken, 89
Parmesan Ham Pasta, 60
Parmesan Potato Rounds, 223
Pasta and Veggies in Garlic
    Sauce, 168
Pasta Ham Hot Dish, 79
Pasta Veggie Medley, 201
Pasta with Marinara Sauce, 174
Peach Cake Dessert, 247
Peanut Chicken Stir-Fry, 111
Peanutty Chicken, 127
Pears with Raspberry Sauce, 237
Pecan Brussels Sprouts, 200
Pecan Chicken, 125
Pecan-Crusted Salmon, 151
Penne from Heaven, 213
Pepper-Crusted Pork Tenderloin, 79
Pepper Steak Sandwiches, 18
Pepper Steak with Potatoes, 23
Pepperoni Angel Hair, 202
Personal Pizza, 39
Pesto Chicken Pasta, 107
Philly Cheese Steak Pizza, 25
Picante Biscuit Bake, 184
Picante Omelet Pie, 176
Pineapple Angel Dessert, 235
Pizza Mac Casserole, 44
Pork 'n' Green Chili Tortillas, 75
Pork 'n' Snow Pea Stir-Fry, 64
Pork Chops with Apple Stuffing, 80
Pork Chops with Onions and
    Apples, 63

Pork Fajita Pasta, 69
Pork Lo Mein, 56
Pork Parmesan, 65
Pork with Apples and Sweet
    Potatoes, 70
Pork with Garlic Cream Sauce, 68
Pork with Pineapple Salsa, 74
Potatoes O'Brien, 215
Pronto Chili, 39

Quick Barbecued Chicken, 112
Quicker Boiled Dinner, 36

Ranch Stew, 42
Ranch Turkey Pasta Dinner, 98
Raspberry Almond Rounds, 231
Raspberry Chocolate Puffs, 242
Raspberry Cupcake Dessert, 227
Raspberry Pork Chops, 63
Raspberry Thyme Chicken, 91
Ravioli Primavera, 166
Reuben Monte Cristos, 27
Rich Cheesecake Bars, 244

Salsa Tuna Salad, 137
Santa Fe Chicken, 130
Saucy Beef Casserole, 46
Sausage Corn Chili, 54
Sausage Hash, 78
Sausage Jumble, 66
Sausage Stroganoff, 65
Sausage-Topped Polenta, 71
Sauteed Summer Squash, 216
Savory Beef and Noodles, 14
Savory Rice Pilaf, 204
Scalloped Basil Tomatoes, 221
Scrambled Egg Sandwich, 168
Scrumptious Spaghetti, 179
Seafood Fettuccine, 141
Seasoned Broccoli Spears, 193
Seasoned French Fries, 207
Sesame Asparagus, 203
Skillet Beef Stew, 46
Skillet Steak and Corn, 41
Sloppy Joe Burgers, 17
Sloppy Joe Casserole, 37
Smoked Turkey Sausage
    with Pasta, 108
Smothered Chicken, 89
Soft Chicken Tacos, 95
Southern Fried Chicken, 129
Southwest Skillet Corn, 192
Spaghetti with Homemade Turkey
    Sausage, 112
Spanish Rice, 200
Spanish Spirals, 37
Spiced Ham Steak, 50
Spicy Cajun Stew, 56
Spicy Creamed Corn, 196
Spicy Flank Steak, 29

Spicy Grilled Steaks, 22
Spinach Burritos, 179
Spinach Feta Turnovers, 177
Spinach Lasagna Roll-Ups, 182
Spinach Pancake Quesadillas, 166
Spinach Pork Tenderloin, 82
Spinach Ravioli Bake, 77
Spinach Tomato Linguine, 172
Spinach Turkey Bake, 125
Spiral Stromboli, 81
Steak Diane, 10
Stir-Fried Asparagus, 190
Stir-Fried Beef on Lettuce, 34
Stir-Fried Shrimp and Mushrooms, 148
Stuffed Walleye, 159
Sunshine Halibut, 154
Sweet and Sour Pork Chops, 49
Sweet 'n' Sour Sausage Stir-Fry, 111
Swiss Mushroom Chicken, 105

Swiss Spinach Salad, 194
Swiss Tuna Bake, 158

Taco Salad, 203
Taco Sandwich, 19
Tangy Carrot Coins, 208
Tangy Turkey Kabobs, 129
Tarragon-Almond Green
    Beans, 199
Tart Cherry Crisp, 247
Tasty Turkey Skillet, 122
T-Bones with Onions, 35
Teriyaki Chicken Sandwiches, 86
Teriyaki Sirloin Steak, 11
Teriyaki Tenderloin, 72
Thanksgiving in a Pan, 121
Three-Cheese Rice Lasagna, 174
Toasted Cheese Supreme, 61
Tomato Pea Couscous, 197
Tomato Spiral Toss, 165

Tortellini Carbonara, 55
Tuna Cheese Melts, 149
Tuna Patties, 154
Turkey Florentine, 110
Turkey Salad on Wheat, 101
Turkey Tetrazzini, 121

Veggie Burgers, 170
Veggie Cheese Squares, 183

Walnut Cream Pasta, 171
Walnut Ham Linguine, 59
Walnut-Rippled Coffee
    Cake, 246
Wild Rice Shrimp Saute, 157

Zesty Steak Salad, 13
Zippy Burgers, 18
Zucchini Corn Saute, 201
Zucchini Pie, 183

General Recipe Index

APPLES
Apple Salad, 191
Chicken with Apple Cream
    Sauce, 109
Cinnamon Baked Apples, 241
Crispy 'n' Crunchy Salad, 190
Pork Chops with Apple Stuffing, 80
Pork Chops with Onions and
    Apples, 63
Pork with Apples and Sweet
    Potatoes, 70

APRICOTS
Apricot Ham Steaks, 48
Apricot Salsa Chicken, 113

ARTICHOKES
Artichoke Beef Steaks, 33
Artichoke Chicken, 130
Artichoke Orzo Pilaf, 215
Artichoke Tossed Salad, 193

ASPARAGUS
Asparagus Frittata, 169
Creamy Asparagus on Toast, 181
Sesame Asparagus, 203
Stir-Fried Asparagus, 190

BACON
Bacon Cheddar Quiche, 53
Bacon Cheese Frittata, 72
Bacon Cheeseburger Pasta, 21
Bacon-Feta Stuffed Chicken, 132
Bacon-Wrapped Chicken, 118
Tortellini Carbonara, 55

BEANS
Bean and Ham Pasta, 67

Black Bean Burritos, 164
Black Bean Nacho Bake, 180
Chili Casserole, 184
Colorful Bean Salad, 187
French-Style Green Beans, 187
Maple Baked Beans, 208
Meatless Chili Bake, 180
Paprika Potatoes 'n' Beans, 212
Tarragon-Almond Green Beans, 199

BEEF (also see Corned Beef;
    Ground Beef; Steak)
Chipped Beef on Toast, 8
Grilled Roast Beef Sandwiches, 16
Italian Beef Sandwiches, 12
Mozzarella Beef Sandwiches, 8
Pepper Steak Sandwiches, 18
Philly Cheese Steak Pizza, 25

BLUEBERRIES
Bonnie Blue-Barb Pie, 246
Frosty Blueberry Dessert, 231

BROCCOLI & CAULIFLOWER
Broccoli Brown Rice Pilaf, 221
Broccoli Coleslaw, 194
Broccoli Corn Bake, 222
Cheese Sauce over
    Cauliflower, 205
Cheesy Broccoli Macaroni, 218
Curried Chicken 'n' Broccoli, 101
Orange Broccoli, 198
Seasoned Broccoli Spears, 193

CABBAGE & SAUERKRAUT
Corned Beef and Cabbage
    Sandwiches, 9

Corned Beef Stir-Fry, 30
Oriental Pork Cabbage Stir-Fry, 62
Reuben Monte Cristos, 27

CARROTS
Buttery Peas and Carrots, 198
Carrot Burgers, 176
Lemon-Glazed Carrots, 214
Tangy Carrot Coins, 208

CASSEROLES
Beef
Chili Bow Tie Bake, 33
Corn Bread Taco Bake, 43
Golden Burger Spirals, 40
Pizza Mac Casserole, 44
Saucy Beef Casserole, 46
Sloppy Joe Casserole, 37
Meatless
Black Bean Nacho Bake, 180
Chili Casserole, 184
Meatless Chili Bake, 180
Microwave Mac 'n' Cheese, 173
Picante Biscuit Bake, 184
Three-Cheese Rice Lasagna, 174
Pork
Au Gratin Taters 'n' Chops, 76
Bacon Cheese Frittata, 72
Pasta Ham Hot Dish, 79
Spinach Ravioli Bake, 77
Poultry
Bow Tie Turkey Bake, 102
Cashew Chicken, 116
Cheddar Chicken Spirals, 103
Chicken 'n' Chips, 117
Chicken and Shells Dinner, 126
Chicken Stir-Fry Bake, 105

CASSEROLES
Poultry (continued)
Chicken Veggie Casserole, 100
Curried Chicken 'n' Broccoli, 101
Fiesta Chicken 'n' Stuffing, 87
Spinach Turkey Bake, 125
Thanksgiving in a Pan, 121
Turkey Tetrazzini, 121
Seafood
Swiss Tuna Bake, 158

CHEESE
Au Gratin Taters 'n' Chops, 76
Bacon Cheddar Quiche, 53
Bacon Cheese Frittata, 72
Bacon Cheeseburger Pasta, 21
Bacon-Feta Stuffed Chicken, 132
Broiled Chicken Cordon Bleu, 86
Cheddar Chicken Spirals, 103
Cheese Sauce over Cauliflower, 205
Cheeseburger Chowder, 31
Cheesecake Waffle Cups, 226
Cheesy Broccoli Macaroni, 218
Cheesy Rice with Peas, 216
Chicken Parmigiana, 119
Chili-Cheese Mashed Potatoes, 188
Chocolate Cream Cheese Pie, 240
Feta Tomato-Basil Fish, 139
Flavorful Mac and Cheese, 52
Jalapeno Swiss Burgers, 24
Microwave Mac 'n' Cheese, 173
Mozzarella Beef Sandwiches, 8
Mushroom Cheeseburgers, 12
No-Bake Cheesecake, 234
Open-Faced Crab Melts, 135
Parmesan Chicken, 89
Parmesan Ham Pasta, 60
Parmesan Potato Rounds, 223
Philly Cheese Steak Pizza, 25
Pork Parmesan, 65
Rich Cheesecake Bars, 244
Spinach Feta Turnovers, 177
Swiss Mushroom Chicken, 105
Swiss Spinach Salad, 194
Swiss Tuna Bake, 158
Three-Cheese Rice Lasagna, 174
Toasted Cheese Supreme, 61
Tuna Cheese Melts, 149
Veggie Cheese Squares, 183

CHERRIES
Microwave Cherry Crisp, 232
Tart Cherry Crisp, 247

CHICKEN
Main Dishes
Aloha Chicken, 99
Apricot Salsa Chicken, 113
Artichoke Chicken, 130
Bacon-Feta Stuffed Chicken, 132
Bacon-Wrapped Chicken, 118

Baked Garlic Chicken, 104
Barbecued Chicken Pizza, 97
Broiled Chicken Cordon Bleu, 86
Cashew Chicken, 116
Cheddar Chicken Spirals, 103
Chicken a la King, 93
Chicken Amandine, 108
Chicken 'n' Chips, 117
Chicken and Shells Dinner, 126
Chicken Mushroom Fettuccine, 90
Chicken Parmigiana, 119
Chicken Salsa Pizza, 93
Chicken Stir-Fry Bake, 105
Chicken Stroganoff, 94
Chicken Tarragon, 126
Chicken Veggie Casserole, 100
Chicken with Apple Cream Sauce, 109
Chicken with Mushroom Sauce, 120
Chicken with Peach Stuffing, 104
Crispy Chicken, 114
Crumb-Coated Chicken Thighs, 122
Curried Chicken 'n' Broccoli, 101
Easy Italian Chicken, 106
Fiesta Chicken 'n' Stuffing, 87
Golden Chicken and Autumn
   Vegetables, 118
Golden Glazed Fryer, 123
Honey Chicken Stir-Fry, 115
Honey Garlic Chicken, 107
Honey-Lime Grilled Chicken, 132
Honey-Mustard Chicken, 98
Lemon Grilled Chicken, 131
Mustard Chicken Breasts, 92
One-Dish Chicken with
   Vegetables, 128
Parmesan Chicken, 89
Peanut Chicken Stir-Fry, 111
Peanutty Chicken, 127
Pecan Chicken, 125
Pesto Chicken Pasta, 107
Quick Barbecued Chicken, 112
Raspberry Thyme Chicken, 91
Santa Fe Chicken, 130
Smothered Chicken, 89
Soft Chicken Tacos, 95
Southern Fried Chicken, 129
Swiss Mushroom Chicken, 105
Salad
Family-Favorite Chicken Salad, 85
Sandwiches
Cajun Chicken Club, 96
Chicken Salad Clubs, 85
Colorful Chicken Croissants, 88
Corny Chicken Wraps, 84
Teriyaki Chicken Sandwiches, 86

CHOCOLATE
Brownie Sundaes, 227
Chocolate Caramel Pie, 238
Chocolate Cookie Cake, 244
Chocolate Cream Cheese Pie, 240

Chocolate Fudge Mousse, 228
Chocolate Ice Cream Syrup, 241
Chocolate Marshmallow
   Squares, 237
Crunchy Fudge Drops, 238
No-Bake Chocolate Torte, 233
Raspberry Chocolate Puffs, 242

CORN
Baby Corn Romaine Salad, 186
Broccoli Corn Bake, 222
Corny Chicken Wraps, 84
Sausage Corn Chili, 54
Skillet Steak and Corn, 41
Southwest Skillet Corn, 192
Spicy Creamed Corn, 196
Zucchini Corn Saute, 201

CORNED BEEF
Corned Beef and Cabbage
   Sandwiches, 9
Corned Beef Stir-Fry, 30
Quicker Boiled Dinner, 36
Reuben Monte Cristos, 27

CRANBERRIES
Cranberry-Orange Turkey Cutlets, 97
Cranberry Peach Crisp, 239
Festive Pork, 58

DESSERTS
Ambrosia Tarts, 229
Baked Ginger Pears, 240
Banana Butterfinger Pudding, 234
Bonnie Blue-Barb Pie, 246
Boston Cream Pie, 245
Brownie Sundaes, 227
Butterscotch Parfaits, 229
Candy Bar Cookie Squares, 243
Caramel Pear Crumble, 243
Cheesecake Waffle Cups, 226
Chocolate Caramel Pie, 238
Chocolate Cookie Cake, 244
Chocolate Cream Cheese Pie, 240
Chocolate Fudge Mousse, 228
Chocolate Ice Cream Syrup, 241
Chocolate Marshmallow
   Squares, 237
Cinnamon Baked Apples, 241
Citrus Shortcake, 228
Cookie Ice Cream Sandwiches, 236
Cranberry Peach Crisp, 239
Crunchy Fudge Drops, 238
Frosty Blueberry Dessert, 231
Frosty Peanut Butter Pie, 230
Lemon Berry Trifle, 232
Melon Ambrosia, 235
Microwave Cherry Crisp, 232
Mocha Pie, 248
No-Bake Cheesecake, 234
No-Bake Chocolate Torte, 233
Peach Cake Dessert, 247

Pears with Raspberry Sauce, 237
Pineapple Angel Dessert, 235
Raspberry Almond Rounds, 231
Raspberry Chocolate Puffs, 242
Raspberry Cupcake Dessert, 227
Rich Cheesecake Bars, 244
Tart Cherry Crisp, 247
Walnut-Rippled Coffee Cake, 246

EGGS
Asparagus Frittata, 169
Bacon Cheddar Quiche, 53
Bacon Cheese Frittata, 72
Creamy Asparagus on Toast, 181
Fluffy Harvest Omelet, 178
Fluffy Scrambled Eggs, 164
Hot 'n' Spicy Omelet, 167
Picante Omelet Pie, 176
Scrambled Egg Sandwich, 168
Veggie Cheese Squares, 183
Zucchini Pie, 183

FISH
Main Dishes
Almond Sole Fillets, 134
Angel Hair Tuna, 144
Angler's Delight, 161
Baked Halibut, 161
Basil Caesar Salmon, 155
Basil Walnut Fish Fillets, 147
Breaded Orange Roughy, 138
Broiled Orange Roughy, 140
Cajun-Style Catfish, 145
Citrus Cod, 152
Crab-Topped Fish Fillets, 156
Creole Tuna, 142
Feta Tomato-Basil Fish, 139
Garlic Salmon Linguine, 141
Glazed Orange Roughy, 147
Golden Catfish Fillets, 142
Herbed Orange Roughy, 148
Herbed Salmon Steaks, 160
Italian Fish Fillets, 151
Italian Orange Roughy, 158
Microwave Red Snapper, 136
Microwaved Cod, 143
Oven Fish 'n' Chips, 162
Oven-Fried Catfish, 157
Pecan-Crusted Salmon, 151
Stuffed Walleye, 159
Sunshine Halibut, 154
Swiss Tuna Bake, 158
Tuna Patties, 154
Salad
Salsa Tuna Salad, 137
Sandwiches
Open-Faced Tuna Burgers, 138
Tuna Cheese Melts, 149

FRUIT (also see specific kinds)
Ambrosia Tarts, 229

Fruit-Filled Puff Pancake, 175
Lemon Berry Trifle, 232

GRILLING RECIPES
Beef
Italian Flank Steak, 15
Jalapeno Swiss Burgers, 24
Mushroom Cheeseburgers, 12
One-for-All Marinated Beef, 22
Spicy Grilled Steaks, 22
T-Bones with Onions, 35
Teriyaki Sirloin Steak, 11
Zippy Burgers, 18
Pork
Maple-Glazed Kabobs, 73
Pork Chops with Onions and
    Apples, 63
Poultry
Golden Glazed Fryer, 123
Honey-Lime Grilled Chicken, 132
Italian Turkey Burgers, 114
Lemon Grilled Chicken, 131
Quick Barbecued Chicken, 112
Tangy Turkey Kabobs, 129

GROUND BEEF
Main Dishes
Almost Stuffed Peppers, 28
Bacon Cheeseburger Pasta, 21
Barbecue Macaroni Beef, 14
Barbecued Onion Meat Loaves, 30
Beef and Pepper Linguine, 34
Beef Fried Rice, 15
Chili Bow Tie Bake, 33
Corn Bread Hamburger Pie, 28
Corn Bread Taco Bake, 43
Creamy Herbed Meatballs, 38
Golden Burger Spirals, 40
Meat Loaf Pie, 38
Meatballs Monte Carlo, 44
Minestrone Macaroni, 26
Mini Italian Meat Loaves, 40
One-Dish Spaghetti, 29
Onion Salisbury Steak, 27
Personal Pizza, 39
Pizza Mac Casserole, 44
Saucy Beef Casserole, 46
Savory Beef and Noodles, 14
Sloppy Joe Casserole, 37
Spanish Spirals, 37
Sandwiches
Chili Burgers, 11
Jalapeno Swiss Burgers, 24
Mushroom Cheeseburgers, 12
Pizzeria Burgers, 71
Sloppy Joe Burgers, 17
Taco Sandwich, 19
Zippy Burgers, 18
Soups & Stews
Cheeseburger Chowder, 31
Cold Day Chili, 24

Mexicana Skillet Stew, 43
Pronto Chili, 39
Ranch Stew, 42

HAM
Main Dishes
Apricot Ham Steaks, 48
Bean and Ham Pasta, 67
Breaded Pork Roll-Ups, 66
Broiled Chicken Cordon Bleu, 86
Flavorful Mac and Cheese, 52
Hurry-Up Ham 'n' Noodles, 68
No-Fuss Ham Patties, 53
Parmesan Ham Pasta, 60
Pasta Ham Hot Dish, 79
Spiced Ham Steak, 50
Walnut Ham Linguine, 59
Sandwiches
Barbecued Ham Buns, 49
Greek Ham Wraps, 57
Italian Subs, 50
Spiral Stromboli, 81
Toasted Cheese Supreme, 61

MEAT LOAVES & PATTIES
Barbecued Onion Meat Loaves, 30
Meat Loaf Pie, 38
Mini Italian Meat Loaves, 40
No-Fuss Ham Patties, 53
Tuna Patties, 154

MEAT PIES
Bacon Cheddar Quiche, 53
Corn Bread Hamburger Pie, 28
Meat Loaf Pie, 38

MEATBALLS
Creamy Herbed Meatballs, 38
Meatballs Monte Carlo, 44
Onion Turkey Meatballs, 117

MEATLESS
Main Dishes
Asparagus Frittata, 169
Black Bean Burritos, 164
Black Bean Nacho Bake, 180
Blintz Pancakes, 177
Chili Casserole, 184
Creamy Asparagus on Toast, 181
Easy Pasta Alfredo, 173
Fluffy Harvest Omelet, 178
Fluffy Scrambled Eggs, 164
Fruit-Filled Puff Pancake, 175
Hot 'n' Spicy Omelet, 167
Meatless Chili Bake, 180
Microwave Mac 'n' Cheese, 173
Microwaved Italian Eggplant, 167
Pasta and Veggies in Garlic
    Sauce, 168
Pasta with Marinara Sauce, 174
Picante Biscuit Bake, 184

Indexes

MEATLESS
Main Dishes (continued)
Picante Omelet Pie, 176
Ravioli Primavera, 166
Scrumptious Spaghetti, 179
Spinach Burritos, 179
Spinach Lasagna Roll-Ups, 182
Spinach Pancake Quesadillas, 166
Spinach Tomato Linguine, 172
Three-Cheese Rice Lasagna, 174
Tomato Spiral Toss, 165
Veggie Cheese Squares, 183
Walnut Cream Pasta, 171
Zucchini Pie, 183
Sandwiches
Carrot Burgers, 176
Jelly Pancake Sandwiches, 171
Scrambled Egg Sandwich, 168
Spinach Feta Turnovers, 177
Veggie Burgers, 170

MICROWAVE RECIPES
Beef
Barbecued Onion Meat Loaves, 30
Chipped Beef on Toast, 8
One-Dish Spaghetti, 29
Pepper Steak with Potatoes, 23
Dessert
Microwave Cherry Crisp, 232
Meatless
Microwave Mac 'n' Cheese, 173
Microwaved Italian Eggplant, 167
Spinach Pancake Quesadillas, 166
Three-Cheese Rice Lasagna, 174
Pork
Bacon Cheddar Quiche, 53
Barbecued Ham Buns, 49
Pork 'n' Snow Pea Stir-Fry, 64
Poultry
Bow Tie Turkey Bake, 102
Cheddar Chicken Spirals, 103
Chicken Stroganoff, 94
Curried Chicken 'n' Broccoli, 101
Fiesta Chicken 'n' Stuffing, 87
Mustard Chicken Breasts, 92
Seafood
Almond Sole Fillets, 134
Cajun Shrimp with Potatoes, 152
Microwave Red Snapper, 136
Microwaved Cod, 143
Sides
Alfredo Potatoes, 209
Hearty Baked Potatoes, 210
Maple Baked Beans, 208
Microwave Acorn Squash, 212
Pecan Brussels Sprouts, 200
Seasoned Broccoli Spears, 193

MUSHROOMS
Chicken Mushroom Fettuccine, 90
Chicken Stroganoff, 94

Chicken with Mushroom Sauce, 120
Mushroom Beef Tenderloin, 20
Mushroom Cheeseburgers, 12
Sausage Stroganoff, 65
Stir-Fried Shrimp and
   Mushrooms, 148
Swiss Mushroom Chicken, 105

NUTS & PEANUT BUTTER
Almond Sole Fillets, 134
Basil Walnut Fish Fillets, 147
Cashew Chicken, 116
Chicken Amandine, 108
Frosty Peanut Butter Pie, 230
Peanut Chicken Stir-Fry, 111
Peanutty Chicken, 127
Pecan Brussels Sprouts, 200
Pecan Chicken, 125
Pecan-Crusted Salmon, 151
Raspberry Almond Rounds, 231
Tarragon-Almond Green
   Beans, 199
Walnut Cream Pasta, 171
Walnut Ham Linguine, 59
Walnut-Rippled Coffee Cake, 246

ONIONS
Barbecued Onion Meat Loaves, 30
Onion Salisbury Steak, 27
Onion Turkey Meatballs, 117
Pork Chops with Onions and
   Apples, 63
T-Bones with Onions, 35

ORANGE
Basil Orange Chops, 69
Citrus Cod, 152
Citrus Garlic Shrimp, 150
Citrus Shortcake, 228
Cranberry-Orange Turkey
   Cutlets, 97
Orange Broccoli, 198
Sunshine Halibut, 154

PANCAKES
Blintz Pancakes, 177
Fruit-Filled Puff Pancake, 175
Jelly Pancake Sandwiches, 171
Spinach Pancake Quesadillas, 166
PASTA
Angel Hair Tuna, 144
Artichoke Orzo Pilaf, 215
Asian Beef Noodles, 32
Bacon Cheeseburger Pasta, 21
Barbecue Macaroni Beef, 14
Barbecue Shrimp over Pasta, 153
Bean and Ham Pasta, 67
Beef and Pepper Linguine, 34
Bow Tie Turkey Bake, 102
Cheddar Chicken Spirals, 103
Cheesy Broccoli Macaroni, 218
Chicken and Shells Dinner, 126

Chicken Mushroom Fettuccine, 90
Chicken Stroganoff, 94
Easy Pasta Alfredo, 173
Flavorful Mac and Cheese, 52
Garlic Salmon Linguine, 141
Golden Burger Spirals, 40
Herbed Egg Noodles, 204
Hurry-Up Ham 'n' Noodles, 68
Italian Pasta and Peas, 211
Lemon Angel Hair, 207
Mexican Pork and Pasta, 75
Microwave Mac 'n' Cheese, 173
Minestrone Macaroni, 26
Noodle Rice Pilaf, 219
One-Dish Spaghetti, 29
Orzo Shrimp Stew, 144
Parmesan Ham Pasta, 60
Pasta and Veggies in Garlic Sauce, 168
Pasta Ham Hot Dish, 79
Pasta Veggie Medley, 201
Pasta with Marinara Sauce, 174
Penne from Heaven, 213
Pepperoni Angel Hair, 202
Pesto Chicken Pasta, 107
Pizza Mac Casserole, 44
Pork Fajita Pasta, 69
Pork Lo Mein, 56
Ranch Turkey Pasta Dinner, 98
Ravioli Primavera, 166
Sausage Stroganoff, 65
Savory Beef and Noodles, 14
Scrumptious Spaghetti, 179
Seafood Fettuccine, 141
Smoked Turkey Sausage
   with Pasta, 108
Spaghetti with Homemade Turkey
   Sausage, 112
Spanish Spirals, 37
Spinach Lasagna Roll-Ups, 182
Spinach Ravioli Bake, 77
Spinach Tomato Linguine, 172
Tomato Pea Couscous, 197
Tomato Spiral Toss, 165
Tortellini Carbonara, 55
Turkey Tetrazzini, 121
Walnut Cream Pasta, 171
Walnut Ham Linguine, 59

PEACHES
Chicken with Peach Stuffing, 104
Cranberry Peach Crisp, 239
Peach Cake Dessert, 247

PEARS
Baked Ginger Pears, 240
Caramel Pear Crumble, 243
Pears with Raspberry Sauce, 237

PEAS
Buttery Peas and Carrots, 198
Cheesy Rice with Peas, 216

Creamed Sweet Peas, 206
Italian Pasta and Peas, 211
Pork 'n' Snow Pea Stir-Fry, 64
Tomato Pea Couscous, 197

PEPPERS
Almost Stuffed Peppers, 28
Beef and Pepper Linguine, 34
Chili-Cheese Mashed Potatoes, 188
Fabulous Beef Fajitas, 45
Gingered Pepper Steak, 17
Jalapeno Swiss Burgers, 24
Pepper Steak Sandwiches, 18
Pepper Steak with Potatoes, 23
Philly Cheese Steak Pizza, 25
Pork 'n' Green Chili Tortillas, 75
Pork Fajita Pasta, 69

PINEAPPLE
Aloha Chicken, 99
Pineapple Angel Dessert, 235
Pork with Pineapple Salsa, 74

PIZZAS
Barbecued Chicken Pizza, 97
Chicken Salsa Pizza, 93
Personal Pizza, 39
Philly Cheese Steak Pizza, 25

PLAN-AHEAD RECIPES
Beef
Italian Flank Steak, 15
One-for-All Marinated Beef, 22
Teriyaki Sirloin Steak, 11
Desserts
Chocolate Caramel Pie, 238
Frosty Blueberry Dessert, 231
Frosty Peanut Butter Pie, 230
Melon Ambrosia, 235
Mocha Pie, 248
No-Bake Cheesecake, 234
No-Bake Chocolate Torte, 233
Pork
Marinated Pork Loin, 76
Teriyaki Tenderloin, 72
Poultry
Lemon Grilled Chicken, 131
Spaghetti with Homemade Turkey
    Sausage, 112

PORK (also see Bacon; Pork Chops;
    Ham; Sausage)
Festive Pork, 58
Herbed Pork Medallions, 60
Maple-Glazed Kabobs, 73
Marinated Pork Loin, 76
Oriental Pork Cabbage Stir-Fry, 62
Pepper-Crusted Pork Tenderloin, 79
Pork 'n' Green Chili Tortillas, 75
Pork 'n' Snow Pea Stir-Fry, 64

Pork Lo Mein, 56
Pork with Apples and Sweet
    Potatoes, 70
Pork with Garlic Cream Sauce, 68
Pork with Pineapple Salsa, 74
Spinach Pork Tenderloin, 82
Teriyaki Tenderloin, 72

PORK CHOPS
Au Gratin Taters 'n' Chops, 76
Basil Orange Chops, 69
Breaded Pork Roll-Ups, 66
Cajun Chops, 59
Dilly Pork Chops, 51
Golden Pork Chops, 80
Honey-Mustard Pork Scallopini, 54
Pork Chops with Apple Stuffing, 80
Pork Chops with Onions and
    Apples, 63
Pork Fajita Pasta, 69
Pork Parmesan, 65
Raspberry Pork Chops, 63
Sweet and Sour Pork Chops, 49

POTATOES & SWEET POTATOES
Alfredo Potatoes, 209
Au Gratin Taters 'n' Chops, 76
Baked Sweet Potato Chips, 209
Balsamic Roasted Red Potatoes, 224
Cajun Shrimp with Potatoes, 152
Chili-Cheese Mashed Potatoes, 188
Creamed New Potatoes, 217
Easy au Gratin Potatoes, 218
Garlic Mashed Potatoes, 217
Hearty Baked Potatoes, 210
Oven Fish 'n' Chips, 162
Paprika Potatoes 'n' Beans, 212
Parmesan Potato Rounds, 223
Pepper Steak with Potatoes, 23
Pork with Apples and Sweet
    Potatoes, 70
Potatoes O'Brien, 215
Sausage Hash, 78
Seasoned French Fries, 207

RASPBERRIES
Pears with Raspberry Sauce, 237
Raspberry Almond Rounds, 231
Raspberry Chocolate Puffs, 242
Raspberry Cupcake Dessert, 227
Raspberry Pork Chops, 63
Raspberry Thyme Chicken, 91

RICE
Beef Fried Rice, 15
Broccoli Brown Rice Pilaf, 221
Cheesy Rice with Peas, 216
Italian Rice, 197
Noodle Rice Pilaf, 219
Savory Rice Pilaf, 204
Spanish Rice, 200

Three-Cheese Rice Lasagna, 174
Wild Rice Shrimp Saute, 157

SALADS
Apple Salad, 191
Artichoke Tossed Salad, 193
Baby Corn Romaine Salad, 186
Basil Cherry Tomatoes, 188
Broccoli Coleslaw, 194
Colorful Bean Salad, 187
Crispy 'n' Crunchy Salad, 190
Family-Favorite Chicken Salad, 85
Greek Tossed Salad, 195
Honeydew Shrimp Salad, 136
Melon with Sweet Lime
    Dressing, 189
Mock Caesar Salad, 191
Salsa Tuna Salad, 137
Swiss Spinach Salad, 194
Taco Salad, 203
Zesty Steak Salad, 13

SANDWICHES
Cold Sandwiches
Chicken Salad Clubs, 85
Colorful Chicken Croissants, 88
Corned Beef and Cabbage
    Sandwiches, 9
Greek Ham Wraps, 57
Turkey Salad on Wheat, 101
Hot Sandwiches
Asian Turkey Burgers, 94
Barbecued Ham Buns, 49
Cajun Chicken Club, 96
Carrot Burgers, 176
Chili Burgers, 11
Corny Chicken Wraps, 84
Grilled Roast Beef Sandwiches, 16
Italian Beef Sandwiches, 12
Italian Subs, 50
Italian Turkey Burgers, 114
Jalapeno Swiss Burgers, 24
Jelly Pancake Sandwiches, 171
Mozzarella Beef Sandwiches, 8
Mushroom Cheeseburgers, 12
Open-Faced Crab Melts, 135
Open-Faced Tuna Burgers, 138
Pepper Steak Sandwiches, 18
Pizzeria Burgers, 71
Pork 'n' Green Chili Tortillas, 75
Reuben Monte Cristos, 27
Scrambled Egg Sandwich, 168
Sloppy Joe Burgers, 17
Spinach Feta Turnovers, 177
Spiral Stromboli, 81
Taco Sandwich, 19
Teriyaki Chicken Sandwiches, 86
Toasted Cheese Supreme, 61
Tuna Cheese Melts, 149
Veggie Burgers, 170
Zippy Burgers, 18

Indexes

SAUSAGE
Barbecue Kielbasa, 55
Italian Sausage Skillet, 64
Mexican Pork and Pasta, 75
Pizzeria Burgers, 71
Sausage Corn Chili, 54
Sausage Hash, 78
Sausage Jumble, 66
Sausage Stroganoff, 65
Sausage-Topped Polenta, 71
Spicy Cajun Stew, 56
Spinach Ravioli Bake, 77
Spiral Stromboli, 81

SEAFOOD (also see Fish)
Barbecue Shrimp over Pasta, 153
Cajun Shrimp, 135
Cajun Shrimp with Potatoes, 152
Citrus Garlic Shrimp, 150
Crab-Topped Fish Fillets, 156
Garlic Lime Shrimp, 146
Honeydew Shrimp Salad, 136
Open-Faced Crab Melts, 135
Seafood Fettuccine, 141
Stir-Fried Shrimp and
    Mushrooms, 148
Wild Rice Shrimp Saute, 157

SIDES
Acorn Squash Slices, 224
Alfredo Potatoes, 209
Artichoke Orzo Pilaf, 215
Baked Sweet Potato Chips, 209
Balsamic Roasted Red Potatoes, 224
Broccoli Brown Rice Pilaf, 221
Broccoli Corn Bake, 222
Buttery Peas and Carrots, 198
Cheese Sauce over Cauliflower, 205
Cheesy Broccoli Macaroni, 218
Cheesy Rice with Peas, 216
Chili-Cheese Mashed Potatoes, 188
Creamed New Potatoes, 217
Creamed Spinach, 211
Creamed Sweet Peas, 206
Easy au Gratin Potatoes, 218
French-Style Green Beans, 187
Garlic Mashed Potatoes, 217
Hearty Baked Potatoes, 210
Herbed Egg Noodles, 204
Italian Pasta and Peas, 211
Italian Rice, 197
Lemon Angel Hair, 207
Lemon-Glazed Carrots, 214
Maple Baked Beans, 208
Microwave Acorn Squash, 212
Mixed Vegetable Casserole, 222
Noodle Rice Pilaf, 219
Orange Broccoli, 198
Oven-Roasted Root Vegetables, 220

Paprika Potatoes 'n' Beans, 212
Parmesan Potato Rounds, 223
Pasta Veggie Medley, 201
Pecan Brussels Sprouts, 200
Penne from Heaven, 213
Pepperoni Angel Hair, 202
Potatoes O'Brien, 215
Sauteed Summer Squash, 216
Savory Rice Pilaf, 204
Scalloped Basil Tomatoes, 221
Seasoned Broccoli Spears, 193
Seasoned French Fries, 207
Sesame Asparagus, 203
Southwest Skillet Corn, 192
Spanish Rice, 200
Spicy Creamed Corn, 196
Stir-Fried Asparagus, 190
Tangy Carrot Coins, 208
Tarragon-Almond Green Beans, 199
Tomato Pea Couscous, 197
Zucchini Corn Saute, 201

SOUPS (also see Stews)
Cheeseburger Chowder, 31
Chicken Chili, 102
Cold Day Chili, 24
Pronto Chili, 39
Sausage Corn Chili, 54

SPINACH
Creamed Spinach, 211
Spinach Burritos, 179
Spinach Feta Turnovers, 177
Spinach Lasagna Roll-Ups, 182
Spinach Pancake Quesadillas, 166
Spinach Pork Tenderloin, 82
Spinach Ravioli Bake, 77
Spinach Tomato Linguine, 172
Spinach Turkey Bake, 125
Swiss Spinach Salad, 194
Turkey Florentine, 110

STEAK
Artichoke Beef Steaks, 33
Asian Beef Noodles, 32
Cube Steak Diane, 21
Fabulous Beef Fajitas, 45
Gingered Pepper Steak, 17
Italian Flank Steak, 15
Mushroom Beef Tenderloin, 20
One-for-All Marinated Beef, 22
Pepper Steak with Potatoes, 23
Skillet Steak and Corn, 41
Spicy Flank Steak, 29
Spicy Grilled Steaks, 22
Steak Diane, 10
Stir-Fried Beef on Lettuce, 34
T-Bones with Onions, 35
Teriyaki Sirloin Steak, 11
Zesty Steak Salad, 13

STEWS
Mexicana Skillet Stew, 43
Orzo Shrimp Stew, 144
Ranch Stew, 42
Skillet Beef Stew, 46
Spicy Cajun Stew, 56

TOMATOES
Basil Cherry Tomatoes, 188
Feta Tomato-Basil Fish, 139
Scalloped Basil Tomatoes, 221
Spinach Tomato Linguine, 172
Tomato Pea Couscous, 197
Tomato Spiral Toss, 165

TURKEY
Asian Turkey Burgers, 94
Bow Tie Turkey Bake, 102
Breaded Turkey Breasts, 90
Cranberry-Orange Turkey
    Cutlets, 97
Italian Turkey Burgers, 114
Lemon Honey Turkey, 124
Onion Turkey Meatballs, 117
Ranch Turkey Pasta Dinner, 98
Smoked Turkey Sausage with
    Pasta, 108
Spaghetti with Homemade Turkey
    Sausage, 112
Spinach Turkey Bake, 125
Sweet 'n' Sour Sausage Stir-Fry, 111
Tangy Turkey Kabobs, 129
Tasty Turkey Skillet, 122
Thanksgiving in a Pan, 121
Turkey Florentine, 110
Turkey Salad on Wheat, 101
Turkey Tetrazzini, 121

VEGETABLES (also see specific kinds)
Chicken Veggie Casserole, 100
Fluffy Harvest Omelet, 178
Golden Chicken and Autumn
    Vegetables, 118
Mixed Vegetable Casserole, 222
One-Dish Chicken with
    Vegetables, 128
Oven-Roasted Root
    Vegetables, 220
Pasta and Veggies in Garlic
    Sauce, 168
Pasta Veggie Medley, 201
Ravioli Primavera, 166
Veggie Burgers, 170
Veggie Cheese Squares, 183

ZUCCHINI & SQUASH
Acorn Squash Slices, 224
Microwave Acorn Squash, 212
Sauteed Summer Squash, 216
Zucchini Corn Saute, 201
Zucchini Pie, 183

The Busy Family Cookbook